SMITHSONIAN

PEOPLE
AND PLACES
A VISUAL ENCYCLOPEDIA

NEW EDITION

Senior Editors Ruth O'Rourke-Jones, Pauline Savage
Design Laura Gardner Design Studio
US Editor Jill Hamilton
Managing Editor Lisa Gillespie
Managing Art Editor Owen Peyton Jones
Senior Producer Meskerem Berhane
Pre-producer Gillian Reid
Publisher Andrew MacIntyre
Art Director Karen Self
Design Director Phil Ormerod
Publishing Director Jonathan Metcalfe
Jacket Designer Tanya Mehrotra
DTP Designer Rakesh Kumar
Jackets Editorial Coordinator Priyanka Sharma
Managing Jackets Editor Saloni Singh
Jacket Designer Surabhi Wadhwa-Gandhi
Jacket Editor Emma Dawson
Jacket Design Development Manager Sophia MTT

Consultant Dr Susan Pattie, University College London

FIRST EDITION

Senior Editor Penelope Arlon
Senior Art Editor Claire Patané
Editorial Team Lorrie Mack, Zahavit Shalev
Design Team Laura Roberts, Venice Shone,
Cathy Chesson, Tory Gordon-Harris
Editorial Assistant Fleur Star
Picture Research Lorna Ainger, Kathy Lockley
Publishing Manager Sue Leonard
Managing Art Editor Clare Shedden
Production Shivani Pandey
DTP Designer Almudena Díaz
DTP Assistant Pilar Morales

Written and researched by Penelope Arlon,
Lorrie Mack, Zahavit Shalev

Consultant Team:
Dr Dena Freeman: Chief Consultant and Africa
Dr Leo Howe: East Asia
Dr Mark Jamieson: North America
Dr James Leach: Australia and the Pacific
Dr Perveez Mody: West Asia
Dr Valentina Napolitano: South America
Dr David Sneath: West Asia
Dr Jaro Stacul: Europe
Bryan Alexander: Arctic

This American Edition, 2019
First American Edition, 2003
Published in the United States by DK Publishing
1450 Broadway, Suite 801, New York, NY 10018

Copyright © 2003, 2019 Dorling Kindersley Limited
DK, a Division of Penguin Random House
19 20 21 22 23 10 9 8 7 6 5 4 3 2 1
001–312865–Aug/2019

A catalog record for this book
is available from the Library of Congress
ISBN: 978-1-4654-8376-8 (paperback)
ISBN: 978-1-4654-8177-1 (hardback)
DK books are available at special discounts when purchased in bulk for sales promotions,
premiums, fund-raising, or educational use. For details, contact: DK Publishing Special Markets,
1450 Broadway, Suite 801, New York, NY 10018 or SpecialSales@dk.com

Printed and bound in Dubai

A WORLD OF IDEAS:
SEE ALL THERE IS TO KNOW

www.dk.com

Smithsonian
Institution

THE SMITHSONIAN

Established in 1846, the Smithsonian is the world's largest museum and research
complex, dedicated to public education, national service, and scholarship in the
arts, sciences, and history. It includes 19 museums and galleries
and the National Zoological Park. The total number of artifacts, works of art,
and specimens in the Smithsonian's collection is estimated at 154 million.

THERE ARE MANY, MANY different groups of people in the world—so many, in fact, that they could not possibly all fit into one book. **People and Places: A Visual Encyclopedia** gives an initial understanding of the enormous diversity of cultures in the world today and celebrates the common bonds that link us all together.

CONTENTS

WE HUMANS ARE VERY SOCIAL ANIMALS, sharing basic physical and

OUR WORLD

emotional needs. Yet we are also many different peoples around the world. This book is created to introduce you to people that

SHARING THE SAME PLANET

Learning from each other

Each of us is both an individual and a member of social and cultural groups. We have our own personality and also our heritage, family, and environment. Together, all these factors makes us who we are. Learning more about how other people live helps us imagine other ways of existing in our world, other possible solutions to the problems we share, and other ways to value the Earth and the many peoples who inhabit it.

Scouts from all around the globe gather at the World Scout Jamboree. Meeting people from different cultures helps us understand our world.

COMMUNICATION

Everyone loves using the internet. When we think about how new this technology is, we understand how much and how fast our world has changed everywhere. We get news instantly, we chat with loved ones far away, businesses flourish in unexpected places, and people educate themselves online. Unfortunately, people can also spread disturbing, hateful messages online and try to influence others to be afraid. We have a lot to learn about how best to use our new resource.

you might not meet in your daily lives, people with whom we share our planet, people whose lives show us the many creative ways we have adapted to our different environments and situations. Some patterns of life are now quickly disappearing and it is important to appreciate how each person and each cultural group contributes to our understanding of human life.

COLONIZATION

A hundred years ago, there were many colonial empires where a powerful country ruled over other peoples and their lands. The colonized people fought for freedom and became independent countries. Many maintained ties with the former colonial power, and the influence can be seen today in architecture, for example.

GLOBALIZATION

People travel but so do fashions, products, and ideas. The internet and social media speed this up and many things are adopted around the world. We all become more alike but often with the loss of indigenous peoples' ways of life. Globalization can also bring better medical support, education, and awareness of human rights.

TECHNOLOGY

New technologies are being developed around the world, often building on each other's inventions. Many make life easier with increased access to water and energy, or they provide new jobs, more comfort, or help solve problems and cure diseases. They can also bring problems, as older forms of work and lifestyles disappear, forcing people to move into cities. Our world becomes a smaller place with less variety and flexibility, and with fewer skills for making or fixing things, or working with our hands.

Solar technology can provide clean energy for people.

WORLD MAP

THERE ARE 195 INDEPENDENT COUNTRIES on Earth today. There are over 61 dependent territories that are administered by any one of: France, Australia, Denmark, New Zealand, Norway, the UK, the US, and the

INTERNATIONAL BORDERS OF THE WORLD

Largest country
Russia
6,599,921 sq miles (17,098,242 sq km)

Longest single land border
Canada/US
5,526 miles (8,893 km)

Smallest country
Vatican City
0.17 sq miles
(0.44 sq km)

Largest desert
Sahara, Africa
3,500,000 sq miles (9,065,000 sq km)

Driest inhabited place
Kufra, Libya
<0.00 in (<0.00 cm) of rain per year

Wettest inhabited place
Mawsynram, India
467 in (1,187 cm) rain per year

ARCTIC OCEAN

Arctic Circle

US (Alaska)

Great Bear Lake

Great Slave Lake

Bering Sea

Aleutian Is (to US)

CANADA

Hudson Bay

Baffin Bay

Greenland (to Denmark)

Jan Mayen (to Norway)

ICELAND

Faroe Islands (to Denmark)

UNITED KINGDO

IRELAND

Lake Winnipeg

Lake Superior

Lake Michigan

Lake Huron

Lake Ontario

Lake Erie

UNITED STATES

PACIFIC OCEAN

St. Pierre & Miquelon (to France)

ATLANTIC OCEAN

Azores (to Portugal)

PORTUGAL

SPA

Gibraltar (to UK)

Ceuta (to Spain)

Melilla (to Spain)

Madeira (to Portugal)

MOROCCO

Midway Islands (to US)

Tropic of Cancer

US (Hawaii)

Guadalupe (to Mexico)

MEXICO

Gulf of Mexico

Bermuda (to UK)

Canary Islands (to Spain)

WESTERN SAHARA (occupied by Morocco) (Disputed)

MAURITANIA

Johnston Atoll (to US)

Revillagigedo Islands (to Mexico)

THE BAHAMAS

CUBA

Turks & Caicos Is (to UK)

Puerto Rico (to US)

Virgin Is (to US)

British Virgin Is (to UK)

Anguilla (to UK)

ANTIGUA & BARBUDA

Guadeloupe (to France)

DOMINICA

Martinique (to France)

ST. LUCIA

ST. VINCENT & THE GRENADINES

BARBADOS

GRENADA

TRINIDAD & TOBAGO

CAPE VERDE

SENEGAL

THE GAMBIA

GUINEA BISSAU

GUINEA

MALI

BURKINA FASO

SIERRA LEONE

CÔTE D'IVOIR (IVORY COAST)

LIBERIA

GHANA

Kingman Reef (to US)

Palmyra Atoll (to US)

Clipperton Island (to French Polynesia)

Cayman Is (to UK)

HAITI

DOM. REP.

JAMAICA

BELIZE

GUATEMALA

HONDURAS

ST. KITTS & NEVIS

Montserrat (to UK)

Curaçao (to Neth.)

EL SALVADOR

NICARAGUA

Aruba (to Neth.)

COSTA RICA

PANAMA

VENEZUELA

GUYANA

SURINAME

French Guiana (to France)

Baker & Howland Is (to US)

Equator

COLOMBIA

Galapagos Is (to Ecuador)

ECUADOR

Fernando de Noronha (to Brazil)

Ascension (to UK)

ATLANTIC OCEAN

Jarvis Is (to US)

KIRIBATI

PERU

BRAZIL

Tokelau (to NZ)

SAMOA

Wallis & Futuna (to France)

American Samoa (to US)

Cook Islands (to NZ)

TONGA

Niue (to NZ)

French Polynesia (to France)

PACIFIC OCEAN

Pitcairn, Henderson, Ducie & Oeno Islands (to UK)

Lake Titicaca

BOLIVIA

PARAGUAY

St. Helen (to UK)

Trindade (to Brazil)

Tropic of Capricorn

Kermadec Islands (to NZ)

Easter Island (to Chile)

Sala y Gomez (to Chile)

San Felix Island (to Chile)

San Ambrosio Island (to Chile)

CHILE

ARGENTINA

URUGUAY

Tristan da Cunha (to UK)

Gough Island (to Tristan da Cunha)

Chatham Islands (to NZ)

Juan Fernandez Islands (to Chile)

Falkland Islands (to UK)

South Georgia & South Sandwich Islands (to UK)

South Orkney Islands

South Shetland Islands

SOUTHERN

Antarctic Circle

Peter I Island (to Norway)

Ronne Ice Shelf

A

0 km 1000 2000

0 miles 1000 2000

Netherlands. Every piece of land is owned by a country with the exception of Antarctica. Australia, Argentina, Britain, Chile, France, New Zealand, and Norway have all laid claim to sections of it, but the 1961 Antarctic Treaty, signed by 12 nations, agrees that no one country can own it. The extreme climate has meant that no one has ever permanently settled there and the only settlements today are scientific bases.

Language spoken by the most people
Mandarin Chinese
918 million

Most populous country
China
1,426,279,708 people

Most populous city
Tokyo
37,000,000 people in metropolitan area

Smallest island country
Nauru
8.2 sq miles (21 sq km)

Largest island country
Indonesia
735,358 sq miles (1,904,569 sq km)

Most populous island
Java
141,000,000 people

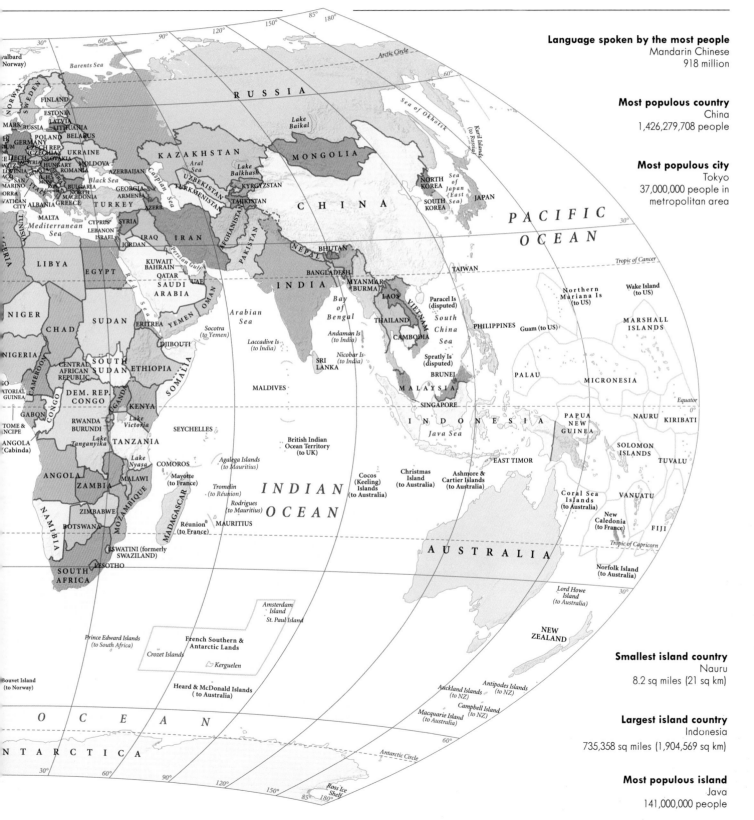

LIFE ON EARTH

On October 31, 2011, the 7 billionth person was born on Earth, and by 2018 there were over 7,600,000,000 people in the world. Our population

WHAT ARE PEOPLE'S LIVES LIKE?

FOOD

If the world's food were divided equally among the people of the globe, everyone would have enough to eat— but unfortunately this is not the case. As people in North America and Western Europe consume more than is good for them, millions of people in southern Asia and sub-Saharan Africa go to bed hungry every night.

EDUCATION

An increasing majority of the world's school-age children are in school, but the quality of this education varies greatly according to location and economic status. The good news is that most people in the world are able to read to some extent, and that more of the world's young people are learning to read every year.

HABITAT

More than half of the world's population currently lives in cities, rather than rural environments, and this figure is expected to rise. This presents unique challenges, since urban expansion can often be damaging both to the environment and to people's health. By 2025, two-thirds of the world's people will live in cities.

is growing so rapidly—both because more babies are surviving birth and infancy and because people are living longer—that we'll probably reach 10 billion by 2055. People belong to many different nationalities, they speak many different languages, and practice different religions, but deep down they strive for the same things: enough food and water, a peaceful and safe place to live, and a happy, healthy life.

RELIGION

The world's religions are as diverse as its peoples. Although the most common religions are Christianity, Islam, or Hinduism, there are many other faiths—from ancient religions such as Judaism and Buddhism, to indigenous beliefs such as animism, to more recent faiths such as Hare Krishna and Mormonism.

LANGUAGE

It is estimated that there are about 6,500 languages spoken in the world. The most common are Chinese (in its various dialects), English, Hindi, and Spanish. As global communication improves, an increasing number of people are learning to speak these major languages, and many of the less common ones are slowly disappearing.

HEALTH

Everyone wants to stay healthy, but in many areas of the world,\ this can be very difficult. While people in the US struggle to find affordable healthcare, many people in developing regions are coping with more basic problems, such as finding safe drinking water and combating infectious diseases such as malaria.

PEOPLE AND CULTURE

LOOKING AT THE WORLD AS A WHOLE, it is fascinating to see the incredible varieties of people within each continent. In the

WHAT MAKES AN ETHNIC GROUP?

Belonging to a group

There are many reasons why people feel that they belong to an ethnic group. They often have lots of things in common, such as shared heritage, language, or culture. Ethnic groups can be large or small, and these days they can live together or can be spread all over the world.

SHARED RELIGION

Religion often creates a sense of cultural distinction and can be a key factor within an ethnic group. Some religions, such as Christianity, can stretch across very diverse ethnic groups, for example from the European communities to South Africa.

THE SOCIAL ANIMAL

People are social beings: those that live near each other create communities and societies. During their lives they socialize, or interact, with many different people from other ethnic groups for various reasons, such as trade.

The Miao people are one of 55 Chinese ethnic minorities. Within the Miao there are many different clans.

forests of Papua New Guinea there are societies who live traditional lifestyles while in nearby Australia the cities buzz with the latest technology and fashions. All cultures are constantly evolving, some faster than others. While this means we lose some aspects of them, such as languages that disappear when there is no one left to speak them, this reflects the liveliness of cultures that grow and adapt to change.

WHO ARE INDIGENOUS PEOPLE?

The word "indigenous" is sometimes used in this book. Indigenous people are those who are "native to," or originate in, a country. Often a country is taken over by another culture or nation and the indigenous population is then governed by different people. This is what happened in Australia where the indigenous people were initially conquered by the British and are now part of the independent Australian nation.

There are very few indigenous people with little contact with the rest of the world. There are, however, some rain forest communities in Papua New Guinea that are relatively isolated.

NATIONALITY

The world is divided into countries that have their own nationality. There can be many ethnic groups within a country, as in Canada, or in some cases, as in Japan, they are almost entirely made up of one.

In many countries children are educated together regardless of their ethnic or cultural differences.

SIMILARITIES

In many countries today people from different ethnic groups live and work together, thus creating the vibrant mix that makes up the modern world. Although people may seem different, we all have a lot of things in common—all people have the need to work, value family and relations, and like to feel a sense of community. People may have their differences, but we are at our core essentially the same—we are all human.

MOVING ON

PEOPLE ARE CONSTANTLY MOVING. THERE ARE MANY reasons why people relocate to a different place. Sometimes people are forced to migrate, by, for example, conflict or a natural

WHY DO POPULATIONS SHIFT?

WAR

Conflict between nations or peoples often leads to people moving to escape danger. Here, millions of Syrians are on the move fearing for their lives. They are refugees in their own country.

IMMIGRATION

Many people are economic migrants and move to find work. There are, for example, Chinese communities in many of the world's major cities.

SLAVERY

From the 16th through to the 19th century many European powers took people from Africa and shipped them all over the world as slaves. The Portuguese shipped over 3.5 million Africans to Brazil and today many of their descendants live in Bahia, Brazil. They have created a new culture based on an African origin with South American and European influences.

Dance troupe in Salvador, Brazil practicing an Afro-Brazilian dance.

disaster, and sometimes people choose to migrate, perhaps for a better life or work. As a result, different people come into contact with each other, languages and ideas spread, and over time ways of life change and in their place new fashions and ideas are formed. These pages look in detail at some of the reasons why people choose to migrate or are forced to move.

Sakurajima volcano, in Japan, hurls rocks down daily on the nearby town. For protection the children wear hard hats to school.

COLONIES

Throughout the 16th to 19th centuries, Europeans conquered huge areas of the world, and large numbers of people moved to some of these areas, such as Australia. Many countries have since become independent but in some cases they have adopted the language of the colonizing power.

NATURAL DISASTER

An earthquake, an eruption of a volcano, or a hurricane can be a reason for people to move. The aftermath of a natural disaster can often bring with it terror and chaos, forcing people to gather up their belongings and leave. In 1995 a volcano on the island of Montserrat in the West Indies erupted and many people had to flee the island. Much of the island is still buried under ash today.

CHANGING POLITICAL BOUNDARIES

Some regimes place tight restriction on movement. Until the late 1980s much of Europe, including East Germany, was ruled by the former communist power, the USSR. The people were unable to move freely until 1989, when the Berlin Wall came down, allowing movement once again.

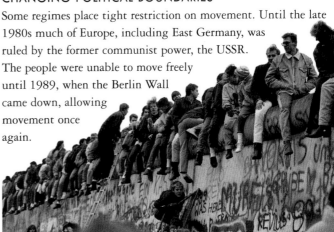

URBANIZATION

Cities often attract people from the surrounding countryside who are looking for work. The city of Dubai, situated on the shores of Dubai Creek in the United Arab Emirates, has become a sprawling place due to businesses growing up around the oil industry. A valuable natural resource will attract people to an area.

THE PEOPLE OF
North and
Central
America

THE CONTINENT OF NORTH AND CENTRAL AMERICA includes 23 countries plus a number of dependent territories.

NORTH AND CENTRAL AMERICA

FROM THE ARCTIC TO THE TROPICS

0 km 400 800
0 miles 400 800

Under pressure
The huge ice sheet pushing down on Greenland has caused the island's center to sink to 1,000 ft (300 m) below sea level.

Coastal record
At 151,394 miles (243,638 km), Canada has the longest coastline of any country in the world.

Deep chill
Recorded in 1971, the coldest-ever recorded temperature in Alaska is -80 °F (-62 °C).

Water power
Over 45 million gallons (180 million liters) of water rush over Niagara Falls every minute.

Lots of latitude

Some parts of Greenland, Canada, and Alaska lie far inside the Arctic Circle, while the southern tip of Panama extends almost as far as the equator.

Distant relation
The 50th state of the US, Hawaii, is far to the west of the continent, halfway to Australia.

Map labels

ASIA

ARCTIC OCEAN

Bering Strait

Beaufort Sea

Greenland (to Denmark)

Baffin Bay

Bering Sea

UNITED STATES

ALASKA

Victoria Island

Davis Strait

Baffin Island

Gulf of Alaska

YUKON

NORTHWEST TERRITORIES

NUNAVUT

Hudson Strait

Labrador Sea

Hudson Bay

NEWFOUNDLAND & LABRADOR

BRITISH COLUMBIA

CANADA

ALBERTA

MANITOBA

QUEBEC

PRINCE EDWARD ISLAND

St. Pierre & Miquelon (to France)

SASKATCHEWAN

ONTARIO

NEW BRUNSWICK

NOVA SCOTIA

WASHINGTON

MONTANA

NORTH DAKOTA

MINNESOTA

MAINE

VERMONT

NEW HAMPSHIRE

MASSACHUSETTS

RHODE ISLAND

CONNECTICUT

OREGON

IDAHO

WYOMING

SOUTH DAKOTA

WISCONSIN

MICHIGAN

NEW YORK

PENNSYLVANIA

PACIFIC

NEVADA

UTAH

UNITED STATES

NEBRASKA

IOWA

OHIO

INDIANA

ILLINOIS

WEST VIRGINIA

NEW JERSEY

DELAWARE

MARYLAND

DISTRICT OF COLUMBIA

CALIFORNIA

COLORADO

KANSAS

MISSOURI

KENTUCKY

VIRGINIA

ATLANTIC OCEAN

OF AMERICA

ARIZONA

NEW MEXICO

OKLAHOMA

TENNESSEE

NORTH CAROLINA

SOUTH CAROLINA

ARKANSAS

MISSISSIPPI

ALABAMA

GEORGIA

Gulf of California

TEXAS

LOUISIANA

FLORIDA

MEXICO

Gulf of Mexico

THE BAHAMAS

CUBA

HAITI

Cayman Islands (to UK)

JAMAICA

Navassa Island (to US)

British Virgin Islands (to UK)

Virgin Islands (to US)

Turks & Caicos Islands (to UK)

DOMINICAN REPUBLIC

Puerto Rico (to US)

Anguilla (to UK)

ANTIGUA & BARBUDA

Guadeloupe (to France)

DOMINICA

Martinique (to France)

ST. KITTS & NEVIS

Montserrat (to UK)

ST. LUCIA

BARBADOS

ST. VINCENT & THE GRENADINES

GRENADA

BELIZE

Caribbean Sea

Aruba (to Neth.)

Curaçao (to Neth.)

Bonaire (to Neth.)

TRINIDAD & TOBAGO

GUATEMALA

HONDURAS

EL SALVADOR

NICARAGUA

SOUTH AMERICA

COSTA RICA

PANAMA

OCEAN

HAWAII

Greenland (the largest island in the world) belongs to Denmark, for example, and the small islands of St. Pierre and Miquelon, near the east coast of Canada, belong to France. Several of the Caribbean islands (such as Martinique and Guadeloupe) also belong to France, while others are territories of the Netherlands (for example, Aruba), the United Kingdom (Cayman Islands), or the US (Virgin Islands).

Facts and figures

LANGUAGES
English is the most widely spoken language in North America, while Spanish dominates in Central America. French features prominently because it is spoken widely in the Caribbean, as well as being one of Canada's two official languages. Indigenous languages are also spoken.

RELIGIONS
Because of the high incidence of immigration in this region, virtually every world religion is practiced here somewhere. The most widely practiced religion is Catholicism with over 70 million Roman Catholics, followed by Protestantism, then Judaism, and Islam.

URBAN POPULATION
The vast majority of people live in towns, cities, and their surrounding areas. The most populated cities in North America are New York City with 8.6 million inhabitants and Los Angeles with 4.1 million. In Central America, Mexico City is the largest, with 12.3 million.

POPULATION BY COUNTRY
Despite having the biggest land mass in the region (and the second biggest in the world), Canada has just over 37 million people. The most populous country in the region is the US, with nearly 327 million. Mexico is the next most populous, with over 129 million people.

CLIMATE

The climates in this region range from the frozen Arctic in the north of Canada and Alaska to the humid tropical climate of Central America. Hurricanes are a hazard on the southeast coast of the US and in the Caribbean. People in these areas learn to live with the risk and know when to evacuate.

NORTH & CENTRAL AMERICA FACTS

PLACES
Number of countries ....30 (plus dependencies)
Highest point ....Mt. McKinley (Denali), Alaska, 20,321 ft (6,194 m)
Lowest point ....Badwater, Death Valley, California, -282 ft (-86 m)
Biggest country ....Canada, 3,855,103 sq miles (9,984,670 sq km)
Smallest country ....St. Kitts and Nevis, 101 sq miles (261 sq km)

PEOPLE
Total population ....547 million
Proportion living in urban areas 82%

The People of North America

COVERING A VAST LAND MASS that has attracted immigrants from every corner of the globe, this region—which stretches from Greenland to Mexico—is home to a greater and more diverse variety of intermingled peoples, cultures, and religions than anywhere else on Earth.

CITY LIFE

The great cities of North America all provide important public spaces that define both their physical and their human landscapes. During the winter months, and especially at Christmas, New Yorkers flock to the huge skating rink in Central Park.

FESTIVALS

While festivals in Mexico are largely based on religion, in the US and Canada, the major celebrations, such as the 4th of July in the US and Canada Day, are designed to build a feeling of belonging to a new nation. Below, Mexican Catholics mark the festival of Our Lady of Guadalupe (December 12) outside the grand 18th-century Basilica de Guadalupe in Mexico City.

Changes of scene

Combining old customs and modern trends, treasured handicrafts and modern technology, formal ceremonies and casual entertainments—all nourish the richly diverse cultures of North America. New arrivals to North America add their own color and detail to the constantly changing scene.

MOVING WITH THE TIMES

Today, the indigenous peoples of North America combine a wide range of elements from the modern world with their own customs and traditions. Here, a Canadian Inuit family navigates the forbidding conditions around their home on a high-speed snowmobile.

AMERICAN INDIANS

American Indians are descended from many different groups across the continent but often come together to celebrate their histories and traditions. Here at the Red Earth Festival in Oklahoma City, two children display symbols of the Kiowa, Cherokee, Comanche, Choctow, and Navajo peoples.

CULTURAL

North American cityscapes reflect the many influences that shape them. In Toronto, Canada's largest city, the City Hall and adjoining square sit between its bustling Chinatown and the glass towers of the business district. The dramatic complex was designed and built in the 1960s by the Finnish architect Viljo Revell.

PLAYING TO WIN

Baseball is more than a sport: it has become an international symbol of the US. From major-league events, to college- and high-school play-offs and casual street games, baseball and other sporting activities play a major part in North American life. Across the country—even in the far-flung state of Hawaii—children don the uniform of their local Little League team to express their passion for their national game.

THE UNITED STATES OF AMERICA is a place where people from many

THE PEOPLE OF THE US

countries have come together to form a diverse culture. Even before the country's independence

A RICH "MELTING POT" OF CULTURES

A symbol of freedom

The Statue of Liberty was erected on an island in New York Harbor in 1886 as a symbol of the city's role as a gateway to the "land of the free and the home of the brave." North of the statue lies Ellis Island, where more than 12 million immigrants first landed in their new country to be processed.

INDEPENDENCE DAY

On July 4, 1776, after the American War of Independence, the Declaration of Independence final text was approved. Each year on this date Americans celebrate their freedom with barbeques, picnics, family gatherings, and fireworks.

CHINATOWN

Chinese people began to arrive by the 1850s, attracted by jobs and the Gold Rush—many built the railroads out to the west. Today over 500,000 Chinese Americans live in New York City. Each year Chinatown hosts the Chinese New Year parade, which occurs the day after the first new moon of the year.

IRISH AMERICANS

In 1845 the great potato rot and subsequent famine in Ireland started a mass migration to the US. Starving families who could not pay landlords faced no alternative but to leave the country in hopes of a better future.

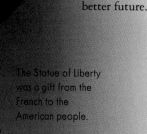

The Statue of Liberty was a gift from the French to the American people.

in 1776, immigrants started to arrive in enormous numbers, attracted by a better life, or the "American Dream." These days America still accepts over one million immigrants annually. The mix of cultures has enriched the country and has become its defining quality. In cities such as New York, pockets of established ethnic communities manage to maintain the culture of their homeland as well as lead American lives.

HISPANIC COMMUNITY

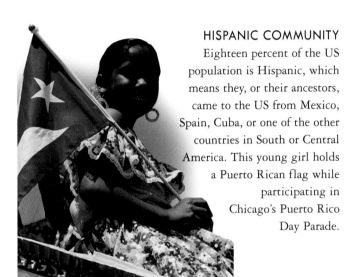

Eighteen percent of the US population is Hispanic, which means they, or their ancestors, came to the US from Mexico, Spain, Cuba, or one of the other countries in South or Central America. This young girl holds a Puerto Rican flag while participating in Chicago's Puerto Rico Day Parade.

AFRICAN AMERICANS

During the 17th and 18th centuries, around 388,0000 people were shipped to the US from Africa as slaves. The descendants of these slaves have made great contributions to American life in all areas—government, the arts and sciences, and sports.

ITALIAN AMERICANS

The first wave of Italians, many of them from northern Italy, arrived in the US in the 1830s. Between 1880 and 1920, poverty forced more than 4 million Italians to come to the US. Now, for 11 days each September, about one million people converge on the neighborhood known as Little Italy in New York City for the Feast of San Gennaro—a massive festival to celebrate the patron saint of Naples, Italy.

AMERICAN JEWS

The first Jewish immigrants to the US arrived around 1650. From the late 1800s, Jews came in greater numbers from Europe and Asia, some looking for work but also often fleeing terrible persecution. About 7 million Jews live in America today and one of the largest synagogues in the world is Temple Emanu-El in New York City. Above, men dance to klezmer music at a party.

St. Patrick's Day is celebrated on March 17 each year. On this day the Chicago River is dyed green for the celebrations!

The Marathon

THE LARGEST RACE ON EARTH

THE VERY FIRST NEW YORK MARATHON was held on September 13, 1970. One hundred and twenty seven runners started, only 55 finished, and less than 100 people watched. By the year 2018, more than 50,000 people finished the race successfully, and it is considered the world's largest marathon. The course is 26 miles (42 km) and covers all five of New York City's boroughs. People from all over the world take part, and the money raised for charity has a huge impact worldwide.

East coast

THE FIRST REGION OF THE US to be colonized by Europeans, the northeast coast takes in the cosmopolitan buzz of New York City, the historic centers of Boston and Philadelphia, and the picturesque landscapes of New England, with its fiery fall foliage, popular winter resorts, and traditional industries such as farming and fishing.

NEW YORK, NEW YORK

Times Square, where it meets the lights of Broadway, forms the heart of New York City, an international center of business and culture, and one of the world's most exciting cities. Broadway was originally an American Indian woodland path.

NATURAL HERITAGE

Most of the pretty, old buildings in New England (like this rural Vermont church) are made of wood. There are two main reasons for this: the early British settlers were familiar with timber-frame construction, and the forested landscape provided plenty of free building material.

MAPLE SYRUP

For hundreds of years, New Englanders have been using the sweet sap from the local trees to make maple syrup. There is only one short season a year when sap can be collected, and the earlier in this season the sap is drawn, the higher its sugar content, and therefore its quality.

LIBERTY BELL

According to legend, on July 8, 1776, the Liberty Bell was rung in Philadelphia calling for people to gather to hear the reading of the Declaration of Independence. Later, in 1837, abolitionists adopted the Liberty Bell as a symbol against slavery. After the Civil War, the Bell became an icon of unity and of the fight for religious freedom and civil rights.

JAMESTOWN

Jamestown, founded in 1607, was the first permanent English colony in the "New World." The settlement has been rebuilt to show how settlers, American Indians, and later colonial people lived. Actors in period dress demonstrate crafts and give tours.

BOSTON SKYLINE

The largest city in New England, Boston was named after the town of the same name in Lincolnshire, England. Established in 1630, today it is the capital and principal port of Massachusetts and a leading center of education, with 35 colleges and universities (including Harvard) in the greater Boston area.

Harvest from the sea

Fishing is a major industry along the northeast coast, which is particularly famous for shellfish of all kinds. Lobster is the best-known product, but crawfish, crab, and clams are important as well. Clam chowder, a thick, nourishing soup enjoyed all over the world, was invented in Maine.

LOBSTER FISHING

In the state of Maine alone there are over 7,000 licensed lobstermen. The trade tends to run in families, with some men "lobstering" exactly the same waters as their fathers and grandfathers before them.

1 Setting traps
Lobsters are caught in bait-filled traps. Once they have been lured inside they cannot escape. Most lobstermen check their traps every 3-4 days.

2 All at sea
Each trap (which can weigh as much as a small person when it is full of lobsters) is pulled up by hand. The men who do this develop very muscular forearms.

3 Good catch
The youngest commerical lobsters are called "chickens"; the largest are known as "jumbos."

Lobstermen tie colored buoys to their traps so they can easily find them.

The Gulf coast

CROWNING THE GULF OF MEXICO, this region (which overlaps with that of the southern states) includes Florida, Alabama, Mississippi, and Louisiana. Here, the Gulf itself—and the waterways connected to it—dominate many aspects of culture and industry, from local foods and festivals to water sports, fishing, and tourism.

MIAMI STYLE

Surrounded by the heavy-duty glitz of Miami, South Beach is famous for its multicolored Art Deco buildings, now immaculately restored to their original condition. The pink-and-chrome perfection of a classic 1950s car perfectly matches the hotel's style, if not its period.

CALLE OCHO CARNIVAL

Miami's vast Cuban population is centered around Eighth Street. Their annual festival, the biggest Latino celebration in the US, is called *Calle Ocho*—Eighth Street in Spanish.

WALT DISNEY WORLD

This huge theme park in Orlando, Florida, is the world's most visited vacation resort. The Magic Kingdom and adjoining attractions combine imaginative rides, fairytale characters, educational centers, and themed hotels.

The inviting beaches that line Alabama's coast are rarely crowded.

MAGNOLIA STATE

Dominated by the vast and powerful river that shares its name, the state of Mississippi was once wealthy and prosperous, its huge cotton industry providing a firm economic foundation. Today, although Mississippi is still a major cotton producer, it also depends on the revenue it receives from oil and and natural gas. Another important source of income is the tourist trade: every year, thousands of visitors come here to see the birthplace of Elvis Presley (Tupelo, Mississippi) and the Delta Blues, and to ride on one of the paddle wheel steamers that have been negotiating the great waterway for generations.

JAMBALAYA

Particularly associated with Louisiana, Cajun food is spicy and rich. One of the best-known dishes, jambalaya, is made from rice fried up with spices, vegetables, sausages, shrimp, and crawfish, known locally as "poor man's lobster."

The *American Queen*, one of the world's largest paddle wheelers, travels along the Mississippi near Natchez.

STORMY WEATHER

This region is vulnerable to violent storms called hurricanes. People are advised to make their homes as safe as possible, wach for warning signs, and—if necessary—leave the area quickly.

TEEMING WATERS

The seas around the Gulf coast provide fishermen with striped bass, herring, shad, and lesser-known species such as menhaden, bluefish, weakfish, and butterfish. There are plenty of catfish farms near the mouth of the Mississippi, and oyster, shrimp, and crawfish farms all along the Gulf.

Small fish used as live bait thrash around in this fine net.

Southern states

FROM COTTON FIELDS to country music and curly wrought iron, the images connected with the American South are uniquely characterful and romantic. Carrying a huge historical legacy as the defender of slavery and the Confederacy during the American Civil War, this region is also home to such modern phenomena as the oil industry and jazz music.

LAND OF COTTON

The US is the world's third-leading producer of cotton. Most of this yield is grown in the south, where Spanish colonists introduced the first cotton plants. Originally, cotton was picked by hand, but today the job is done mechanically. In cotton country, the fluffy harvest is known as "white gold."

Children in New Orleans make music in the street.

DRILLING FOR OIL

First discovered in Texas in 1901, oil has provided vital revenue to the state ever since; at the beginning of the 21st century, this region was supplying over one-third of the country's oil.

HORSE RACING IN KENTUCKY

The celebrated Kentucky Derby was first held in 1875. Each year, thousands of enthusiasts fill the main spectator area (the infield) shown here; wealthy patrons use the grandstand. The event's success inspired the local breeding of thoroughbreds for which the state is now famous.

Music

Many major musical styles were born in the South, including gospel, jazz, blues, rock and roll, and country. Music permeates the region's culture, and inspires much of its tourism—thousands of people every year visit New Orleans, Nashville, and Memphis for their musical associations alone.

GOSPEL SOUNDS

Nurtured in southern churches, gospel music resonates with the passion and expressiveness of early African American spirituals. The name "gospel" comes from the Old English "god," meaning good and "spel," meaning story or news.

NEW ORLEANS

Affectionately nicknamed "The Big Easy" or "the city that care forgot," New Orleans symbolizes charm, pleasure, and general indulgence. Founded by French explorers in the 18th century, it was later colonized by the Spanish, and it's this influence that is most evident in the city's distinctive architecture.

Friends and neighbors join in by beating the rhythm on empty cardboard boxes.

New Orleans is famous for its *Mardi Gras* celebrations, when merrymakers fill the streets.

COUNTRY NOTES

The hub of the country-music universe is Nashville, Tennessee. Influenced by the ballad and folk traditions of early European immigrants, country music uses melodic guitar, fiddle, and voice to express basic emotion. Since it first became popular in the early 20th century, the style has spawned several related genres, such as country-rock, western, bluegrass, and rockabilly music.

Western states

BIRTHPLACE OF SUCH POWERFUL American icons as the cowboy and the movie star, the western region of the US also contains some of the most breathtaking landscapes in the world: the Rocky Mountains, the Grand Canyon, the Death Valley desert, and the stunning national parks of Yellowstone and Yosemite.

CINEMA CITY

Gwyneth Paltrow poses for photographers at Hollywood's annual Academy Award ceremony. California's film industry has spread the influence of American culture to almost every corner of the world.

WATER WONDERLAND

California's climate and location make it ideal for water sports, such as surfing, kiteboarding, and windsurfing. It is a hub of innovation for many action sports, including skateboarding.

WINTER SCENE

Colorado is one of North America's premier destination for skiers. Famous for its celebrity visitors and residents, the pretty resort of Aspen (shown here) is totally surrounded by mountains.

LAS VEGAS

The extravagant glamor of Las Vegas has made this Nevada city one of the world's gambling meccas. Here, fabulous hotels offer 24-hour gaming in opulent, carnival-like casinos, where there are no windows or clocks to remind players of the outside world.

WEST COAST METROPOLIS

San Francisco is built on rugged terrain that dominates its landscape. The cable car was designed in 1873 by Scots-born Andrew Hallidie to replace the carriage-pulling horses that were often injured on the treacherous slopes.

WINE LAND

Northern California, the heart of America's wine country, produces a number of vintages that equal Europe's finest. Here, skilled workers in the Napa Valley harvest Cabernet Sauvignon grapes for one of the region's celebrated red wines.

THE FIFTH OF MAY

Latinos living in the US celebrate their countries' friendship at the Cinco de Mayo (May 5) festival. Held in various cities (this one is San Diego), it honors a Mexican victory over the French in 1862.

As part of the *Cinco de Mayo* festival, dancers in long ruffled dresses take to the streets, twirling gracefully to traditional guitar music.

THE ALOHA STATE

Admitted to the union in 1959, modern-day Hawaii provides a tourist paradise. It is the only state that grows coffee. Here, adorned with flowery *leis* around their necks, local girls perform their ancient ritual dance, the *hula*.

Back at the ranch

One of the industries on which Arizona was founded, cattle ranching is still important to the state's economy. Today, in addition to working ranches, there are many that cater to tourists wanting to experience cowboy life first hand. This one is in the Coconino National Forest.

RIDE 'EM COWBOYS

Virtually everywhere cattle ranching is established, its essential skills—often in extreme and specialized form—are displayed as some kind of entertainment. Here, at the Green Days Rendezvous Rodeo in Wyoming, a courageous cowboy rides a bucking bronco.

The wild ones
SAVING OREGON'S FERAL HORSES

WHEN EARLY PIONEERS BEGAN RAISING HORSES in the Oregon
desert, a number of spirited creatures regularly broke through their
restrictive fencing and headed for the open range. Also, when
times were so hard that desperate ranchers could not afford to buy
feed, they would release their prize stock to fend for themselves
rather than allow them to starve. For decades, the wild herds
doubled in size every few years, and thousands were captured by
opportunists and sold off for slaughter. Finally, in 1971, Congress
passed the Wild Free-Roaming Horses and Burros Act, which
assigned responsibility for their care to the state Bureau of Land
Management. Today, the BLM manages the rangeland so it
is able to support the herds, and makes sure that sick and injured
animals are cared for. Every year, they also gather in hundreds of
healthy horses and burros (donkeys) and find permanent homes for
them under the hugely successful "Adopt-a-Horse" program.

The midwest

SOMETIMES CALLED "HEARTLAND US," the midwestern region includes the legendary plains that roll across states like Nebraska and North and South Dakota, the fertile farming lands that typify Kansas, Idaho, Iowa, Oklahoma, and Wisconsin, and the Great Lakes' states lying farther east, with their huge industrial centers.

TWIN CITIES

Spanning the Mississippi River, the Minnesota cities of Minneapolis and St Paul are collectively known as the Twin Cities. Traditionally called "the last city of the east," St. Paul sits directly opposite Minneapolis (shown here), "the first city of the west."

Iowa is a predominantly agricultural state containing hundreds of small farming communities like this one.

ALL THAT JAZZ

The establishment of a strong jazz and blues culture in the midwestern cities came from the African American migration from the southern states in the 1920s. Here, the tradition is carried on in a Chicago jazz club.

TORNADO ALLEY

The region between the Rocky and Appalachian Mountains frequently experiences tornadoes. "Tornado Alley" is not defined clearly but runs from Texas in the south, through Oklahoma, Kansas, Nebraska, and east South Dakota. Twisters form when cold dry air, warm dry air, and moist air meet. People here practice drills and have warning systems in place for when a tornado forms.

Farming country

The image of the agricultural midwest is so firmly established that it has its own place in popular culture: Rodgers and Hammerstein's *Oklahoma* celebrates corn that grows "as high as an elephant's eye," while the farmlands of Kansas play a featured part in both *The Wizard* of Oz and *Little House on the Prairie*.

MAJOR CROPS

Although a wide range of crops is grown in this area, the three most important are wheat, soybeans, and corn. Historical evidence suggests that grain has been planted here since about 1840.

1 Wheat
Kansas—"the wheat state"—is the country's leading producer of the grain, with roughly one third of the state's farms devoted to this crop alone.

2 Soybeans
More than a third of the world soybean crop comes from the United States, and most of this is grown in the Midwest. This large farm is in Wisconsin.

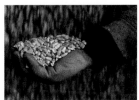

3 Corn
Around 60 percent of the corn grown worldwide comes from the midwest region, a huge strip of which is known as "the Corn Belt."

DAIRY FARMING

Widely known as "Dairyland," Wisconsin produces huge quantities of milk. In addition to milk, vast amounts of butter and cheese are made here, often by farming families descended from the Swedish and German immigrants who poured into the state at the end of the 19th century.

Organic farming as practiced by these Wisconsin-based enthusiasts is the fastest-growing agricultural sector in the country.

ONLY

ONLY

Alaska
LIVING IN THE NORTHERNMOST PART OF THE US

THE ARCTIC IS AN UNLIKELY PLACE FOR PEOPLE TO LIVE. The extreme weather and temperature conditions make it very difficult to survive there. The first people to master survival and the art of living off the land in these extreme conditions included the Aleuts, Inupiat and Yuit, Athabascans, Tlingit, and Haida. Life for the people, however, started to change following the purchase of Alaska by the US in 1867. In the 20th century, technology made it possible for others to live comfortably in Alaska, and people started to arrive when it was discovered that the area was rich in natural oil and gas as well as gold. The oil and mining companies moved in and the trans-Alaska oil pipeline was built, which carries millions of gallons of oil every day across the country. Challenges in Alaska today include protecting the rights of native peoples, as well as the natural environment while moving forward in the modern world.

AMISH

THE PLAIN PEOPLE

THE AMISH HAVE SWISS-GERMAN ANABAPTIST ORIGINS in the 1690s. Closely related to the Mennonites, the Amish order was named after an early leader, Jakob Ammann, who drew up their defining principles, which include: living apart from the world, remaining close to the land, supporting

GETTING AROUND
The Amish are not permitted to own motorized vehicles, so they drive horse and buggies instead of cars. This limits the distance they can travel easily from their stable, fairly insular, communities. If necessary, they will ride in someone else's car to make a journey or take a plane, train, or bus for longer distances.

Home on the farm

Amish people live in small farming communities. Their pretty white homes are cozy and practical, with light, power, and heat from wood or coal stoves, and natural, propane, or bottled gas. There are no private telephones, but groups of neighbors often install a single, communal phone for emergencies.

ALL FOR ONE
When people need a new house or barn, their friends all join together to help them build it.

1 Making plans
Amish Elders plan a barn-building session for a newlywed couple. The construction itself is called a "raising"; the whole gathering is called a "frolic."

2 Team effort
During the morning, neighborhood men assemble the frame of the traditional barn. Amish women contribute by preparing meals for the workers.

3 Final result
Completing a barn can take a week or more, but barn framing itself can be done in a day. Amish barns with their steeply pitched roofs have not changed for a century.

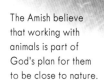

The Amish believe that working with animals is part of God's plan for them to be close to nature.

LIVING ON THE LAND
The Amish work mainly in agriculture or related trades like blacksmithing and saddlery. Although their farm machinery is often modern in design, it is horse powered. Some of the yield they produce is consumed within the community, but much of it is traded with outsiders (or English or Yankees as the Amish call them).

one another, and shunning any form of adornment. This last rule has led to the Amish being known as "the plain people." Seeking religious freedom, the Amish began to migrate to the United States in the early 18th century. Today there are no Amish communities residing in Europe and more than 63 per cent of Amish families still live on farms where their ancestors settled in Pennsylvania, Indiana, and Ohio.

HOME LIFE
Families are often large and closely knit. Discipline is strong, but Amish parents recognize the need for adolescents to see the outside world before choosing the Amish lifestyle. Usually two years long, this is called *rumm-shpringa*, meaning running around.

NIMBLE FINGERS
Apart from fabric and things like underwear and men's shirts and suits, which tend to be bought from specialist stores, an Amish family's clothing is made by the women. Their sewing machines are powered by treadle rather than electricity. The Amish are also known for their patchwork and quilting skills—their quilts are highly prized and sold to bring in extra money.

Young girls learn how to sew from their mothers.

Amish clothing is plain and dark. Children dress similarly to their parents.

LEARNING BY EXPERIENCE
Children go to Amish schools until they're about 14. After that, they gain the skills they need through training on the job: boys are apprenticed on a farm or in a workshop; girls work at home.

American Indians

EXPERTS AGREE THAT THE NATIVE PEOPLES OF North America originally came from Siberia, trekking across an Ice-Age land

THE FIRST INHABITANTS OF THE US

BRAVE WORDS

In World War II, Navajo radio operators used their language (Diné) as a code, and the enemy never broke it. Here "code talker" Dan Akee displays his Congressional Medal of Honor. Today, Navajo is the most commonly spoken of the remaining American Indian languages.

Proud nations

American Indians are usually categorized according to the regions they first settled: Plains, Northeast Woodlands, Southwest, and others. Within each category, there are a number of separate groups, or nations. Across the country though, these groups are linked by a pride in their heritage, and a fierce determination to keep their cultures alive.

PAINTING IN THE SAND

As part of their healing ritual, the Navajo people of the Southwest create delicate and beautiful sand paintings. Once, these were destroyed as soon as they were created, but now many are preserved, or their designs captured on special rugs and textiles.

PRESERVING HERITAGE

Part of the Smithsonian Institution museum complex on the National Mall, the National Museum of the American Indian (NMAI, see left) has an amazing collection of Native artifacts but also hosts many interactive events, educational programs and offsite traveling exhibitions. The NMAI brings together the narratives and objects of the many American Indian nations and they have had a voice in the planning and now the programming of the museum.

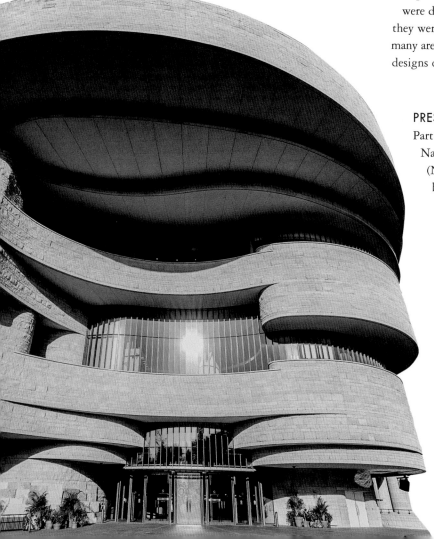

Navajo craftspeople make intricate silver-and-turquoise jewelry and weave brightly colored textiles.

bridge to present-day Alaska. Later, they spread across the continent and formed separate groups. Today, people of American Indian origin are integrated into wider society. Some American Indian people live on reservations where they can also practice ancestral rituals and customs in shared communities. Many create beautiful traditional crafts, which they sell to the public as a way of earning a living.

IMAGE AND REALITY
With the Cheyenne, the Sioux Nation defeated the 7th US Cavalry at Little Big Horn in 1876, killing their leader, General Custer. This famous battle was soon followed by revenge when the US Cavalry massacred the Sioux at Wounded Knee. These iconic battles have inspired many Hollywood movies and the images of Indians in movies are often based on these Plains people.

WEARING THE PAST
Historical Sioux dress involves many of the elements associated with American Indian clothing: feathered headdresses, fringed leather, beadwork, quillwork, and moccasins. Today, most American Indians wear casual clothing for every day, and save their full regalia for ceremonial occasions or tourist display.

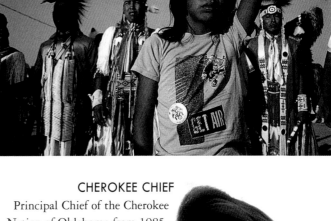

PRINCIPAL PEOPLE
Native to the Southeast region, the Cherokee Nation—who, in their own language, call themselves the "principal people"—practice a number of traditional crafts. Perhaps the best known is the making of patterned baskets, but they are also skilled potters, carvers, and weavers.

CHEROKEE CHIEF
Principal Chief of the Cherokee Nation of Oklahoma from 1985 to 1995, Wilma Mankiller was the first female in modern history to lead a major American Indian people. Her family name is an old military title given to the honored figure entrusted with protecting a Cherokee village. She died in 2010.

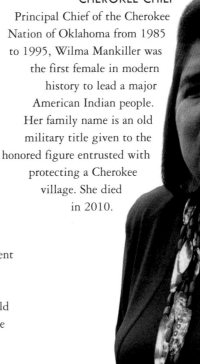

LIVING HISTORY
This recreated Cherokee settlement in North Carolina is a popular tourist attraction, and helps the people preserve their centuries-old heritage. Here, a young Cherokee girl uses traditional skills and designs to weave a collection of colorful belts.

THERE ARE MORE PEOPLE IN MEXICO THAN in any other

MEXICANS

Spanish-speaking country in the world, including Spain, and its population continues to increase rapidly. Of

MULTI-COLOURED CULTURE

the total number, about 60 percent

New World mix

In common with much of South America, Mexico has a culture that blends influences from its indigenous population with those of the Spanish who defeated the Aztecs and colonized the country during the 16th century. Mexico remained under Spanish rule for 300 years, achieving total independence only in 1821.

LOOKING TOWARD THE PAST
Deceptively modern in feel, these shops in the city of Oaxaca have been built in an early colonial style distinguished by simple shapes, flat roofs, and wide doors and windows with contrasting borders.

ART FOR ALL

During the 20th century, Mexican artists led a movement to bring art to the people by putting it on public buildings. This mosaic, on the University Library in Mexico City, tells the pre-Hispanic history of Mexico.

Locals like to buy fresh fruit and vegetables daily at markets such as this one in Merida, Yucatan.

are of Amerindian and Spanish descent, 20 percent are American Indian, and 10 percent are European. Mexico was one of the cradles of early agriculture and raising crops has been an important part of life until recent years. Today, relatively few people in Mexico are involved in agriculture; some work in industry, while more than half of the population are employed in the service sector.

INDUSTRY
Vehicles and electronic equipment are two of Mexico's top exports to the US. Parts are assembled in this small southern factory.

WEAVING
Many traditional textiles are woven on backstrap looms, named for the belt support that fits around the weaver's waist.

THE CULTURE OF THE HORSE
Mexican horsemen are called *charros,* and their special skills and rituals are known as *charrería. Charreadas* are rodeo-style events that involve impressive displays of horsemanship, and related skills like lassoing from the saddle, all performed in elaborate costume.

Today, most performing *charros* are wealthy ranchers.

MARIACHI MUSIC
Often associated with romance (the name comes from the French word for marriage), *mariachi* bands date from the 19th century. They play at weddings and parties, and ardent suitors hire them to serenade their *enamoradas* (lovers).

FAMILY LIFE
Mexican families tend to be large, and extended family members all living under the same roof for financial benefit. Today many women work outside the home and with paid or family help, also maintain the household.

THE DAY OF THE DEAD
According to ancient Amerindian belief, the dead come back to visit their loved ones on one day each year: *Día de los Muertos,* or Day of the Dead. Despite strong efforts, the Spanish were unable to destroy this belief or the rituals associated with it, but they did give it a Catholic veneer by moving it to All Saints' Day, November 1. Here, a family group keeps a graveside vigil on that day.

CANADIANS

A CULTURAL MOSAIC

CANADA IS THE SECOND-LARGEST COUNTRY in the world and has a strong national and cultural identity of its own. Apart from bountiful natural resources, stunning landscapes, and a famously tolerant, law-abiding

Mix and blend

Most Canadians are of English, Scottish, Irish, or French descent but immigration still brings in new ethnicities from around the world. There are large Italian, German, and Chinese communities established here, along with those of native (First Nation) groups and other cultures. Canada has two official languages, English and French, and is proud of its multicultural mix of peoples.

PLAYING TO WIN
While lacrosse is Canada's national sport, ice hockey inspires a public passion that makes it top unofficial contender. Here, with the speed and energy that characterize the game, a Canadian player competes against the USSR in the Calgary Olympics.

INDUSTRIAL STRENGTH
During the 20th century, manufacturing overtook agriculture and the exploitation of natural resources to dominate Canada's economy. Here, a skilled worker adjusts components at a Ford car plant in Ontario.

CITY FISHING
With the Vancouver skyline as a backdrop, two intrepid fishermen position their nets in English Bay, near the city center. Canada's waters, both inland and coastal, are ideal for fishing, a hugely popular recreational activity as well as an important commercial venture.

A TASTE OF EUROPE

In the province of Quebec, not only the language is French; the culture and the urban landscapes that support it also feel very European. This typical street scene in the old part of Quebec City, for example, could almost be set somewhere in France.

society, it offers one of the highest standards of living anywhere in the world. Canada was first colonized in the 17th and 18th centuries by France and Britain. While both influences are evident today,

modern Canada is a parliamentary democracy and a member of the British Commonwealth, with Queen Elizabeth II as its head of state. The maple leaf is its national symbol.

GROWTH INDUSTRY

Lumber is one of Canada's most important natural resources; for the western province of British Columbia, lumber (and related trades like the pulp-and-paper business) constitutes the main industry.

1 Tree felling
On Lyell Island, in BC's Queen Charlotte group, a logger cuts down a large tree. Evergreen trees from British Columbia make up about half of all Canada's lumber.

2 Cheap transportation
Felled logs are usually transported to the timber or paper mill by water. Here, the driver of a "winder boat" rounds up loose logs on their way for processing.

3 Cutting up
Instead of being transported to a mill, cut tree trunks are sometimes trimmed into posts or planks on a portable sawmill taken to the forestry site.

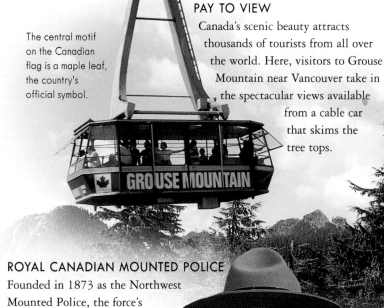

The central motif on the Canadian flag is a maple leaf, the country's official symbol.

PAY TO VIEW

Canada's scenic beauty attracts thousands of tourists from all over the world. Here, visitors to Grouse Mountain near Vancouver take in the spectacular views available from a cable car that skims the tree tops.

ROYAL CANADIAN MOUNTED POLICE

Founded in 1873 as the Northwest Mounted Police, the force's "Royal" title was conferred in 1904. In 1920, their responsibilities were expanded to include the enforcement of federal laws countrywide, and they became the RCMP. Today, the familiar uniform is purely ceremonial.

MUSICAL RIDE

Developed in 1908, Mounties performed their first formal show in front of the Prince of Wales displaying their riding skills of intricate figures choreographed to music. Today this display is performed across the country during the summer.

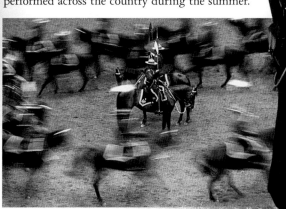

Toronto

CANADA'S COSMPOLITAN HUB

TORONTO'S STRIKING SKYLINE TOWERS OVER THE SHORES of Lake Ontario. Canada's largest city has nearly 3 million inhabitants and is one of the most cosmopolitan in the world. It has attracted immigrants throughout its history and today around half of the population belongs to ethnic minority groups. While there are significant Chinese and South Asian populations, no single group dominates. This diversity is reflected in the city's districts such as Little India, Chinatown, Greektown, and Little Jamaica. Although Canada is officially bilingual, few Torontonians speak French at home as their main language. Around 200 languages are spoken in the city, including Chinese and Italian, but English is the most widely spoken.

FIRST NATIONS

CANADA'S NATIVE PEOPLES

modern-day Canada, only about four percent identify as aboriginal. This category is divided into three: the First

The world of the Iroquois

The Iroquois are a federation of First Nations people (Mohawk, Oneida, Cayuga, Onondaga, Seneca, and Tuscarora) who originally inhabited the forests of the northeastern United States and southeastern Canada. Today, more than half live in Canada. The Iroquois call themselves *Haudenosaunee*, meaning "people of the longhouse," after their large, traditional dwellings.

BADGES OF HONOR
Two generations of Mohawks attend a traditional ceremony. Although historically Iroquois men wear feathers as a badge of their nation, the style of headdress (and shirt) shown here is usually associated with Plains Indians. Today, many groups have adopted Plains dress to express their pan-Indian identity.

SIX NATIONS POW WOW
Throughout much of North America, the pow wow—a festive meeting between the members of one or more nations—is a native tradition. This one, held at the Six Nations Iroquois Reserve near Brantford, Ontario, features all the singing, dancing, feasting, and color that characterize these celebrations.

ANCIENT SPORT
The ancient Iroquois game of *tewaarathon*, known as lacrosse, is widely enjoyed in many countries. Today, the Iroquois Nationals are the only indigenous team in the world to take part in international sporting competition.

Nations (like the Haida and the Tlingit in the northwest, and the Iroquois, Algonquin, and Cree in the central and eastern regions; the Métis, a mixed-race group that originated from unions between French-Canadian fur traders and indigenous women; and the Inuit in the north. All have very distinctive cultures, but they share a strong bond and pride in their indigenous heritage.

WITHOUT FEAR

Since many apparently lack a fear of heights, Iroquois men often work on building sites. Iroquois crews have helped build such celebrated projects as the Empire State Building, the Golden Gate Bridge, and the world's tallest free-standing structure—the CN Tower in Toronto (left).

Haida life

The Haida have always had rich natural food resources, enabling them to trade with other groups. Elaborate social ceremonies, many concerned with skills and status, developed between trading groups. Today some Haida people are skilled artists while many work in commercial fisheries or ecotourism.

BUTTON BLANKETS

These Haida dancers wear ceremonial button blankets, which were once made by sewing shell fragments onto blankets traded from the Europeans. Now, bought buttons and blankets fulfill the same functions.

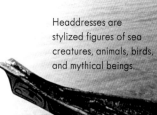

Headdresses are stylized figures of sea creatures, animals, birds, and mythical beings.

TOTEM POLES

For the native people who make them, totem poles are important cultural and historical documents. They are created to record a family's history, or to mark significant milestones like the death of a leader.

1 Carving
The animals carved on a totem tend to be mythical figures that represent families or clans. Human figures often portray the pole's owner.

2 Painting
The totem poles made by the Haida feature some of the most beautiful and intricate painting of all indigenous Northwestern peoples.

3 Raising
The heavy poles are hauled upright by large groups of people. They use four sets of ropes in each direction, and a supporting X-frame.

FLOATING TREES

The Haida also carve and paint beautiful dugout canoes, which they once traded to other Pacific-coast peoples. The giant cedars that make the best canoes grow in the Queen Charlotte Islands off British Columbia. The Haida know this territory—their homeland—as *Haida Gwaii*—"islands of the people."

INUIT

THE RETURN OF "OUR LAND"

IN 1999 THE CANADIAN GOVERNMENT GAVE BACK part of the Northwest Territories to the Inuit. The new land, called Nunavut, which means "our land," has been occupied by the Inuit for 4,000 years. For centuries the Inuit lived

IGLOOLIK

Igloolik is a small town on an island in Foxe Basin. In 1932 the Hudson Bay Trading Company built the town as a trading post and the Inuit were lured away from their nomadic settlements to the western luxuries of the town. Although you can eat western food, even junk food, in Igloolik, they still like to rely on meat from the land, such as caribou (wild reindeer), walrus, seal, whale, and birds.

LANGUAGE—INUKTITUT

The Inuit language, *Inuktitut*, is widely used in the North with varying dialects. In *Inuktitut* there are 125 different words for snow and ice! This is actually essential when snow conditions are vital for survival.

Inuktitut characters	Inuktitut word	Meaning
ᐊᐳᑦ	aput	snow
ᓯᑯ	siku	ice
ᖃᓐᓂᖅ	qanniq	falling snow
ᐱᖅᓯᖅ	piqsiq	snow lift by wind (blizzard)
ᐊᐅᕕᖅ	auviq	snow ideal for igloos

Here are some familiar *Inuktitut* words:

Igloo—house

Anorak—windproof coat

Kayak—long, thin boat suitable for one person

CARIBOU SPOOKS

The Inuit sometimes build a structure, called an *Inukshuk* (see right), on raised ground to help them navigate. They also use it as a caribou spook in the hope that the caribou will think it is a man and run in the opposite direction, toward the hunter.

THE IGLOO MYTH

Contrary to popular belief, the Inuit do not live in igloos. The snow houses that we know as igloos are only temporary shelters for hunters. However, igloo actually means "house" in *Inuktitut* so technically they do live in igloos!

1 **Building an igloo** The hunter must find a site containing snow that is perfect for making an igloo. Blocks of snow of the same size are cut using a snow knife.

2 **Starting the wall** The skillful builder stands the bottom blocks upright, slightly leaning inward. He shapes and fits each block, so that there are no gaps between them.

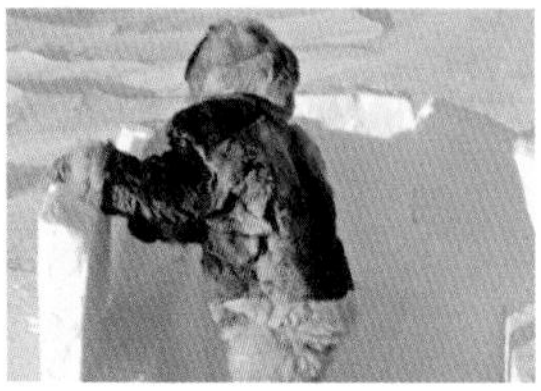

3 **The finished shelter** As the walls rise, the angle of each block increases, and a large fitted cap-block completes the domelike structure.

without much outside contact and developed a tough way of life that suited their frozen environment. Since their integration into the political structure of Canada, their lives have modernized in many aspects.

However, the Inuit make efforts to keep their traditions—old beliefs combine with Christianity, dogsleds run alongside skidoos, and raw meat is eaten along with prepacked meals.

The modern hunt

The Inuit still hunt out on the ice for valuable meat and fur, and can be away from home for a month or more. They use snowmobiles or dogsleds, and guns. The hunters talk to each other over radios, known as *uvaq*, which means "over," named after the word they heard so often during transmissions.

ON THIN ICE
The hunter takes a flat-bottomed boat out onto the ice floe so that when he has shot an animal in the water he can paddle to retrieve it. It is essential to use a boat because the ice can break up easily.

An igloo may keep out some cold, but in temperatures of -40°F (-40°C), the inside will still be a chilly 14°F (-10°C).

LIFE ON THE LAND
It is a difficult and not very prosperous life as a full-time hunter. However, there are some families who have returned to the land to live in camps all year round. The Canadian Government now helps financially in an effort to try to regain some of the Inuit traditions.

MOST OF THE PEOPLE WHO LIVE ON THE WORLD'S biggest island

GREENLANDERS

(it's more than three times the size of Texas) are descended from

MODERN LIFE IN A FROZEN WORLD

Inuit groups and from

Proud land

Although it's part of Denmark, Greenland has had wide-ranging powers of self-rule since 1979. Elected every four years, the Greenlandic parliament, called the *Landsting*, oversees most domestic legislation, including the country's modern and efficient health, welfare, and education systems.

MIXED FEELINGS

On the first day of school, children wave their national flag—the flag of Denmark. Greenland is very dependent on Denmark: most of its money comes from the Danish government, who also run its foreign affairs and legal system. Some people resent this, though, and want their country to be totally independent.

SUMMER CRAFT

Hunting is an important industry in Greenland. Some Inuits still catch seals, walruses, and small whales from traditional boats called kayaks. To make them light enough for one man to carry, these were originally covered with seal skin. Today, this has been replaced by plastic-coated canvas.

RELIABLE TRANSPORTATION

These strong huskie dogs are harnessed up to pull an old-fashioned sled. While snowmobiles are sometimes used to travel across icy terrain, they are not allowed in many places because the noise they make frightens animals and scares away game. For this reason, and because machines tend to break down and run out of fuel, traditional transportation is often the best.

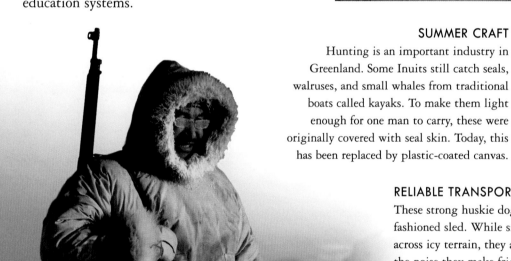

RULES OF HUNTING

Federal law dictates which animals can be hunted with guns. Hunters, who are mainly Inuit (Greenlandic Inuit are called *Inughuit*) cannot shoot narwhal, for instance, but they can shoot *nanuq*, the great polar bear. There are also limits on the numbers that can be killed. Such legislation not only protects species, it acknowledges the Inuit view that animals have spirit owners who demand respect.

Scandinavians: Greenland is a largely self-governing territory owned by Denmark. Since almost all the land is permanently covered with thick ice, only about 57,000 people live there, mainly scattered along the southernwest fringe. Greenland has two official languages: Danish and Greenlandic, an Inuit dialect peppered with Danish words. Many locals, however, feel strongly that only Greenlandic should be recognized.

COMMUNITY LIFE

Greenlanders live mainly in urban centers like the pretty harbor town of Ilulissat. Within each town or city, there are conventional roads, but these do not usually link one center with another—people travel long distances by air. Housing is modern and well insulated, and shopping is done in ordinary supermarkets. Most produce is imported, however, and meat from seabirds, seals, and whales is sold alongside beef and lamb.

FISHY PROFITS

Greenland's fishing industry produces 95 percent of its commercial revenue. There are more than 200 species of fish and seafood in the island's waters, but the principal trade is in cold-water shrimp and halibut. Fishermen sell most of their produce through wholesale companies like this one, where halibut is being packed for shipment.

HISTORIC CRAFT

Greenland attracts large numbers of tourists, many of whom take home traditional *tupilak* figures carved by the Inuit from soapstone, caribou antler, or whale tooth. Typical examples like these represent mythical creatures from Inuit legend.

COLORFUL CLOTHING

Greenlandic dress is one of the few national costumes that involve long pants for women. Featuring intricate motifs, beading, and sometimes even lace, the outfit always includes high boots: white ones for young unmarried girls, red for those who are married, and blue or yellow for older women.

The People of Central America & the Caribbean

THE NARROW LAND MASS and the sprinkling of islands that lie between North and South America are home to a wide variety of peoples. Most of them are are a mix of indigenous peoples and later arrivals.

Red, gold, and green are the colors of Rastafarianism.

RASTAFARIANS

The ancestors of today's Afro-Caribbeans were taken to the islands from Africa as slaves. The Rastafarian religion, founded in Jamaica in 1930, includes the belief that Emperor Haile Selassie of Ethiopia is the Messiah, and that his followers will one day return to their homeland. The word Rastafarian comes from "Ras Tafari," Haile Selassie's given name.

PANAMA CANAL

Opened on August 15, 1914, the Panama Canal took nearly 8,000 miles (13,000 km) off the journey from New York to San Francisco, and brought money and jobs to Central America. Its construction, paid for by the US and France, took 34 years and more than 30,000 lives were lost.

COLONIAL AND CONTEMPORARY

Most large cities in Central America blend the modern and their historic past with hallmarks of the modern world such as glass-walled buildings and massive public sculptures. Shown here is downtown San José, the capital city of Costa Rica.

Danger in paradise

The beautiful Caribbean islands (this idyllic beach is in Cuba) attract
thousands of visitors and tourism is a major part of local economies.
The same landscapes are also vulnerable to severe weather conditions
such as hurricanes, which can destroy lives and property.

The islands of the Caribbean
feature white sandy beaches
fringed with graceful palm trees.

HOME AND AWAY

British colonists introduced
the game of cricket to the
islands they settled. In
Barbados, West Indian
players like these, are now
among the best in the world.

GROWING THINGS

A wide range of fruit
and vegetables is grown in
the region. Some of this
produce is sold for export,
but much of it ends up
in colorful street markets
like this one on Grand
Bahama Island.

CELEBRATION

Catholicism is the dominant
religion in Central America.
To celebrate Good Friday in
Antigua, Guatemala, the
streets are covered with
alfombras, or "carpets" made
from painted sawdust.

MAKING MUSIC

This region has produced some of the most influential musical
styles of recent years, from the ranchera sounds of Central
America, to styles as diverse as mambo,
rumba, calypso, and reggae from the
West Indies. This traditional steel-
drum band is performing in
Soufriere, Saint Lucia.

Steel drums evoke
the Caribbean
wherever they're
played.

CRÉOLES

TROPICAL MIX

THE ORIGINAL INHABITANTS OF THE WEST INDIES WERE the Carib Indians (after whom the Caribbean Sea was named). Apart from isolated pockets, however, they have long since disappeared, and today the islands are populated mainly by the descendents of unions

COLORFUL CAPITAL
In 2010, a terrible earthquake took the lives of some 230,000 people in Haiti and destroyed many buildings, including this Roman Catholic cathedral in the capital, Port-au-Prince. Clearly European in style, the exterior was painted a bright tropical pink.

Best of both worlds
Créole society reflects both French and African culture. Buildings tend to be European in style, with distinctively tropical touches. On the whole, clothing has a conventional western look that is often interpreted in brilliant sunshine hues. The Créole language is an expressive blend of dialects brought by the ancestors from Africa with French vocabulary.

SPECIAL DAY
Decked out in frothy white dresses with gloves and veils, these young girls in St. Lucia pose proudly for the camera on the day they take their first communion. Catholicism is the dominant religion in the French West Indies, and people take great pride in observing its rites.

SPIRITS OF THE PAST
A follower of the Vodun religion performs a ritual dance. Strongly associated with Haiti, Vodun arrived with West-African slaves. Vodun means "spirit" in the Fon and Ewe languages of West Africa. Followers believe in a supreme god, the creator of the universe, along with lesser deities. In Vodun, female and male priests lead the people and assist in healing.

CASH AND CARRY
Many Créole people are very poor, and women regularly walk for days to sell their wares at the nearest market, bearing heavy loads on their head all the way. These Haitian pedlars in Port-au-Prince have high hopes of selling their precariously stacked supplies of plastic basins and household towels.

between colonists who arrived there in the 15th century and African slaves. The word "creole" originally referred to anyone of European parentage born in the New World. Now, of its several different meanings, the most common, spelled Créole, refers to the people of this heritage who live in the French West Indies (such as St. Lucia, Martinique, Guadaloupe, Dominica, and Haiti), and whose colorful culture reflects their dramatic past.

CREOLE SOUNDS

Music is an integral part of Créole culture, and many local rhythms have become popular worldwide: zouk and beguine from Martinique and Guadaloupe, for example, and meringué from Haiti and Dominica. Another dominant musical style is American jazz, as interpreted with a strong Caribbean flavor by this small but enthusiastic band in Guadaloupe.

TABLE TOURNAMENT

Créole men take their dominoes seriously and often play for money. Here, intense concentration shows on the faces of both competitors and observers at an outdoor match in St. Lucia.

SEDUCTIVE LANDSCAPES

The islands of the West Indies are actually the tops of underwater—often volcanic—mountains. Because of this, the landscape of each one consists of central hills or highlands that slope down to lush coastal plains ending in white sandy beaches. These attract visitors from all over the world, and the resulting tourism is one of the two most important industries in the region; the other is farming.

Exotic blooms that grow wild in the Caribbean provide this young girl with all the carnival finery she needs.

SPRINGTIME CELEBRATIONS

Virtually every Créole island supports its own colorful carnival involving parades, street parties, costumes, masks, dancing, and feasting. Although preparations begin in January, the festivities themselves are crowded into the few days just before Lent. These happy children are all ready to take part in one of the carnival processions on Guadaloupe.

Traveling by tap-tap

THE PAINTED BUSES OF HAITI

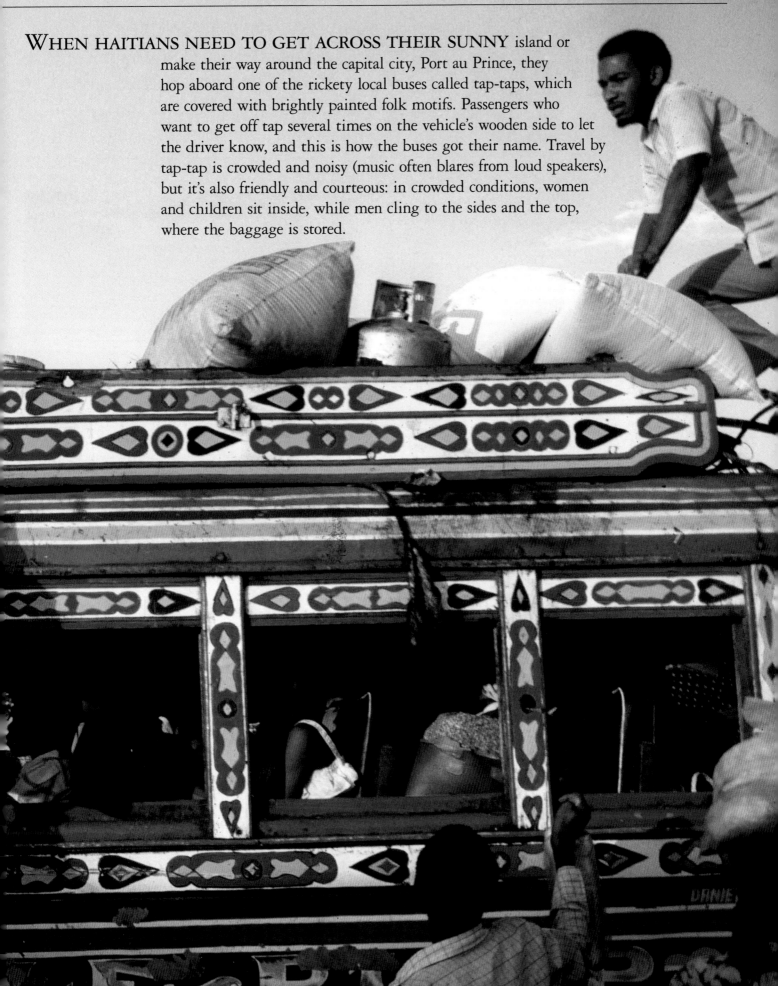

WHEN HAITIANS NEED TO GET ACROSS THEIR SUNNY island or make their way around the capital city, Port au Prince, they hop aboard one of the rickety local buses called tap-taps, which are covered with brightly painted folk motifs. Passengers who want to get off tap several times on the vehicle's wooden side to let the driver know, and this is how the buses got their name. Travel by tap-tap is crowded and noisy (music often blares from loud speakers), but it's also friendly and courteous: in crowded conditions, women and children sit inside, while men cling to the sides and the top, where the baggage is stored.

MISKITU

EMBRACING OTHER WAYS

WHILE SOME GROUPS (SUCH AS THE KOGI IN SOUTH AMERICA) value cultural purity, the Miskitu people of Central America are almost defined by the exotic mix of peoples they've absorbed. Originating from unions between Indians and Afro-

People of the coast

The Miskitu make their home along the Caribbean coast of Nicaragua and Honduras. This territory, known as the Mosquito Coast, is rich in natural resources, yet the people are poor, and many make their living from subsistence farming, fishing, and hunting. They have their own language, also called Miskitu, and many people speak English and Spanish as well.

MISKITU CAYS
These groups of small cays (islands) off the coast also belong to the Miskitu. People don't live on them, but they regularly hunt for turtles, collect coconuts, and shelter from stormy seas there.

In this coastal village, dugout canoes are lined up along the beach.

TURTLE PEOPLE
The Miskitu were once known as the "turtle people" and green turtles are still a major source of food. Hunters kill them on the beach and leave the tide to wash them clean. These turtles are for domestic consumption only— exporting them is illegal.

FAMILY LIFE
Most Miskitu families live in villages. Men do most of the farming and fishing, with women lending help when they can. Children sometimes collect fruit and seafood when it is easily available.

Caribbeans, the Miskitu are an assimilating people—they choose partners from a variety of groups, and consider any children to be Miskitu. During the 1800s, Moravian missionaries brought Protestantism to the people, and this is still the main religion. The origin of the name Miskitu is uncertain. Oral tradition among the Miskitu points to a warrior chief named Miskut, who settled with his people in this area long ago.

BUILDING A TRADITIONAL HOUSE
All Miskitu men know how to build a house, since few women would marry a man without this skill. To protect their families from the region's frequent flooding, they usually build their homes on stilts.

1 Making planks
To prepare the lumber, large pine logs are hoisted up onto a platform. A two-man team then uses a long saw to cut each log into planks.

2 Roofing material
Women gather a special kind of palm leaf called *papta* that is used for thatch. When they get to the site, they will tie it into bundles for the men to work with.

3 Taking shape
At this point in the construction process, the frame is up and work has begun on one of the walls. During the dry season, the roof can safely be left until last.

COOL AND DRY
Miskitu houses allow plenty of cool air to flow underneath, across the open porch, and through the windows. Simple shutters swivel into place when it is cold or rainy.

Traditional buildings have thatched roofs like this one, but some modern homes are roofed with zinc.

MAKING A LIVING
Traditionally, the Miskitu relied on natural resources and trade for their livelihood. Now, they depend more on wage labor, which can be difficult to find.

WORK AND PLAY
These boys from the village of Awastara are playing marbles. Children help with household chores, fishing, and farming and many do not have access to secondary education.

CROWNING THE KING
In the 17th century, inspired by the English, the Miskitu created their own king; called Jeremy I, he was crowned in 1687. The last king was deposed by the army in 1894. Today, to commemorate their royal line, many communities crown a symbolic king for one day a year.

KUNA

FRAGMENTS OF A LOST WORLD

AMONG THE LAST OF THE INDIGENOUS PEOPLES who once populated the Panama coast, the Kuna people now live mainly in the islands of the nearby San Blas archipelago. Some elements of their culture are probably of ancient origin; reflecting a

Independent nation

The land inhabited by the Kuna people is known as the Comarca of Kuna Yala ("Kuna Yala" means "Kuna Land"). Since 1938, it has been a self-governing area within the country of Panama, making this the first indigenous group in modern Central America to exercise political control over its own territory.

WOMEN'S WORLD

Kuna society places great value on women—female children are highly desired, daughters tend to inherit family houses, and a husband moves in with his wife's family. One clear expression of this attitude is the fact that women's dress is much more elaborate, colorful, and symbolic than men's clothing.

DIVING FOR GOLD

One uniquely modern tradition involves the luxury ships that constantly cruise the Caribbean. Kuna youngsters row out to meet them, and the passengers throw coins in their direction.

Gold nose rings indicate a woman's status.

DANCING WITH THE PAST

The Kuna value tradition highly, and their culture provides customs and rituals for most life events. Often, these customs are passed down the generations through chants and dances.

From the time of puberty, Kuna girls have their arms and legs tightly bound in beaded wrappings.

ISLANDS IN THE SUN

Kuna Yala consists of 365 islands like this one, and a strip of land on the adjacent Atlantic coast. With the help of environmental groups, the Kuna have established a 232-sq mile (600 sq km) forest reserve on their territory.

spiritual relationship with nature, for example, they create sanctuaries for plants and animals, called Galu, near many of their settlements. Other customs though—such as the colorful way they dress—did not emerge until the 19th century. The Kuna have their own language, also called Kuna. Spanish is their second tongue, and some people—mostly those who trade with tourists—speak a few words of English.

LOBSTER FISHING
At one time, lobster provided the Kuna with dietary protein as well as export revenue. Now, supplies are dwindling, and lobster has become so expensive that local people can't afford it.

SUGARCANE
Largely agricultural people, the Kuna farm plots of waterside land. Main crops include coconuts, plantains, bananas, and sugarcane, which this matriarch is processing while she puffs on her traditional pipe.

WOVEN CULTURE
One of the best-known Kuna traditions is the making of colorful *molas*—hand-woven panels appliquéd with beautiful patterns or pictures. Although many of them feature authentic folk-art designs, the craft itself is a relatively modern one, inspired by access to both commercial fabrics and, to some degree, images from Western media.

TRADING IN TRADITION
Molas (which were originally intended to be set into women's blouses) are strongly symbolic of Kuna cultural identity, but they are widely valued too by souvenir-hunting tourists and lovers of textile art. Patterns range from graphic shapes and stylized plants and animals to interpretations of poster images, labels, illustrations, and logos. Resourceful traders use the same technique to produce smaller, more saleable items like bags and pot holders.

MAYA

PRESERVING THE PAST

THE ANCIENT MAYA HAD AN EXCEPTIONALLY SOPHISTICATED

civilization. As well as a hieroglyphic script, a written history, an intricate system of mathematics, impressive arts and crafts, and complex architecture, they devised a three-part interlocking calendar based on astronomy.

The modern way

About seven million Maya live in Central America. Like their ancestors, many of them survive by growing corn or other crops on their land, or by producing woven textiles for sale. In some villages, the men have to leave their families to find work in the cities, or on coffee and cotton plantations in other areas.

Some Maya textile designs are hundreds of years old.

FEEDING THE FAMILY

Corn is an essential crop for the Maya people, and it forms a major part of their diet. This busy mother uses ground corn to make *tortillas* (pancakes) over a wood fire, but it can also be served baked, boiled, and made into bread. Supplementing this basic fare are other vegetables (like beans and squash), fruit, and small amounts of meat and fish.

LIVING LEGENDS

Formed by a group of writers, and based in Chiapas in Mexico, the *Sna Jtz'ibajom* theater company brings Maya myths, legends, and history to life through elaborate plays and puppet shows that tour widely. Their name, *Sna Jtz'ibajom*, means "The House of the Writer."

By the 10th century, their widely spread society had split into smaller groups and these were overpowered by the Spanish colonists a few centuries later. However, Maya people survive into the 21st century, maintaining an awareness of their heritage and language. Today, there are more than thirty Maya groups in Central America, principally living in Guatemala, Belize, and southern Mexico.

COMING HOME

Typical Maya houses are made of locally available materials like wattle and daub (rubble and clay), plaster, and wood. They are usually painted white. In areas with heavy rainfall, homes have palm- or grass-thatched roofs that are steeply pitched, with overhanging eaves to protect the walls. The small plot of land this cottage stands on is enclosed with a drystone wall and a length of rush fencing.

The front door has a coat of fresh blue-and-white paint.

MAYA MUSIC

The modern marimba, similar to the xylophone, is part of the Maya musical tradition. Originating from a primitive instrument brought to Central America with early African slaves, it was adopted and developed by the indigenous Maya people.

ANCIENT ARCHITECTURE

This limestone temple is located at the ancient site of Chichen Itza on the Yucatan peninsula in Mexico. The city flourished from 950–1200 CE when it was an important cultural center. Today, the site attracts tourists from all over the world.

FANCY FEMALES

These days, Maya men and boys tend to wear plain western clothing, while women's dress reflects decorative historical elements such as bold borders and colorful embroidery. This barefoot mother-and-daughter pair have chosen traditional skirts and blouses in bright cotton fabrics.

Woven checks are a popular choice.

FIRED EARTH

The entire Mexican village of Amatenango is dominated by its famous women potters. Using the local *terra cotta* clay, and passing on skills from mother to daughter, these Maya women have been producing decorative pots and bowls here for centuries.

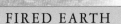

Terra cotta means fired earth.

WINTER FESTIVAL

The people of Chichicastenango, Guatemala, commemorate the arrival of the white man in a ceremonial Dance of the Conquistadors, part of their annual winter-soltice festival. This costumed participant wears the mask of Tecum Uman, last Maya emperor of Guatemala.

THE PEOPLE OF
South America

Latin America *noun* those parts of either American continent where Spanish and Portuguese are the dominant cultures

SOUTH AMERICA

THE CONTINENT OF SOUTH AMERICA COMPRISES 12 countries, plus the dependency of French Guiana. Offshore territories include the Galapagos Islands (Ecuador),

HOME OF THE DISAPPEARING RAIN FOREST

Global position

Joined to Central America by the Isthmus of Panama, South America lies across the equator. Because it is rapidly being destroyed, the vast tropical rain forest around the Amazon River is one of the world's most environmentally sensitive sites.

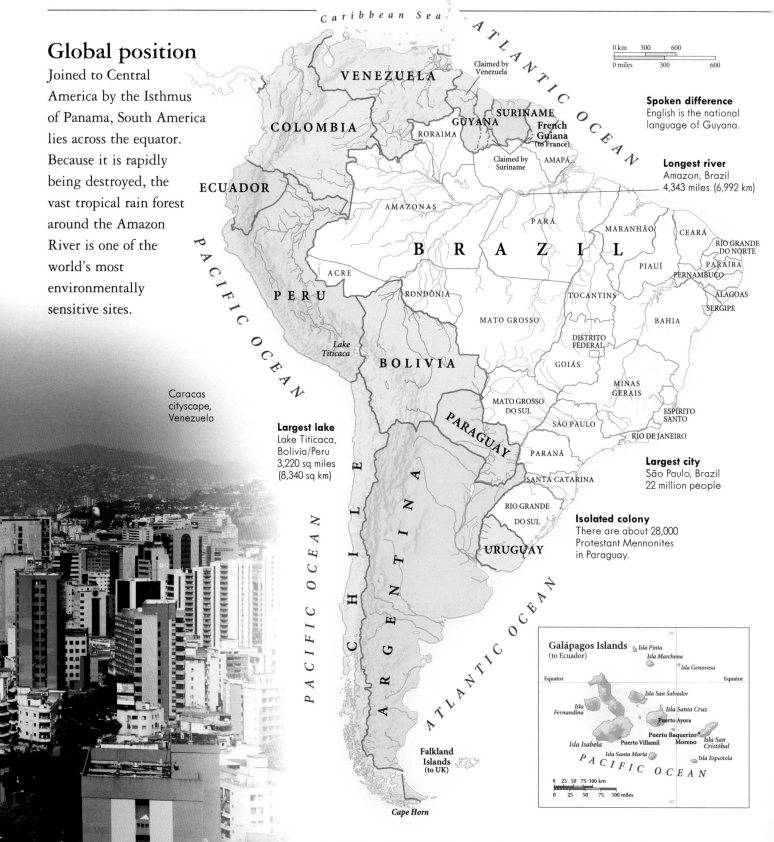

Caracas cityscape, Venezuela

Spoken difference
English is the national language of Guyana.

Longest river
Amazon, Brazil
4,343 miles (6,992 km)

Largest lake
Lake Titicaca,
Bolivia/Peru
3,220 sq miles
(8,340 sq km)

Largest city
São Paulo, Brazil
22 million people

Isolated colony
There are about 28,000 Protestant Mennonites in Paraguay.

0 km 300 600
0 miles 300 600

Caribbean Sea

ATLANTIC OCEAN

VENEZUELA
Claimed by Venezuela
COLOMBIA
SURINAME
GUYANA
RORAIMA
French Guiana (to France)
Claimed by Suriname
AMAPÁ
ECUADOR
AMAZONAS
PARÁ
MARANHÃO
CEARÁ
RIO GRANDE DO NORTE
PARAÍBA
PERNAMBUCO
PIAUÍ
B R A Z I L
ACRE
RONDÔNIA
TOCANTINS
ALAGOAS
SERGIPE
BAHIA
MATO GROSSO
DISTRITO FEDERAL
Lake Titicaca
PERU
GOIÁS
MINAS GERAIS
BOLIVIA
MATO GROSSO DO SUL
ESPÍRITO SANTO
SÃO PAULO
PARAGUAY
PARANÁ
RIO DE JANEIRO
PACIFIC OCEAN
SANTA CATARINA
RIO GRANDE DO SUL
URUGUAY
C H I L E
A R G E N T I N A
PACIFIC OCEAN
ATLANTIC OCEAN
Falkland Islands (to UK)
Cape Horn

Galápagos Islands
(to Ecuador)
Isla Pinta
Isla Marchena
Isla Genovesa
Equator
Isla San Salvador
Isla Fernandina
Isla Santa Cruz
Puerto Ayora
Puerto Baquerizo Moreno
Isla San Cristóbal
Isla Isabela
Puerto Villamil
Isla Santa María
Isla Española
PACIFIC OCEAN
0 25 50 75 100 km
0 25 50 75 100 miles

the Juan Fernández Islands and Easter Island (Chile), the Fernando de Noronha Archipelago (Brazil), and the Falkland Islands, a British dependency claimed by Argentina as the Islas Malvinas. In terms of both size and population, the biggest country is Brazil. Most people in South America are descended from indigenous Indians, Portuguese or Spanish colonists, African slaves, or a mixture of these groups.

Facts and figures

LANGUAGES
Reflecting the region's colonial past, European languages are the most widely spoken. Portuguese dominates in Brazil with 205 million speakers. Across the continent, 182 million people speak Spanish. Indigenous tongues such as Quechua and Guarani are also spoken.

RELIGIONS
South America is unusual in its religious uniformity. Roman Catholicism, another colonial legacy, dominates with 353 million followers. In Andean countries, it is often blended with indigenous beliefs, such as in La Diablada, a carnival in Bolivia, where people dress as devils.

URBAN POPULATION
South America's cities are constantly growing in population. Most of the big urban centres are near the coast. Brazil's largest cities are São Paulo with 22 million inhabitants and Rio de Janeiro, 13 million. Buenos Aires in Argentina has over 3 million.

POPULATION BY COUNTRY
Almost half the continent's population live in Brazil—there are 211 million Brazilians. In contrast, French Guiana has the smallest number of people with just 297,000 inhabitants. Colombia is the second most populated country in South America with 50 million people.

CLIMATE

The climate in South America ranges from warm, wet, tropical around the northern coastlines and the Amazon Basin, to cold and dry in southern Chile and Argentina, as well as high parts of the Andes. The Amazon rain forest is home to more species than anywhere in the world, as well as 350 indigenous peoples.

SOUTH AMERICAN FACTS

PLACES
Number of countries ....12 (plus dependencies)
Highest point ....Cerro Aconcagua,
Argentina, 22,831 ft (6,959 m)
Lowest point ....Valdés Peninsula,
Argentina, -131 ft (-40 m)
Biggest country ......Brazil, 3,227,095 sq miles (8,358,140 sq km)
Smallest country ....French Guiana, 31,737 sq miles (82,200 sq km)

PEOPLE
Total population ....431 million
Proportion living in urban areas 80%

The People of South America

THIS LONG, VAGUELY TRIANGULAR continent was first settled thousands of years ago by adventurous migrants from North America. Descended from the same prehistoric race as the Inuit, First Nations, and American Indian peoples, they wandered across the spectacularly varied landscape they discovered, and eventually inhabited almost every part of it.

HIGHLAND PEOPLE

These Andean shepherds in Bolivia belong to the large Aymara Amerindian group. This people—and their language, which is also called Aymara—live mainly in the highlands of Bolivia, Chile, and Peru.

SPACE-AGE CITY

While many South American cities have a historical look, Brasilia, the capital of Brazil, is a strikingly modern metropolis. Here, a tiny human figure enhances the monumental proportions of the city's Congress and Senate Building, designed by Brazilian architects Oscar Niemeyer and Lucio Costa.

FIGHTING FOR THEIR HOME

The number of people living in isolation from the industrial world is dwindling rapidly. Many of those who are left make their home in the vast Amazon rain forest, which is under serious threat from developers who cut down its trees and plunder the region's natural resources.

This Matses Indian boy lives in a small village near the Galvez River in Peru.

AFRICAN ORIGINS

When the European colonizers arrived (see opposite), they built huge plantations and brought over millions of slaves from Africa to work on them. Large numbers of people descended from slaves still live in many parts of South America, particularly in the northeast.

Of African descent, this mother and child are Maroons from Suriname.

European influences

During the 16th century, the human landscape of South America changed dramatically with the arrival of colonists from southern Europe. Their influence spread quickly and completely, and today many aspects of culture in South America are still dominated by ideas and traditions that originated in Spain and Portugal.

MUSIC
Now an important part of South American music, the guitar was brought over by early Spanish explorers. Their instruments helped them pass the time on long voyages.

LIQUID HISTORY
Early Europeans who settled in South America brought with them wine-making skills from Spain and Portugal. The vines they planted are now the basis of flourishing wine industries in countries such as Chile and Argentina.

LACES AND NETS
The skill of lace making arrived in Brazil with the wives of Portuguese fishermen who settled there. The Portuguese word for lace makers is *rendeiras*.

A MATTER OF FAITH
Roman Catholicism replaced the original belief systems of nearly all the indigenous peoples in South America. This dominance is reflected in the elaborate church architecture that is a feature of virtually every town and city on the continent. Built on the site of an old Inca temple, for example, this cathedral in Cuzco, Peru clearly reflects Spanish influences.

OLD-WORLD DRESS
The traditional clothing worn by Taquile islanders in Lake Titicaca developed from the garments worn by Spanish settlers when they first arrived in Peru.

RELIGIOUS FESTIVAL
Here, the Otavalens of Ecuador gather for worship on Palm Sunday. Their bright costumes constrast dramatically with the jungle of pale green leaves they have brought to church to mark this special day.

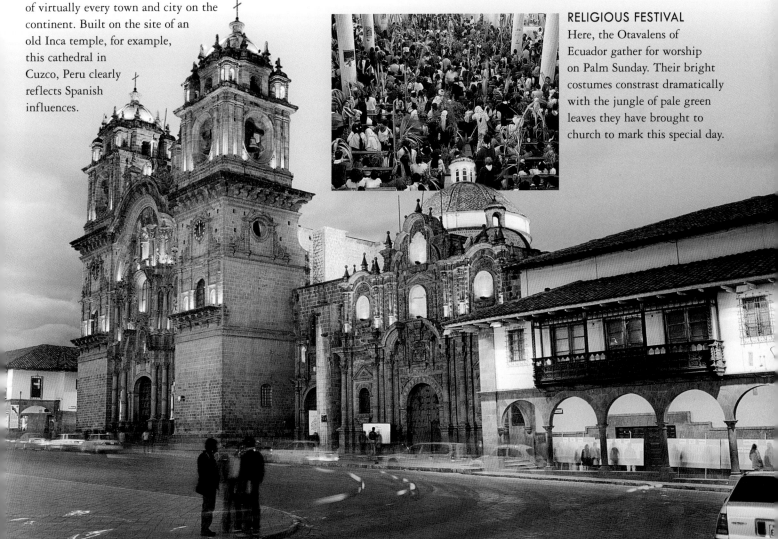

KOGI

GUARDIANS OF OUR WORLD

NATIVES OF THE HIGH SIERRA NEVADA de Santa Marta mountains in northern Colombia, the Kogi are one of the few indigenous Amerindian groups who were not conquered by the Spanish. Descended from the sophisticated Tairona civilization that flourished

MINIATURE WORLD
The 6,600 sq miles (17,000 sq km) of the Sierra Nevada are home to an astonishing variety of ecosystems, from turquoise waters and coral reefs to deserts, plains, rain forests, and glaciers.

ON THE MOVE
Kogi families do not stay in one place, but move between different levels, according to the natural rhythm of the seasons and the fertility of the land. Horses provide the main means of transportation in this steep landscape, which is criss-crossed with narrow paths instead of roads.

The place of creation

The land of the Kogi is set apart from the rest of the continent, in a mountain range near the Caribbean coast. These people have spent centuries exploring the realms of mind, body, and spirit. They believe that if the rest of humanity (what they call the "younger brother") does anything to harm their sacred homeland, then the whole world will be doomed as well.

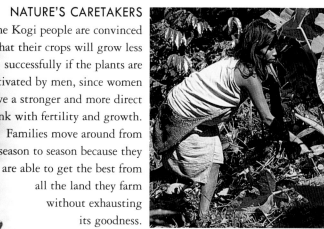

NATURE'S CARETAKERS
The Kogi people are convinced that their crops will grow less successfully if the plants are cultivated by men, since women have a stronger and more direct link with fertility and growth. Families move around from season to season because they are able to get the best from all the land they farm without exhausting its goodness.

SHELL SEEKER
An elder gathers shells on the beach for use in one of the main Kogi rituals: the chewing of coca leaves by adult males. Burned shells produce fine white lime powder. When mixed with leaves and saliva in the mouth, it helps the chemical stimulant in the plant be absorbed.

over 1,000 years ago, the Kogi believe their mountain to be the "place of creation" and "the heart of the world." They see themselves as "elder brothers of humanity," and accept the care of our planet as their sacred responsibility. A deeply spiritual people, they place great value on communicating with everything around them—including animals, plants, and even rocks—by thought and intuition as well as with words and actions.

GUIDES AND RULERS

The leading figures in Kogi life are called "mamas" (from "*mamos*" meaning sun)—they are always male. Acting as healers, priests, and judges, these figures are chosen from birth. They undergo 18 years of training, much of it spent in caves, where they are deprived of daylight. This mama is holding a *poporo*—a hollowed-out gourd used to hold lime powder.

SYMBOLIC BUILDINGS

The construction of Kogi huts is closely linked with the people's spirituality. For instance, because their belief system states that the universe has nine levels, every roof has nine layers of thatch, which are meticulously laid in alternating directions.

SHOPPING BAGS

Kogi women grow cactus fiber, then weave it into bags called *mochilas*. Worn slung across the chest by the men, these bags hold coca leaves, which are shared with other men as part of the greeting ritual.

SEPARATE LIVES

Kogi families gather in villages when they want to exchange news or make community decisions. When they are there, the men spend much of their time in the nuhue ("men's house" or "world house"), the largest and finest building. Even when they are working their land, Kogi families live separately—the men in one hut, and women and children in another one close by.

OTAVALENS

TUCKED HIGH IN THE ECUADORIAN ANDES, the valley town of Otavalo has been attracting visitors to its market for hundreds of years. The local people, known as Otavalens, speak Quichua, one of the languages of the old

TRADITIONAL TRADERS

A lasting culture

The Otavalens have prospered through the commercial availability of fine, colorful woven textiles they sell at markets in the northern Andes mountains. They have kept a powerful sense of their own identity. Not only their language but also their houses, their clothing, their crafts, and their basic culture are rooted in native tradition.

TEAM SPIRIT

Working outdoors on a simple elevated frame, these country laborers are using a two-man handsaw to turn huge eucalyptus logs into long, straight planks. The lumber they are producing is intended for the roofs of village houses in the Otavalo valley.

Otavalan men dress their hair in a long braid or *shimba* that hangs down almost to their waist.

HOME COOKING

Ecuador is a fertile land whose rich soil nourishes a plentiful supply of fruit and vegetables. This girl prepares *calabash*, a long gourd that has been grown in these parts for thousands of years. Although inedible when fully grown, the young gourd can be cooked in a wide variety of ways.

PANPIPES

Popular throughout the Andes, native panpipes are made from reeds of different lengths tied together with plant fiber. This Otavalan man is playing a relatively small set, but some larger versions have as many as 30 pipes.

Inca empire, and many of their customs and rituals are rooted in this ancient and powerful culture. Later, they were heavily influenced by the Spanish colonists, who exploited their traditional craft and weaving skills, taught them new ones, and provided access to extensive markets in other parts of the world. Today, the Otavalen people are among the most prosperous indigenous groups in South America.

Saturday shopping

There are two main markets in Otavalo—one that supplies food, animals, and household goods to the local people, and one that sells textiles and crafts to the tourists. Saturday is market day, and many of the stalls are open for business before dawn. By midmorning, the local market is closing down, and by noon, even the tourists have drifted away.

PIG FOR THE POT

Otavalen shoppers take special care when it comes to choosing one of their most important purchases—live guinea pigs, known as *cuys*. These animals, which slightly resemble large rabbits with small ears, are kept almost like pets until a special occasion arises. Then they are killed and cooked for the celebration feast.

WORKING TRADITION

Both clothing and domestic textiles play an important part in Otavalo craft heritage. Here, a busy tailor makes practical use of a modern sewing machine in his market stall. Behind him hangs a selection of colorful rugs woven from the wool of llamas and alpacas. Both of these Andean creatures are distant relatives of the camel.

This flower seller, like many other traders, travels a long way to buy and sell goods at Otavalo market.

HATS ON

The Otavalens, in addition to being skillful weavers since pre-Incan times, are also accomplished hat-makers. The narrow-brimmed fedora, of felted wool, is worn daily by men as part of their traditional costume.

YAGUA
AIMING POISON DARTS

NATIVE TO THE AMAZON RIVER BASIN in northeastern Peru, the Yagua are one of the last rain forest people to use blowgun-fired darts for hunting and defense. The darts are tipped with curare, an ancient and deadly poison brewed up from forest roots and leaves. Curare kills almost instantly by causing widespread paralysis—as soon as it hits the lungs, the victim suffocates. The long blowguns themselves take several days to make, and involve a number of different tree and plant materials, but the Yagua get maximum mileage from the specialized skills involved. Like many other isolated groups, they are a focus of increasing interest for intrepid tourists. Taking full advantage of this, their craftspeople have begun to turn out suitcase-sized model blowguns (supplied without poison darts), which they sell to earn ready cash.

YANOMAMI

THE YANOMAMI PEOPLE OF THE AMAZON BASIN are one of the largest and most remote rain forest groups in South America, where they have lived for thousands of years. Their way of life consists of hunting and

CARETAKERS OF THE RAIN FOREST

Ancient world

The large Yanomami population (there are thought to be tens of thousands) live in hundreds of villages scattered through the dense rain forest near the Brazil–Venezuela border. Most live deep inside the forest, while some have settled along the banks of major rivers, including the Negro and the Orinoco.

COMMUNITY LIFE

Between 40 and 400 people live in each Yanomami village; the journey between villages can take from a few minutes to several days. Neighboring settlements are independent, yet they keep in constant touch.

MAGIC LIQUID

To make beer from *manioc* (also called sweet cassava), the creamy white root is first mashed, then chewed by village women until it is mixed with their saliva. At this stage, all the women spit it into one large jar where, after a few days, it begins to ferment. Eventually, it turns into a potent drink that is highly valued for both social and ceremonial purposes. This man hopes his bowl of beer will ward off evil spirits.

FAMILY HOMES

Yanomami communities, which are usually made up of extended family groups, live in huge dwellings called *yanos*; some house up to 400 people, but most are smaller than this. Each *yano* is built in the shape of a large ring, with an open courtyard in the middle for group celebrations and ceremonies.

FOOD AND DRINK

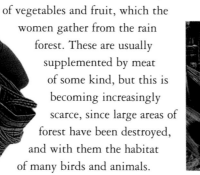

This girl carries fruit from the spiny palm tree in a bundle on her back. The Yanomami diet consists mostly of vegetables and fruit, which the women gather from the rain forest. These are usually supplemented by meat of some kind, but this is becoming increasingly scarce, since large areas of forest have been destroyed, and with them the habitat of many birds and animals.

HOME COMFORTS

Inside the *yano*, each family has its own area, which is centered around an open fire. Most people sleep in hammocks hung in layers from the ceiling, but some younger Yanomami sleep under the stars.

fishing, gathering wild food, and the small-scale farming of subfertile plots. Today the future of the Yanomami is uncertain. Prior to the discovery of gold in the 1980s, and since then, they have endured violence, greed, and infectious diseases at the hands of big business interests intent on exploiting the land. Both multinationals and poor migrants have also caused serious damage to the environment in their desperate search for gold.

RITUAL FOR THE DEAD
The Yanomami include fierce displays in many of their rituals. During funeral ceremonies, for example, warriors perform fantastic dances. Later, the deceased's body is burned and the ashes, along with ground-up bones, are mixed with soup and drunk by friends and family. In this way, they believe, the dead person becomes part of the living.

Ritual warriors cover their heads with white down.

LIVING OFF THE LAND
There isn't much room for farming in the rain forest, but clearing small plots allows the people to grow basic crops. Since most communities move on every few seasons to get the best from the soil, this task is repeated regularly. The working party shown here includes a youngster observing the process; knowledge has to be passed on in practical ways because the Yanomami have no written language.

DECORATIVE PIERCING
Like some people in western cultures, the Yanomami use piercing as a form of adornment. According to custom, thin wooden sticks are used; males perforate their bottom lip in the middle only, while females add an extra stick on each side.

KAYAPÓ

SPEAKING TO THE WORLD

LIKE MANY NATIVE PEOPLE IN THE AMAZON BASIN, the Kayapó Indians fear for their 11 million hectares of tropical rainforest and savanna home, which is being destroyed by the reckless harvesting of its trees. To communicate this to the world, they have appointed a unique messenger—a chief called Raoni who travels tirelessly from continent to continent pleading their case. As well as meeting world leaders, Chief Raoni uses social media to build awareness. His appearance makes him hard to ignore: on his head is a circle of perfectly matched parrot feathers, handed down through generations like a precious crown. Dominating his face completely is his huge lower lip, stretched since childhood over a series of bigger and bigger balsawood disks. For the Kayapó, this extraordinary feature is an ancient symbol of strength, a quality they value highly.

BRAZILIANS

AS WELL AS BEING THE LARGEST COUNTRY IN South America by far (it's even bigger than the continental United States), Brazil has one of the world's longest coastlines. Settled in the 16th

LIFE IN THE LAND OF CARNIVAL

City mix

More than 80 percent of Brazilians live in cities— the largest are São Paulo and Rio de Janeiro. Most people are of South American heritage but many belong to immigrant communities from Europe, Africa, and the Middle and Far East. There is a large Jewish population and there are more Japanese in São Paulo than in any city outside Japan. Each city contains wealthy districts and very poor areas.

STREET LIFE
Clinging to the steep hills behind it, Rio de Janeiro's shantytowns or *favelas* are a triumph of human spirit over deprivation. Assembled from found materials like plastic, sheet metal, and odd bricks, these precarious structures support a complex and lively street culture.

AIMING FOR A GOAL
Soccer was introduced to Brazil by Scottish engineers at the end of the 19th century. Since then, the game has become not just a symbol of patriotic pride, but almost a national obsession, and Brazilian players are among the best in the world. The small boys kicking a ball around this São Paulo *favela* know that becoming a sporting hero is one way to escape their bleak surroundings.

CARNIVAL
The exuberant street festival known as Carnival is the most important event in the Brazilian calendar. Once a year, in the days leading up to Ash Wednesday, thousands of costumed revelers pour through the cities, singing, dancing, and playing musical instruments. The most famous of all Brazilian Carnivals is in Rio de Janeiro; here, a fantastic fruity float makes its way down one of the wide thoroughfares.

century by Portuguese colonists and given its independence in 1822, the Federative Republic of Brazil consists of 26 states plus a federal district that, since 1960, has been the setting for their capital, Brasilia, built for that purpose. Together, they accommodate the region's highest population. "Brazil" is believed to come from a Portuguese word for the distinctive red color of brazil wood—*brasa* means "glowing coals."

MAKING COFFEE

Drunk in virtually every country on Earth, coffee is second only to oil as an international commodity, and Brazil is its leading producer worldwide. The raw crop undergoes several stages before it can be exported.

1 Picking
The cherries (fruit) on the coffee plant turn dark red when they are ready to be harvested. Hand picking is labor intensive, but it produces a high-quality crop.

2 Winnowing
Using a large sieve, the cherries are tossed into the air to remove dirt and leaves. This process (called winnowing) prepares them for drying and husking.

3 Tasting
Specialized tasters process a few of the beans into coffee, then sample it for acidity, body, aroma, and flavor before the rest of the batch is blended and roasted.

FRUIT FOR SALE

Although the Brazilian economy is no longer dominated by agriculture (manufacturing and service industries are also very important), one-third of its workforce is still employed on the land. Some of the country's most profitable exports are fruit crops, especially oranges and bananas.

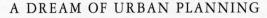

A DREAM OF URBAN PLANNING

Curitiba in southern Brazil is one of the world's most efficient cities. Uniquely friendly to the environment (two-thirds of the garbage is recycled), it also provides extensive social welfare; here, street children are employed in an urban park.

"MARVELOUS CITY"

People who live in Rio de Janeiro call it the *Cidade Maravilhosa*, or marvelous city. Overlooking Rio, arms outstretched in welcome, stands the famous statue of Christ the Redeemer, conceived and built in the Art Deco style by engineer Heitor da Silva Costa, and inaugurated in 1931.

BAHIANS

GRANDCHILDREN OF SLAVERY

ALONG THE NORTHERN COAST OF BRAZIL lies a fertile crescent of land where, in the 16th and 17th centuries, Portuguese settlers established large and wealthy plantations of sugar cane, coffee, and tobacco. To work in the fields, more than

CRUEL HISTORY
Salvador, Bahia's capital, was once the capital of Brazil. Its ultrafashionable Pelourinho district was originally named for the slave-beating sites located here—*pelourinho* means pillory, or whipping post.

Unique hybrid
A large majority of Bahian people are of African origin, although, like the rest of Brazil, there is a very mixed ethnic population. While the region's culture is rooted in an African past, it has a unique Afro-Brazilian identity that draws visitors from all over the world. Today, tourism is Bahia's leading industry.

CARNIVAL
The Salvador carnival, with its exuberant music, dancing, and feasting, is the largest street festival in the world. When it's on, up to three million people— tourists as well as locals—flock into the city. As part of the celebrations, percussion groups called *Blocos Afros* take to the streets.

SUGARCANE
Ropelike stalks of sugarcane are piled high in a Salvador market. For the workers, the task of harvesting canes is just as back-breaking as it was for their ancestors because it is still largely done by hand with a machete.

FOOD FOR FRIENDS
Preparing meals by hand is important, since every dish is believed to carry energy from the person who made it. Like many migrant cuisines, Bahian food was created from local produce prepared in the traditional style of the mother country. Here, fish and seafood are particularly plentiful.

3.5 million slaves—more than nine times the number that went to the United States—were shipped in from West Africa and sold through teeming human markets. Although slavery was abolished in Brazil in 1888, the direct descendants of these early workers still dominate the present-day state of Bahia. In its early days, this region was known as "the province of the bay"; the name "Bahia" comes from baia, the Portuguese word for bay.

Candomblé

The slaves who landed in Bahia were forbidden from practicing their African faith. In order to keep hold of their beliefs, therefore, they resorted to disguise—ancient gods were hidden behind Catholic saints, and familiar customs dressed up as Christian ritual. The new religion that grew out of this fascinating mix is called Candomblé. Today, it defines not only the spirituality, but also the culture of Bahian life.

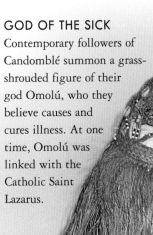

FIRE DANCE

African gods are called orixás. Passing a bowl of fire from head to head is part of the Candomblé ritual devoted to Xango, the fire orixá. Dancing is another important element of the ceremony: when the movements become wild and frenzied, some believers go into a trance.

GOD OF THE SICK

Contemporary followers of Candomblé summon a grass-shrouded figure of their god Omolú, who they believe causes and cures illness. At one time, Omolú was linked with the Catholic Saint Lazarus.

SISTERS IN FAITH

Allied to Candomblé is a female society called the Sisterhood of the Good Death. Devoted to the Assumption of the Virgin, its followers (who are all over 40) express their spirituality through street processions, samba dancing, and feasting. This sister is clothed in white, the color of Candomblé.

Worship takes place in terreiros, or houses of Candomblé.

CAPOEIRA

Cushioned by soft earth, young Bahian men practice capoeira, a blend of martial arts and dancing that warrior slaves brought with them from Africa. This move—where one person tosses the other into a midair somersault—is performed on beaches and streets all over the state.

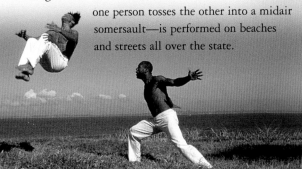

UROS

PEOPLE OF THE WATER

AT THE PERUVIAN END OF LAKE TITICACA lie more than 40 tiny, floating islands built by the Uros people. Unlike ordinary islands, which are part of Earth's surface, these are manmade from the hollow totora reeds that thrive in the shallow waters of the lake. The lives of the 1,200

Floating nests

The Uros islands look like huge straw nests floating in the bright blue waters of Lake Titicaca. Each one is formed from layer on layer of totora reeds, woven by hand into mats and bound tightly together. The reeds rot very quickly, however, so new ones are constantly being added on top to renew the surface.

REED HOMES

Uros families live in huts made completely from totora reeds. Wooden stakes support the bases, which are raised slightly off the ground. The walls and the roof are formed from sheets of bound reeds known as *quesana*. A few of these huts are fitted with solar panels as a power source.

1 Collecting
The reeds that the Uros people use are pulled away from the bottom of the lake by its moving waters. This woman is collecting them in her reed boat.

2 Drying
Before they can be woven, the long reeds are laid out to dry in the sun. This doesn't take long, since its strong rays are intensified by the lake's glassy surface.

3 Weaving
Here, reeds are bound into bundles that form one of the small, simple boats the Uros people use to transport themselves and their possessions.

WOVEN CURRENCY

Like many South American peoples, the Uros weave beautiful textiles. They sell these to the tourists and trade them on the mainland for clothing and household supplies.

TROUBLE UNDERFOOT

The Uros people are very used to walking on the spongy, uneven surface of their islands. Unwary visitors and children, however, can easily fall through a weak patch. The ground is constantly being renewed, but accidents do happen.

Uros Indians who inhabit the islands are bound up completely with these reeds. They not only use them to form the ground they walk on, but also bind them together to construct simple shelters, weave them into mats, build rafts and boats with them, burn them as fuel, drink a healing tea made with their flowers, and even prepare their soft hearts as an asparagus-like vegetable to accompany their meals.

MENDING NETS
A few decades ago there was a thriving fishing industry in the Uros Islands, but this, like many other traditional trades and customs, has been eroded by technology and tourism. Today, any fish the people catch is mainly for their own meals, or to use as barter on the mainland.

NATURAL PRESERVATION
Fresh fish would quickly spoil in the strong sun, so the Uros people preserve some of their catch by cleaning it, then spreading it out on the ground to dry.

COLD AND BRIGHT
Because Lake Titicaca is so far above sea level—about 12,500 ft (3,800 m)—it is chilly all year round, so the people wrap up well in woolen clothing. Hats keep their heads warm and protect them from the sun.

Observation platform

AYACUCHO

DESCENDED FROM AN ANCIENT PRE-INCA PEOPLE called the Huari, the Ayacucho (the name means "purple soul"), like the Otavalens, share their name with an Andes region and city. During the colonial era, the territory

BUILDING ON THE PAST

Inspiring setting

Inhabitants of a city that features some of the most outstanding colonial architecture in South America, the urban Ayacucho population, like so many others, reflects two main influences—from their Amerindian ancestors and from the Europeans who dominated their land for so long. The craft objects for which they are best known include brilliantly hued textiles, stone and wood carving, and fine filigree silver.

POSITIVE ATTITUDE

Guerrilla warfare led by the Shining Path began in 1980 and continued for many years resulting in the deaths of thousands of people in the Ayacucho area. People are trying hard to move on from these bitter memories and focus on the color and vitality that define their city today.

Ayacucho women wear the bright skirts, white blouses, and felt hats typical of Andes dress.

EASTER LAMB

In the strongly Roman Catholic Ayacucho culture, Easter is the most important celebration, and Holy Week (*Semana Santa*) dominates the life of the people. During this time, the scent of incense is everywhere, prayers are murmured constantly, and solemn processions fill the streets. As her contribution, this young girl is carrying a living symbol of the Lamb of God.

flowered as a center of commerce and culture. In 1824, the bloody conflict that liberated Peru from Spain was fought here, and remembered as the Battle of Ayacucho. Again during the 1980s, the people were caught up in violence between the army and terrorists rebelling against it. Today though, the warmth of the Ayacucho people, together with their exquisite craft skills, have made their home a hugely popular visitor attraction.

COLORFUL SCENES

The Ayacucho are known for producing *retablos*, painted wooden boxes framing papier mâché scenes—religious or historical. This simple one shows a Palm Sunday gathering, but some are very complex, with several stories like a house.

MAKING MERRY

In Ayacucho, February is carnival time, when the streets overflow with dancers, singers, musicians, and high-spirited revellers. Here, a brilliantly costumed troup of players (note the glowering devil on the left) makes its leisurely way through the crowd.

SOLID HERITAGE

Many of the city's important buildings were constructed using rose-colored stone, quarried locally, which is called the "marble of Peru." The structure that dominates this cityscape is the Cathedral.

MODERN INFLUENCES

Ayacucho people in urban areas enjoy wearing traditional dress on special occasions. Most of them, however—especially children—prefer modern clothing for every day.

OF ALL THE COUNTRIES IN SOUTH AMERICA, Argentina reflects the strongest European (as opposed to Amerindian) influence. This is due not only to early Spanish colonization but

ARGENTINES

NEW-WORLD NATION: OLD-WORLD CULTURE

Land of diversity

South America's second largest country, Argentina has a hugely diverse population. As well as the Hispanic majority, there is a significant Italian sector here, and small, proud, pockets of French, Jewish, British, Japanese, and Polish people. The name Argentina comes from *argentum*, the Latin word for "silver"; early explorers mistakenly thought there were large deposits of the mineral here.

TEATRO COLÓN

The glittering Teatro Colón in Buenos Aires is one of the world's finest opera houses. Since it was built in 1908, the leading opera and ballet stars of every generation have performed here—from Enrico Caruso to Placido Domingo, and from Anna Pavlova to Mikhail Barishnikov.

TWO TO TANGO

Born in the slums of Buenos Aires near the turn of the 20th century, the slow and sensual dance called the tango has since taken the flavor of Argentinian life to almost every country in the world.

NATIONAL INSTRUMENT

Invented in 1830 and shaped like a large, square concertina, the *bandoneón*—an important element of tango culture—is Argentina's national instrument. Its name is believed to come from a combination of "Band", the surname of an important musical-instrument dealer of the day, with the word "acordeón" (accordion). People who play this instrument are known as *bandoneonistas*.

MODERN CITY

The wide Avenida 9 de Julio that runs through the heart of Buenos Aires was named in honor of Argentina's Independence Day. People who live in this huge waterfront city are known as *Porteños*—literally, "people of the port."

also to the heavy immigration of other Europeans in the late 19th and 20th centuries. Today, the impact of this immigration gives Argentina a unique blend of varied cultures from Europe and Hispanic South America. Just over 90 percent of the population lives in its cosmopolitan cities and more than one third of people live in or near the vibrant capital, Buenos Aires.

GATHERING GRAPES

The heart of Argentina's prosperous wine industry is the western province of Mendoza. The country's first vines were planted in this area in order to provide communion wine to colonists from Chile. Here, local grape pickers bring in another year's harvest.

OFF THE HOOF

The production of beef (in the form of both cattle and meat-packing industries) dominates Argentina's economy. Because of this, the *asado*, or barbecue—always a male domain—is an important social ritual. Locals tend to prefer their roasts and steaks well cooked.

ROMANCE OF THE RANGE

Cattle ranching is centered in the flat, fertile, farmland region known as the Pampa. Historically, the work is done by nomadic horsemen called *gauchos*, whose almost mythical status parallels that of the American cowboy. Bucking tradition, a female *gaucho*, or *gaucha*, is herding these Hereford cows.

Artists' colors

PAINTING THE TOWN RED, BLUE, YELLOW, GREEN ...

IN THE SOUTHEASTERN CORNER OF BUENOS AIRES, near the waterfront, lies the historic working-class *barrio*, or neighborhood, of La Boca; *boca* means mouth, and the district was named for the mouth of the Riachuelo River, which winds along its southern edge. Full of ancient cobbled streets and rickety houses made of wood and tin, La Boca grew up as the city's Italian quarter at the end of the 19th century. Soon, the immigrant families who lived here began to adopt an appealing custom from their former hometown, the port of Genoa in Italy, where people brightened their streets with paint left over from the building and refitting of ships in the harbor. Today, many inhabitants of La Boca take great delight in carrying on this tradition—painting every part of the buildings in dazzling crimson, cobalt, aqua, or saffron.

TAQUILEÑOS

LIVING AT THE TOP OF THE WORLD

THE GLITTERING WATERS OF LAKE TITICACA—the highest navigable lake in the world—span the border between Peru and Bolivia. On the Peruvian side is a small but very beautiful island called Taquile, which

Island in the sun

Taquile is an enchanting place whose exquisite setting and gentle way of life attract more and more tourists every year. There are fishermen and farmers here, but most people make their living from the tourist industry. Society is completely communal on Taquile, and everyone, whatever they do, shares in any profits the visitors bring.

CRAFTING BY MEN

Textile crafts provide considerable tourist income for the Taquileños, and many elements of their traditional dress (which they wear every day) are hand made on the island as well. Knitting forms a major part of this heritage—but only the men do it. Here, an industrious worker is turning out one of the stocking caps, or *chulos*, worn by adult males—with red pompoms if they are married, and white ones if they are single. Women also reveal their marital status through their clothing—navy or black skirts if they are married, brightly colored ones if they are not.

POWERED BY THE SUN

Solar panels, attached to many homes, provide electricity to Taquile. Other power sources, such as fossil fuels like gas and coal, are costly and difficult to transport because everything has to be brought to the island by boat. The island has also installed a solar-powered water-pumping station, which means people no longer have to carry water long distances from wells.

ANCIENT ARCHWAY

The main entrance to Taquile is through a graceful archway over 500 steps up from the lake and harbor below. This arch, like most of the paths, ruins, and terraces on the island, is made from warm, reddish local stone.

has been inhabited for over 10,000 years. Named after the Count of Taquila, a Spanish nobleman who once owned it, the island is increasingly a tourist destination. However, many aspects of modern life are absent: electricity is supplied by generators and there are no cars or paved roads. People live by a strict and simple moral code: *Ama suwa* (do not steal), *Ama llulla* (do not lie), and *Ama quella* (do not be idle).

Carnival

There are three main festivals a year on Taquile: the first is around Easter, the second is when the harvest comes in, and the last is at new year. At these times the islanders bring out their finest costumes and jewelry and create joyous celebrations with music, dancing, and feasting.

GIFT FOR THE GODS
Here a group of islanders gather and bless fresh coca leaves, which are used in many ceremonies on Taquile. Leaves are offered to the gods of the lake and surrounding mountains before a departure to ensure each journey they make is a peaceful one.

MANY LAYERS
At carnival time, Taqueliños parade through the island playing festive music and performing special dances. As the women twirl, they reveal the full glory of their costumes, which have up to 16 layered skirts.

MAPUCHE

ADAPTING AND SURVIVING

FOR HUNDREDS OF YEARS, MAPUCHE CULTURE (their name means "people of the Earth") dominated the rugged landscapes of present-day Chile and northern Argentina. When the Spanish arrived, the Mapuche refused to be overpowered, yet they

Masters of their universe

Mapuche territory is harsh, but it is also remarkably varied, from jagged peaks and valleys in the mountains to coastal lowlands and plains. The Mapuche have remained stable and prosperous because they have adapted to these diverse terrains, learned to hunt and farm them skillfully, and established strong community structures based on extended family units called *lofs*.

FEMALE SHAMAN

Mapuche priests or shamans, called *machis*, are usually female. This one stands in front of a small hill that has been a sacred site since before the Spanish arrived. On top is a statue of Caupolican, a revered Mapuche chief.

COLONIAL LEGACY

The introduction of horses and cattle by the Spanish had a huge influence on the Mapuche. Most importantly, horses provided greatly increased mobility, which made them much more effective hunters and fighters. Also, both horses and cattle ran wild on the plains, which led to the livestock trading that is still a major source of income for the Mapuche.

HOME LIFE

Inside a family dwelling, called a *ruca*, meals are prepared over an open fire. Domestic chores like cooking and childcare are the sole responsibility of Mapuche women, who also take charge of preserving valued customs and passing them on.

FAMILY HOUSE

Rucas have steeply pitched roofs covered with reed thatch that extends all the way down the walls. Traditionally, *rucas* are built facing east. According to Mapuche belief, the east, from where the sun, moon, and stars rise, is the source of all life forces.

quickly adapted for their own purposes the unfamiliar horses and cattle their invaders brought with them. Finally losing their independence to military force in the mid-1800s, this proud people still maintain their own strong identity, religion, family structure, and language. The Mapuche call their homeland Waj Mapu, meaning "all the Earth," and their language Mapudungun—"the language of the Earth."

MEN'S WORK

All work outside the home is undertaken by Mapuche men in their role as head of the family. Here, at harvest time, a hard-working farmer gathers sheaves of ripe wheat from one of the small agricultural plots that surround a collection of *rucas*. Wheat, corn, potatoes, beans, squash, and peppers are all widely cultivated crops.

YEARLY BLESSINGS

Once a year the Mapuche celebrate their main festival called *Nguillatun*. At this time, they offer thanks for the community's well-being, pray for its continuing safety, and ask the gods to grant abundant harvests and healthy, fertile livestock.

SOCIAL STRUCTURE

Mapuche society is organized into groups of related families, called *lofs*, rather than into towns and villages. Each *lof* consists of 15–20 families under the leadership of a *lonko*, or head man. Here, two generations of Mapuche males wear simple woolen garments, which, by tradition, are woven by the women and girls of their *lof*.

The bright blue of the boy's shirt (right) represents sky and spiritual purity to the Mapuche.

PLAYING TOGETHER

Team activities like this game of *palin* link Mapuche communities and provide a focus for their identity. Similar to field hockey, *palin* involves a curved stick, or *weño*, and a small ball. Matches are played by friendly opponents, or used to settle differences between quarreling parties.

THE PEOPLE OF
Africa

African *adj* of Africa - *n* a native of Africa; a person of black race, **especially one whose people live now, or lived recently, in Africa.**

AFRICA

CRADLE OF THE HUMAN RACE

THE EARLIEST HUMAN REMAINS are found in Africa, from where we began to emerge about 200,000 years ago. Africa is home to the world's longest river, the Nile, and its biggest hot desert, the Sahara, which

Ceuta
This Spanish enclave in Morocco is significant because it connects Europe and Africa.

0 km 400 800
0 miles 400 800

Suez Canal
Completed in 1869, the Suez Canal joins the Mediterranean Sea with the Red Sea and was a revolution in shipping at the time.

PORTUGAL SPAIN ITALY
Ceuta (to Spain) Melilla (to Spain) CYPRUS SYRIA
Madeira (to Portugal) MOROCCO TUNISIA LEBANON
Canary Islands (to Spain) ISRAEL
JORDAN

Western Sahara (disputed)
ALGERIA LIBYA EGYPT
Lake Nasser

CAPE VERDE
MAURITANIA
SAUDI ARABIA

MALI NIGER SUDAN ERITREA
SENEGAL CHAD YEMEN
THE GAMBIA DJIBOUTI
GUINEA-BISSAU GUINEA BURKINA FASO BENIN
SIERRA LEONE CÔTE D'IVOIRE (IVORY COAST) TOGO NIGERIA ETHIOPIA
LIBERIA GHANA CENTRAL AFRICAN REPUBLIC SOUTH SUDAN SOMALIA

The Sahara

The world's largest hot desert covers a great deal of northern Africa. At 3.5 million sq miles (9 million sq km), the Sahara's area is close to that of the United States, and it is growing every year.

EQUATORIAL GUINEA
SAO TOME & PRINCIPE
GABON CONGO DEM. REP. CONGO UGANDA KENYA
RWANDA Lake Victoria
BURUNDI
Cabinda (to Angola)
TANZANIA SEYCHELLES

ATLANTIC OCEAN

ANGOLA COMOROS
ZAMBIA MALAWI Mayotte (to France)
MOZAMBIQUE MADAGASCAR
ZIMBABWE MAURITIUS
NAMIBIA BOTSWANA Mozambique Channel Réunion (to France)

Namibia
This was the first country in the world to include the protection of the environment in its constitution.

ESWATINI (formerly SWAZILAND)
SOUTH AFRICA LESOTHO

Madagascar
A glance at its shape reveals that Madagascar was once attached to the African mainland.

INDIAN OCEAN

Cape Agulhas
This is Africa's most southerly point.

dominates the northern part of the continent. Despite its natural resources, Africa has had more than its fair share of problems. For years, Europeans colonized it, plundering the continent for their own gain. Since then, Africa has had to contend with wars, natural disasters, crippling debt, and AIDS. It is home to many of the poorest countries in the world. Despite their troubles, Africans are determinedly working toward a better future.

Facts and figures

LANGUAGES
Arabic and its dialects are Africa's most popular language, with around 150 million speakers. Yoruba is one of the languages spoken in Nigeria and has 28 million speakers. Many other languages are spoken by just a few thousand people each.

RELIGIONS
In Africa many people follow one of the major world religions and practice a local African religion. Islam and Christianity are the most widely followed religions. Christianity is most prevalent in sub-Saharan countries, and Islam in the north and the Horn of Africa.

URBAN POPULATION
Fewer than half of Africans live in cities but urban areas and shanty towns on their outskirts are growing rapidly due to migration. The most populous cities are Egypt's capital, Cairo, and Lagos in Nigeria, both with 20 million inhabitants.

POPULATION BY COUNTRY
Nigeria has the greatest population in Africa with 201 million people, followed by Ethiopia with 110 million. The tiny island of Mauritius is the most densely populated country with 1,601 inhabitants per sq mile (618 per sq km).

CLIMATE

Most of Africa experiences consistently high temperatures. However, the amount of rainfall in different areas at different times varies. The savanna of Kenya, for example, has distinct dry and rainy seasons, which bring relief to wildlife and to people who live on and farm the land.

AFRICAN FACTS

PLACES
Number of countries ....54 +dependencies
Highest point ....Kilimanjaro, Tanzania
19,340 ft (5,895 m)
Lowest point ....Lake Assal, Djibouti
-509 ft (-150 m)
Biggest country ....Algeria
919,595 sq miles (2,381,741 sq km)
Smallest country on African mainland ....The Gambia
3,907 sq miles (10,120 sq km)

PEOPLE
Population of continent ....1,312 million
Urban population 40%

The people of Africa

FROM THE DESERT merchants in the north to the Pygmy peoples in the central rain forests, and the nomadic herdsmen of the south, people have always moved around this enormous continent with little regard for national borders. In recent times there have also been very large migrations toward the cities.

A young Kenyan girl with the Nairobi skyline behind her.

BIG CITY
Kenya's capital, Nairobi, is the biggest city in East Africa and has many modern buildings, shops, and museums. Like other cities that grow too quickly, it also has serious problems such as slums where there are no sanitation facilities.

INDEPENDENCE
Much of Africa was colonized by European powers, particularly the English and French, in the 18th, 19th, and early 20th centuries. Some countries retain strong links with former colonial powers. Here, President Buhari of Nigeria greets President Macron of France, who is making a diplomatic visit.

A DEVASTATING DISEASE
Africa is the region that has been most affected by HIV/AIDS, a virus that attacks the immune system and is most commonly passed on through sex. So many adults have died that children are being raised by older relatives. There is no cure, but improved prevention and treatments have cut the number of deaths and new infections.

Rich and varied cultures

The cultures of this vast continent are as diverse as its people and are expressed in crafts such as brightly colored fabrics, sculptures, and jewelry. Myths, religious beliefs, customs, and language are often unique to each particular tribe or nation.

LEARNING LIGHT

Girls in Ivory Coast carry backpacks with solar panels on them as they walk to school. The panels charge lamps in the bags, allowing the girls to study after dark.

MASKS AND RITUALS

In some religious ceremonies, participants don fantastic masks or costumes and allow themselves to be possessed by a spirit or god.

MUSIC AND DANCING

African music and dance often serves a ceremonial purpose. Here, South African women celebrate Nelson Mandela's presidential campaign.

ORAL TRADITION

Writing is rare in African cultures. Important ritual and cultural information is communicated through art or songs, sometimes by spiritual leaders entrusted with this task.

COUNTRY LIFE

Many Africans live by cultivating land or raising animals. Some farmers produce enough food for themselves and maybe a little to sell locally; others work for big farms producing large amounts of cash crops like cocoa, coffee, or bananas for sale abroad.

Many rural Africans today live in huts somewhat like this one.

MOORS

CIRCLING THE SAHARA

SAHARAN MAURITANIA HAS ONE OF THE LOWEST population densities in the world, with four persons per square mile (2.3 square kilometers). Less than 50 years ago nomadism was practiced by almost all Mauritanians, but today the Moors are one of the

The nomadic year

The Moors spend October to December in the north of their territory where there are few wells, but excellent grazing. As winter ends they move south through dunes and dusty plains. There is little movement between June and September but after the fall rains the Moors trek every day to return to the northern pastures.

THE *RHAL*

Every family owns a *rhal*, a wooden platform with carved legs. When the family is on the move the *rhal* is placed upside down on a camel. Cooking pots and containers are hung from its sides, and the women and children sit on it, like a saddle. The *rhal* is the woman's responsibility and, like all her possessions, is kept on the northern side of the tent.

Curved wooden tent poles.

Head coverings protect people from the sun, wind, and sand.

PACKING UP THE CAMP

It only takes the women an hour or two to dismantle the tents for loading onto the camels. Once the tent components and other possessions are piled on board, the women are helped up and the children handed to them. Men walk behind the camels with the cattle. There is no definite destination for the next camp—the men stop when they see an appropriate spot.

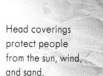

few groups that still lead a semi-nomadic, traditional life. Their movements are determined largely by their animals' need for water and pasture. But, like all nomads, the Moors do not live in total isolation or survive by their animals alone. Their travels invariably bring them into contact with their settled neighbors from whom they buy essentials such as grain, vegetables, weapons, and even wives.

FAMILY GROUPS

Camps usually consist of close family members—in the local language the same word, *khayme*, refers to both camp and family. The camp varies in size from five to 20 tents, depending on how much pasture is available.

ANIMAL HIDES

Hammunat Moors use locally available materials. The women make water containers out of goatskin. The skin is dried, tanned, and then sewn up before the finished container is finally tested to make sure it is watertight.

A TENT OF HER OWN

A bride continues to live with her parents for a year after her marriage. During this time, her mother makes the new couple a tent out of heavy cotton strips sewn together. It will remain the bride's property in the event of a divorce.

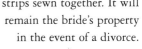

HOME FURNISHINGS

The tents contain blankets, cooking utensils, the *rhal*, and a metal trunk holding clothes, perfumes, and mirrors. The floor is bare or covered with palm mats woven by the women.

MOROCCANS

DUSK FALLS ON MARRAKESH'S CENTRAL SQUARE

BY DAY, MARRAKESH'S DJMA EL FNA is an enormous empty space close to the souks. As dusk falls it is magically transformed. Booths selling nuts and dried fruit open; squadrons of orange juice stalls appear; a dozen or more barbecues roasting enormous quantities of meat are lit sending plumes of smoke into the air; and entertainers of all sorts start to arrive. There are troupes of brightly clad child acrobats; storytellers; musicians; snake charmers; and belly-dancing female impersonators. Crowds amble around, eating and being entertained, while cars skim the perimeter of the square—giving the enchanted fairground the surreal air of a giant traffic island.

EGYPTIANS

AT THE ENTRANCE TO AFRICA

THE LIFEBLOOD OF EGYPT IS THE NILE RIVER, which passes through the center of the country. It has enabled many civilizations to flourish, among them the Ancient Egyptians, Nubians, Greeks, and

Bustling metropolis

Egypt's capital, Cairo, is the city with the second largest population of any in Africa—over 20 million people live here. There has been a city on this site by the Nile delta since Babylonian times, so ancient monuments jostle with the sprawling modern metropolis. Cairo and its environs are home to the Great Pyramid at Giza and to many ancient churches, mosques, and synagogues.

CROWDED CITY

More than two million cars travel the streets of Greater Cairo daily, resulting in an almost continual rush hour with traffic so densely packed it barely moves. Many people walk or use buses and taxis. Street sellers push carts filled with delicious foods.

FRESH BREAD

This pitta-bread seller is carrying the most simple and basic type of bread. Flour and water are mixed together and baked rapidly in a clay oven. Because it has a pocket, the bread can be stuffed with meat and vegetables to form a handy sandwich.

Romans, as well as Muslim, Turkish, and European colonial powers in more recent times. Today, 97.5 million people live in Egypt, making it the most populous Arab country by a long stretch. Most are Muslims and Arabic is the national language. The country has been run as a republic since 1952. Tourism and tolls from the Suez Canal are some of Egypt's biggest industries.

A MIXED POPULATION

The Coptic Christians are Egypt's largest minority. Living mostly in Upper Egypt but with monasteries and churches throughout the country, Copts form about 15 percent of the population. Christians have lived in Egypt since Roman times.

ABU SIMBEL

This temple in the south of Egypt was built by Pharaoh Ramesses II around 1200 BC. In 1968 it was moved so its original site could be flooded to make room for the Aswan Dam, which provides water and electricity for all Egypt.

THE CALL TO PRAYER

Next to every mosque is a tower from which the Muslim faithful are called to prayer five times a day. Traditionally a man called a *muezzin* sings out the *salat* (call), but in some places loudspeakers broadcast a recording instead.

SINGING STAR

Egyptian singer, Umm Kulthum, used to sing with her father at weddings. He disguised her as a boy because female singers were frowned upon at the time. Her strong voice soon won her fame. She went on to make many recordings and films.

GIFTS OF THE NILE

This farmer is using donkey power to raise water for irrigating his crops. For centuries though, Egyptian farmers relied on the annual flooding of the Nile River to water their fields. Since the Aswan Dam was built the floods no longer occur. Instead, rain water is captured and stored in a reservoir until it is needed.

TUAREG

CROSSING THE SAHARA DESERT

FACES SWATHED IN INDIGO-DYED SCARVES that are only removed in private, the Tuareg are a romantic symbol of the harsh, nomadic desert life. Until the mid-20th century, many still traversed the desert as they had done for centuries, although now most have settled down to work the land. Descended from Arabs and Berbers, the Tuareg were the earliest inhabitants of the Sahara region. They served an important function in the global economy by transporting small luxury items such as jewelry and weapons from Africa to the markets of the Middle East and Europe. These days, the nomadic lifestyle is dying. Droughts, civil unrest, and the people's minority status in their own countries have compelled many Tuareg to settle, but inevitably it is progress that has dealt nomadism the cruelest blow. The reason the Tuareg no longer command the desert is simply because their camels are no match for the trucks that effortlessly zip back and forth across the Sahara.

EVEN TODAY WITH AN ELECTED GOVERNMENT, the Ashanti people

ASHANTI

of southern Ghana continue to place great importance on their king, who is known as the *asantehene*. Royal patronage enabled the arts to flourish

A ROYAL TRADITION OF CRAFTWORK

The cloth of kings

Graphically patterned *Kente* cloth has been worn by Ashanti royalty since the 12th century. Because every pattern has a name, often inspired by a famous person, event, or proverb, *kente* cloth is much more than fabric. It is the bearer of Ashanti history, culture, and beliefs.

1 Dyeing yarn
The yarn is boiled together with starch and dye in a large kettle heated over a fire pit. Then it is hung out to dry under the hot Ghanaian sun.

2 Big bobbins
Bobbo, a master weaver, winds the dry yarn onto enormous bobbins. He chooses a design and selects his colors before he sets up the loom and starts weaving.

3 Little bobbins
After school, Bobbo's son winds yarn and learns to weave by helping his father, as Bobbo did before him.

CORONATION PROCESSION

A spectacular procession takes place when a new *asantehene* (king) comes to power. It features the Golden Stool, which is believed to have descended from heaven in the 17th century. The *asantehene* may not actually sit on it but he is is lowered and raised three times over this symbol of Ashanti power. At his enstoollment, as on all state occasions, he wears gold jewelry and a special type of *kente* cloth that is reserved only for kings.

AT THE LOOM

Kente cloth is woven out of doors. A loom with very long warp threads is used so that long, thin strips of fabric are produced. The weaver opens and closes these using a lever controlled by his feet. At the same time, he throws the shuttle holding the weft threads rapidly back and forth between the warp threads.

The wooden loom is built and maintained by the weaver.

THE FINAL STAGE

The long strips of fabric are sewn together to make the actual cloth. A man's robe requires 24 strips on average, while a woman's skirt needs far fewer.

and also gave rise to both power struggles and many ceremonies. There is still a strong and innovative tradition of craftwork among the Ashanti. A new tradition was born in the 1960s when a talented sculptor created the first fantasy coffin in the shape of a fish for his dying uncle, who was a fisherman. In keeping with the lavish and lengthy funerals customary in Ghana, the idea was an immediate and lasting hit.

MARKET TRADERS

These women are selling vegetables at Kumasi Central Market, in the capital of the Ashanti region. The huge open-air market is the largest in West Africa. Many people travel from far and wide to trade there. Available goods range from grains and spices to gold and diamond jewelry, and clothes made fromAshanti *kente* cloth.

FANTASY COFFINS

Specially commissioned coffins in the form of airplanes, chickens, guitars, and even giant Bibles celebrate the achievements of the person who has died and enable them to go on their final journey in style.

A SINGLE PIECE OF WOOD

Stools are a typical Ashanti item and are often made of soft sese or cedar wood. Craftsmen are exceptionally skilled and do not measure the wood; they simply begin carving it with a tool called an adze.

Craftsmen sometimes incorporate images into the design that reflects the perso nality of the owner.

DOGON

ASTRONOMERS AND MYTH-MAKERS

SOUTHEASTERN MALI is home to around 300,000 Dogon people. The majority live in small villages clustered around the foot of the 90-mile (145-km) Bandiagara Cliffs. The Dogon have a

All dressed up

Many different Dogon ceremonies are celebrated, but the most important is the *sigui* ceremony, which is held once every 60 years. Its exact date is calculated to coincide with the moment when Sirius appears between two mountains peaks. At this event power is symbolically handed from one generation to the next and a new *toguna*, or meeting house, is built.

SOLAR-POWERED MEAL

Using a clean and sustainable energy source, solar-powered stoves were introduced to Mali in the 1990s. Here a Dogon woman prepares a meal outside her home in a village in West Mali.

DOGON RELIGIOUS SOCIETIES

All-male religious societies are an important part of Dogon life. The role of the *Wagem* cult is to keep dead ancestors involved in village affairs, while the *Binu* cult has a similar role with regard to members of the spirit world. The *Lebe* cult perform the *bulu*—an agricultural rite. It takes place just before the rains begin and its purpose is to ensure a successful harvest.

THE AWA SOCIETY

During a funeral, members of the *Awa* society lead the souls of the dead to their rightful place in the supernatural world. They wear masks indicating that they have been taken over by the souls of supernatural beings and speak a mysterious language called *sigi so*. Every 60 years the Awa society perform the most important rite of all, the *sigui*, a celebration of renewal.

profound knowledge of astronomy. They determine the time of one of their ceremonies by the position of the distant star, Sirius. Dogon priests have long maintained that Sirius had a companion star—invisible to the naked eye—which western astronomers finally managed to locate in 1995. Dogon stories about the creation and workings of the universe are some of the most complex known to anthropologists.

The toguna or "House of Words" is the spiritual center of Dogon life. It has a low roof so that nobody can stand up and start fighting if there is a disagreement.

THE ONION CROP

The Dogon grow onions as a cash crop. These are pounded, shaped into balls, and dried in the sun. They will be taken by truck as far away as the Ivory Coast to be sold as ingredients for sauces. The pots used to water the crop are made out of clay by Dogon women.

The "chess-board" pattern symbolizes the relationship between the spirit world and the world of the living.

PROBLEMS WITH TOURISTS

Decorative gate posts were a feature of Dogon buildings but many were stolen by art collectors and tourists. These days few are made, and the Dogon have resorted to defacing the remainder so that no one will be tempted to steal them.

WODAABE
DRESSING TO IMPRESS

AT THE ANNUAL WEEK-LONG Gerewol festival, the Wodaabe men of Chad, Nigeria, and Niger compete with one another to find a marriage partner. Each man tries to impress the women the most. The Wodaabe ideal of male beauty is an aquiline nose, bright eyes, and white teeth, so the men's dresses, makeup, and facial expressions are designed to highlight these features. They perform a series of dances to win the attentions of the female judges, who, in this polygamous society, may have as many husbands as they wish.

DINKA

THE DINKA OF SOUTH SUDAN, like their neighbors the Nuer, are a seminomadic people. Although they grow crops and keep various animals, the Dinka particularly treasure their cattle. During the short rainy season

LIFE IN THE CATTLE CAMP

Dinka select cattle for the size of their horns.

Cattle wealth

The Dinka people are very proud of the long-horned cows that represent their wealth. Such is the importance of cattle that the Dinka write songs about their animals and perform dances to honor them. When a Dinka boy wants to marry he offers cattle to the girl's family. And when there is a dispute, cattle are given to the wronged party by a court of Dinka elders.

A HOME FOR EACH SEASON

During the dry season the Dinka and their cattle move to camps by a river, leaving only the old and infirm in the villages. But when the rains come and the riverside grasslands become swampy they return to their villages once more. There they live in small groups of grass-roofed mud houses and cultivate crops such as sorghum and millet.

the Dinka live in villages built on sandbanks emerging out of the swamps and cultivate crops. However, in the dry season, which runs from September to May, all able-bodied Dinka leave the village in search of pasture and water for their animals. Since 1983, southern Sudan has been blighted by civil war. Many people were killed and cattle died. South Sudan became independent in 2012 but fighting continues in the region.

MILK AND BUTTER

Women and children are responsible for milking the cattle and distributing dairy products. The milk is collected in gourds. Some of it is drunk straight away, some is soured for storing, and if there is any extra it is churned to make butter.

A USE FOR EVERYTHING

Of course, milk and butter are valuable as food, but the Dinka find a way to use everything that the cattle produce. Cow urine, which is sterile and antiseptic, is collected and used for cleaning wounds, washing, and tanning hides. The ash from burned cow dung has many uses too, including insect repellent (see below), makeup, and even toothpaste! Although cows are not generally slaughtered, when an animal dies its hide is used to make mats, drums, belts, and ropes. Nothing is wasted, not even horns and bones.

A NATURAL INSECT REPELLENT

Keeping flies and mosquitoes at bay is a priority in the cattle camp. Not only do they irritate both people and animals but they are also capable of spreading diseases.

1 Dung repellent
A young girl collects cow dung at the Wunbel cattle camp in southern Sudan. There is plenty of it available for use as a natural insect repellent.

2 Bonfires
At dusk the dung is burned. People and animals gather around the fires fueled by burning dung. The smoke covers everything and keeps insects away.

3 Using the ash
The Dinka cover themselves with the insect-repelling ash. With typical Dinka concern for their animals, they also rub the ash into the skin of their cows.

Calling the cattle

A Dinka child beats his drum to a specific rhythm to call his family's cows to his *khat*, a specific area in the middle of the camp where they will be tethered for the night. The cows have been trained to recognize and respond to this particular rhythm. The smooth management of thousands of animals in the cattle camp is possible because every family has its own rhythm.

Large drum made out of cowhide.

GAMO

HIGHLAND VILLAGERS OF ETHIOPIA

THERE ARE OVER 1.6 MILLION GAMO PEOPLE in the highlands of southwestern Ethiopia. Their villages are dotted around the lush, green hills, and many are above 10,000 ft (3,000 m). Heavy rains fall from

Family and friends

In the Gamo highlands, families live in compounds containing a number of huts. The main hut has a high, pointed roof so that rain can drain off the outside. Smoke from cooking escapes through the weave in the thatch. It can take five or six hours to cook dinner on the hearth at the back of the hut, so while women cook, men congregate to while away the time smoking and discussing local politics.

THE MAIN FAMILY HOME
The tall family houses are often 20 ft (6 m) or more, and feature a "nose," or little porch at the front. The enormous bamboo poles planted outside this home signify that the man of the house is undergoing initiation as a *halaka*, or elder. Bamboo grows abundantly and is important both for building homes and for rituals.

AN EXTRA ROOM
Frequently, simple round huts are built alongside the main family home. These are lower than the main hut and either house the family's son and his wife, or are used for cooking or storing grain.

1 Making the walls
Making a hut is a lot like making a basket. Vertical lengths of bamboo are planted in the ground and then horizontal lengths woven through them to form walls.

2 The roof
A small circular structure, similar to the kind that forms the bottom of a basket, is woven, placed on top of the walls, and then connected to the wall struts.

3 Layers of thatch
Dense thatch is placed over the roof to form a thick covering that will prevent the rain from entering the hut. A hut like this one can last for several years.

June to September, and lighter rains in February and March. People rely on these to grow crops such as barley, wheat, corn, and sorghum. They also cultivate *enset*. Although it bears no fruit, this plant is related to the banana. It has many uses and is virtually indestructible. Not only does it provide food but its stems can also be made into rope, and its waterproof leaves used to keep off the rain.

Festivals and rituals

New year is celebrated after the heavy rains in September. Sheep are sacrificed, those who have been married or initiated in the previous year participate in special rituals, and everybody greets each other with the exclamation "Yo!". This is the main festival but there are others throughout the year, as well as particular Gamo practices relating to death and marriage.

Men performing a ritual to celebrate the new year.

AFTER A FUNERAL

Only close relatives attend a burial, but the entire community participates in the mourning ritual. Male relatives of the person who has died dress in their war outfits and carry their spears. At a special mourning field they, together with the rest of the community, run around in their battle gear chanting war songs, expressing the warriorlike strength it takes to confront death.

BRIDAL JOURNEY

On marriage, young women move from their parents' home to the home of their husband and his family. This bride makes the journey to her new family in style—riding on a donkey and proudly wearing a leopard skin. Leopards used to roam the lowland areas, where they were hunted and traded. There are not many left these days, but families who own leopard skins wear them at celebrations and weddings to signify power.

SHARING THE WORK

The men who own plots of land rarely tend them alone. Workgroups of 10–15 people spend a day or two on each individual's plot. These men are preparing to plant barley or wheat by hoeing the ground. Lower down the slopes people plant corn or sorghum. Even if the rains fail and the crops do not grow there is no risk of famine because there are hardy *enset* plants—whose roots and stems are edible—to fall back on.

MBENDJELE

PYGMY PEOPLE OF THE RAIN FOREST

AS MANY AS 200,000 DIFFERENT GROUPS live in the forests of central Africa in countries such as D.R. Congo, Gabon, Cameroon, Central African Republic, and Uganda. They are sometimes known collectively as

Women's work

Mbendjele women gather fruit, nuts, mushrooms, tubers, and caterpillars. They are not permitted to kill animals by drawing blood so rather than shoot, they fish or catch and kill small animals by clubbing them. At harvest time women help gather in the crops for their settled neighbors in return for a share of the harvest.

MAKING MUSIC

The Mbendjele, like other Pygmy groups, have a tradition of making music together. They sing complex harmonies with an improvised, yodeling style. Music is woven into daily life and they sing as they walk in the forest to alert wild animals or as they prepare to hunt. These women, in a village near Lake Bunyonyi in Uganda, sing and clap rhythmically.

RAINFOREST KITCHEN

Mbendjele groups move camp frequently. Fortunately, it only takes minutes to set up a new kitchen. Elderly women carry smoking embers wrapped in leaves to the new camp so it is easy to start a fire on arrival. The family machete and cooking pot are carried in a basket. The heavy homemade pestle and mortar are often left at the site for the next time the group returns. Chopping boards and plates are simply readily available wood and leaves.

A CURE FOR ILLNESS

Mokodis are strings woven from tree bark, vines, and other forest materials. They are made by both women and men, and are worn on the affected part of the body to cure illness. Special *mokodis* are tied around the wrist and waist of newborn babies to protect them.

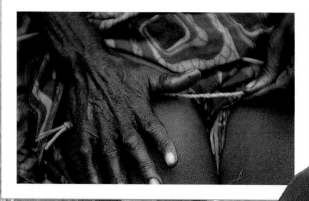

Hunters must be absolutely silent so as not to alarm the animals. They communicate using signs like this one, which means "elephant."

Pygmies. All share a small stature and a profound knowledge of the rain forest—the most diverse habitat on Earth—from which they derive almost everything they need to live. Mbendjele are one such people. They hunt and gather, moving frequently from place to place within the forest so as not to exhaust it. However, they are under increasing pressure from logging and conservation interests to abandon their way of life.

PREPARING FOR THE HUNT

A clan elder takes the gunpowder from a few bird-shot pellets and combines it to make a bullet big enough to kill a pig. Mbendjele people do not own guns, but they sometimes make deals with local people who do, borrowing a gun in return for a share of the kill. Pygmy people do not want to deplete the forest so they only kill large animals such as elephants or buffalos if there is an unusually big crowd of people to feed because of a funeral or celebration.

1 A successful hunt
The Mbendjele are excellent hunters. This hunter returning to the camp is carrying two monkeys and a duiker (a kind of antelope) that he has killed.

2 Sharing the kill
A big feast follows a successful hunt. The animals are quickly cut up and cooked so that everyone in the group can benefit from the nutritious meat.

3 Cooking the meal
In the hot and steamy climate fresh meat, like this duiker head, soon spoils. One method of preservation is smoking it over an open fire.

This sign means "gorilla". Mbendjele believe gorillas are reincarnated humans and never kill or eat them.

This sign means a hunter has spotted a chimpanzee.

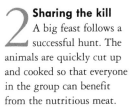

MAASAI

THE MAASAI PEOPLE live along the Great Rift Valley in southern Kenya and northern Tanzania. Although they are seminomadic, and traditionally have not cultivated crops, they are tied to the land by their animals. Land

CATTLE HERDERS OF EAST AFRICA

Men and cattle

The Maasai way of life revolves around keeping animals, particularly cattle. Maasai men are grouped with their contemporaries into age-sets in which they remain for their entire lives. Particular types of work are allocated to each age-set. Every few years, the entire age-set participates in a ceremony at which they move up a stage. Young men between their late teens and early twenties are *moran*, or warriors. During this period of their lives they live with and look after the cattle.

During their time as *moran* the young men learn to recognize every single animal in their care.

JUMPING COMPETITIONS

Everyone sings and dances in Maasai ceremonies. *Moran* show their prowess by rhythmic vertical jumping—the higher the better. They can jump for hours, sustained by the singing and chanting of the rest of the group.

HELPING OUT

Maasai children spend most of their time playing, but they are allowed to look after sheep and goats, which are not as highly prized as cattle. They are encouraged to be respectful and to address all elders, not just their own parents, as "mother" or "father."

ownership was once foreign to the Maasai, yet they now find themselves struggling to gain access to their traditional grazing lands. This is due to the tourist industry, catering to the growing western appetite for safaris.

Many Maasai have responded to this by opening their villages to tourists. Selling craftwork and performing for tourists brings in money, but some Maasai feel it is undignified to sell their culture in this way.

CATTLE BLOOD
High in protein, cattle blood is given to the sick and to women following childbirth. To extract the blood, a vein is opened up in the animal's neck. It is sealed after the blood has been extracted, doing no lasting damage to the animal.

Women and girls

Maasai women build and maintain the home, collect water and firewood, look after children and animals, and do skilled beadwork. More recently, some women have begun growing and selling vegetables. Maasai girls undergo initiation at puberty and are married soon after, often to much older men who have completed their time as *moran*.

BEAUTIFUL BEADWORK
Women buy bright plastic beads from non-Maasai and use them to make distinctive jewelry. Rules dictate which colors may be used and in what combinations. The women in the picture are in a tourist *manyatta* (village) on the edge of the Maasai Mara game reserve, where tourists can watch them as they work.

The end of an era

FROM WARRIOR TO JUNIOR ELDER

THE SOUND OF THE KUDU HORN awakens strong emotions among Maasai warriors, known as *moran*. The one occasion on which it is blown is to summon them to their *eunoto* ceremony, where they cease to be *moran* and graduate to junior elders. Approximately every 10 years, *moran* from Kenya and Tanzania gather for the *eunoto*. As *moran*, the men lived and worked together tending cattle, hunting, and decorating themselves with red ocher. Now, the many restrictions on them will be lifted and they will be allowed to marry, but they will lose the excitement of their former lives. In their red robes and impressively painted, they take a final meal together and process back to the main camp. As the kudu horn is blown, hundreds of *moran* chant and present arms. Later, they will sit on the cowhides on which they were circumcised while their mothers shave off the long hair symbolizing their warriorhood. Many weep and tremble, believing that the best period of their lives has now ended.

CAPETONIANS

WHERE THE WARM WATERS OF THE INDIAN OCEAN collide with the cooler waters of the Atlantic lies picturesque Cape Town, huddled at the foot of Table Mountain. The first inhabitants of this region were the

THE DIVERSE RESIDENTS OF CAPE TOWN

Port city

Cape Town exists because merchant ships traveling between the Netherlands and the East Indies needed somewhere to stock up on food and drink. Members of the Dutch East India Company founded the settlement as a supply station in 1652. Some employees left the company to become farmers. These settlers are the forebears of Afrikaners, a group who dominated South Africa until the 1990s.

Cape Town occupies an area of striking natural beauty.

NATURAL BEAUTY
Capetonians appreciate their city's location and like nothing better than hiking in the surrounding countryside. The region has many national parks as well as Table Mountain which, at 3,563 ft (1,086 m), looks out onto stunning views over the city and the coast.

nomadic San people, then Khoi herders. The Dutch established a colony from 1652, bringing with them slaves from Indonesia, Madagascar, India, and Mozambique, and gradually taking over the land. The territory was handed over to the British in 1806. Later immigrants included Jews escaping violence in Eastern Europe, and economic migrants from India, Africa, and Europe. South Africa did not gain full independence until 1961.

SHANTY TOWN

Many of Cape Town's black residents live in ghettos created during the apartheid era, a time of imposed racial segregation. Some live in shanty towns, unofficial neighborhoods where people build shacks out of anything available.

Two mighty oceans meet at the Cape— the Indian Ocean and the Atlantic.

DEMOCRACY IN ACTION

In 1994, the first election after the fall of apartheid saw millions of people lining up to vote. For many, it was the first election in which they could participate. It is known as the Freedom Election, which swept Nelson Mandela's African National Congress (ANC) to power.

EQUAL RIGHTS FOR ALL

Since the end of the apartheid era in 1994 full racial integration has been South Africa's aim, so mixed schools are becoming more common.

FIRST MOSQUE

Auwal Mosque, the first official mosque in South Africa, opened in 1794. It is in the Bo-Kaap area, home to the Cape Malays, descendants of slaves from all over the Muslim world who were brought here by the Dutch in the 16th and 17th centuries.

ZULUS

MODERN LIVES, TRADITIONAL WISDOM

DURING THE REIGN OF KING SHAKA (1816–1828), Zulus became the mightiest military force in southern Africa. This small group conquered and absorbed many other tribes, resulting in a fifty-fold increase in the land they

Health and illness

Zulus believe bad luck, ill health, and death can often be attributed to sorcery or an offended spirit. The first step when a problem is suspected is to consult an *isangoma*. These healers, almost all of them women, feel called to their profession. They undergo intensive and lengthy training while apprenticed to an experienced practitioner.

UMUTI MARKET

While an *isangoma* diagnoses ill health, a specialist called an *inyanga* makes up medicines (*umuti*) from plant and animal products. Many Zulus prefer these to Western medicines. Here, materials for making *umuti* are laid out for sale on a car.

An *isangoma* carries an *ishoba*—a stick made with the tail of a wildebeest and decorated with beads—as an aid to diagnosis.

Isangomas wear distinctive beadwork in their hair.

controlled, until the British Empire invaded and eventually took their territory. Signs of their warrior past remain in their ritual costumes, which feature animal skins, spears, and shields. Some Zulus live in homesteads known as *umuzis*. Many *umuzis* are on land owned by white farmers, and at least one family member earns a wage. Other *umuzis* are open to the public and their inhabitants make a living from tourism.

GOING TO SCHOOL

Most of South Africa's ten million Zulus live in the countryside of Kwa-Zulu Natal, herding cattle and growing crops. Like all South African children, Zulu children go to school until the age of 15.

Two *isangomas* participate in a healing ritual.

BASKETS AND BEADS

Beadwork is a well-developed Zulu craft. If a woman has, or would like to have, a relationship with a particular man she can send a subtle message to him through her jewelry. Zulu basketwork is much admired too. Baskets are even watertight enough to hold liquids, thanks to the tight weave and to the fact that the liquid in the baskets causes the fibers to swell.

MINING FOR COAL

Many Zulus were forcibly moved under apartheid (a system of racial separation) to areas with few economic opportunities. To earn money, many Zulu men went to live and work in South Africa's coal mines far away from Kwa-Zulu Natal. They often live in dormitories, only returning to see their families once or twice a year.

SAN

OFTEN REFERRED TO AS "BUSHMEN," the many different groups now known as San are the original inhabitants of the Kalahari Desert in South Africa, Botswana, and Namibia. Their lifestyle resembles that of the

HUNTER-GATHERERS OF THE KALAHARI

MONKEY ORANGES

The San are entirely self-sufficient and are skilled at getting every possible use from the little that is available in the bush. The fruit of the monkey orange tree is good for quenching thirst but it also has a number of other uses. The fruit can be used as dye or soap, the bark as medicine, and the leaves to heal wounds.

A FLEXIBLE LIFESTYLE

A San community consists of a few extended families. The group build homes together inside a walled compound. When water and food become scarce, the group leave their homes to fall apart naturally and move to a new site where they build another camp. However, their land is being encroached upon by industries such as diamond mining, making it harder for the San to move wherever they wish.

The San way of life

Survival in the desert requires a number of different skills. Men make weapons and hunt for animals, while women fashion skin bags and use these to gather fruit and nuts. In San society everything is shared and everyone is treated equally. When an animal is killed the meat does not belong to the person who killed it but is shared with the entire group. Although there is no formal leadership, skilled and experienced individuals are highly respected.

ROOTS AND TUBERS

Roots and tubers provide moisture as well as food to the San. Women are expert at finding and digging these up, and are also knowledgeable about their medicinal properties and uses.

SAN CAVE ART

The oldest San cave paintings are thought to be 27,500 years old. The animals represented in the cave paintings may record the experiences of San spiritual leaders. These leaders, or shamans, would hold a trance dance to heal someone or ensure good hunting. The paintings show what the shaman may have seen while in a trance.

earliest, preagricultural societies. The San are hunter-gatherers who live in family groups of 10–30 people. The members of the group live as equals and share everything. They are skilled at hunting animals and at finding food and water in the bush. They keep few possessions so that they can move easily to a new site if their water source dries up. They speak "click languages" that include a range of sounds made with the tongue.

Hunting and trapping

Although the San do much of their hunting with a bow and arrow, they also set traps like this one, which is designed to catch a guinea fowl. San men and women are extremely skilled at this and their traps very rarely fail to catch birds or small animals. The animals most commonly hunted are eland (antelope), wildebeest, gemsbok, giraffe, reptiles, and birds.

PREPARING FOR THE HUNT

Because there are few animals in the bush, hunting is a skilled task and something of a ritual event, reinforcing the relationship between the men in the group.

1 Finding poison
A hunter digs for beetle larvae. They contain a poison which, when it enters an animal's bloodstream, can kill it. One arrow may require the poison of 10 larvae.

2 The mixing bowl
He extracts the poison and mixes it with plant juice and saliva in one of the ball sockets of an eland. The juice acts like glue, making the poison stick to the arrow.

3 Delicate work
The poison is placed on the arrow shaft, not the tip. This is to prevent the hunter from getting poisoned if he accidentally scratches himself with one of his arrows.

PATIENCE AND SKILL

The poisoned arrows do not inflict much immediate damage on a big animal. The hunter must follow the animal's tracks for several days until it succumbs to the poison.

MALAGASY

AFRICAN AND INDONESIAN ROOTS

THE FIRST SETTLERS ON MADAGASCAR CAME, not from Africa, but from Southeast Asia, over 4,000 miles (6,000 km) away. They settled on the central highlands of the island. Later, Africans settled in the

A miniature continent

Thousands of islands litter the Indian Ocean. The largest, Madagascar—which is the world's fourth largest island—lies 250 miles (400 km) off the east coast of Africa. Ecologically, it is one of the most diverse countries on Earth. Almost 98 percent of the land mammals, and a high proportion of plants, reptiles, and birds live only here.

A woman taking a fish home from market by balancing it on her head.

MARKET DAY

Although their main crop is rice, which is consumed locally, farmers on Madagascar grow various crops including coffee, vanilla, cloves, and sugar for export. In order to produce decaffeinated coffee the beans must be treated. However, there is one exception to this rule—the Madagascar coffee species *Mascarocoffea vianneyi* produces naturally decaffeinated beans.

A RICH SOURCE OF FOOD

Coastal Malagasy have always eaten fish, crab, and shrimp, but recently fishing has become more intensive in order to supply fish and shrimp for export. Although this generates much-needed income for Madagascar, there is concern that overfishing might seriously deplete the waters and cause a food shortage.

coastal regions and other immigrants came from the Muslim world. These days 25.6 million Malagasy comprise almost 20 distinct ethnic groups, sharing a language, a nationality, and many similar beliefs and customs. The incredible diversity of Madagascar's human population is matched by the variety of its animals and plants, which evolved in the millions of years after the island broke off from the African mainland.

Some graves in the south of the island are decorated with carved figures and the horns of zebu cattle.

The importance of fady

Complex and varied *fady*, or taboos, exist in every group on Madagascar. For instance, the Mahafaly people in the south of the island consider it unlucky for children to sleep in the same house as their parents. Some *fady* are concerned with the proper way to treat the dead.

CARING FOR THE DEAD

Around half of the Malagasy people follow traditional religions, but even those who are Christian retain the traditional beliefs and practices concerning the *razana*, or dead ancestors. *Razana* must be kept happy or they will bring bad luck to the living.

1 Family reunion
Some years after the death and burial of a relative, the Merina and Betsileo people of the central highlands dig up the body and wrap the bones in a new shroud.

2 A new shroud
The *famadihana*, or "turning of the dead" allows relatives to show respect for a *razana* and ensure that he or she will continue to protect them in the future.

3 Homes for the dead
Not everyone performs the *famadihana*, but all Malagasy take good care of the dead. On Madagascar, tombs are often more lavish than the homes of the living.

VANILLA

Madagascar produces the majority of the world's vanilla—a complex crop to cultivate. Each plant must be pollinated by hand, allowed to grow for six months, and then undergo a series of processes for a further three months.

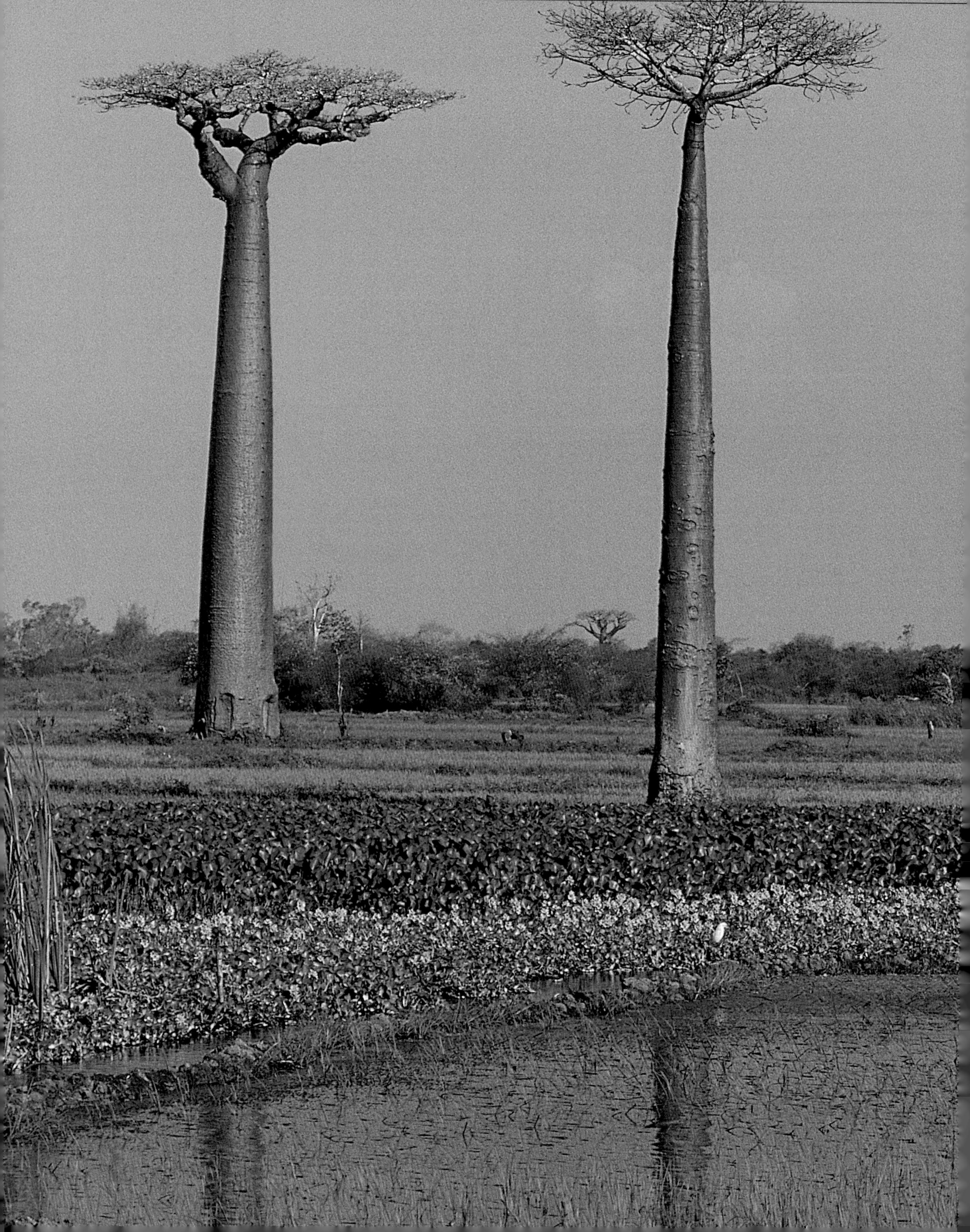

Africa's paddy fields

GROWING RICE IN MADAGASCAR

STRIKING BAOBAB TREES TOWER OVER PADDY FIELDS edged with water hyacinths on the west coast of Madagascar. Rice is the staple food of the island, and is grown on every available piece of land. Ironically, its very cultivation is contributing to a food shortage. Madagascar has always suffered from soil erosion, but the clearing of 80 percent of its forests to provide farmland has accelerated this process. Sadly, the exquisite water hyacinths make matters worse. Choking up rivers and lakes all over Africa, these weeds are responsible for killing fish and smothering crops. They are just another obstacle to Malagasy farmers trying to produce enough food for the islanders.

THE PEOPLE OF
Europe

EUROPE

A CENTRE OF INDUSTRY AND COMMERCE

GOOD AGRICULTURAL LAND, RICH MINERAL resources, technological innovation and a relatively compact size have enabled Europe to prosper. After devastating wars in the 20th century, it has now had many years of

The borders of Europe

To the west, Europe is bordered by the Atlantic Ocean; to the north, by the Arctic; and to the south, by the Mediterranean Sea. The Ural Mountains and the Caspian Sea divide Europe from Asia. Parts of Russia and Turkey are included in both Asia and Europe.

0 km 200 400
0 miles 200 400

Largest Lake
Lake Ladoga, Russia
6,822 sq miles
(17,670 sq km)

Most westerly point
Látrabjarg, Iceland

Novaya Zemlya

Kara Sea

Barents Sea

White Sea

Denmark Strait

ICELAND

Faroe Islands (to Denmark)

Norwegian Sea

Shetland Islands

Outer Hebrides

Orkney Islands

SCOTLAND

NORTHERN IRELAND

IRELAND

UNITED KINGDOM

WALES ENGLAND

North Sea

DENMARK

Channel Islands (to UK)

English Channel

BELGIUM

LUXEMBOURG

NETHERLANDS

GERMANY

Bay of Biscay

FRANCE

SWITZERLAND

LIECHTENSTEIN

ANDORRA

MONACO

PORTUGAL

SPAIN

Mallorca
Eivissa Menorca
Balearic Islands

Corsica

Sardinia

Gibraltar (to UK)

Mediterranean Sea

NORWAY

SWEDEN

FINLAND

Gulf of Bothnia

Åland

Vänern

Vättern

Gotland

Baltic Sea

RUSSIA

ESTONIA

LATVIA

LITHUANIA

POLAND

CZECH REPUBLIC (CZECHIA)

SLOVAKIA

AUSTRIA

HUNGARY

SLOVENIA

CROATIA

ITALY

SAN MARINO

BOS. & HERZ.

MONTENEGRO

VATICAN CITY

Sicily

MALTA

Ionian Sea

SERBIA

KOSOVO (disputed)

NORTH MACEDONIA

ALBANIA

Aegean Sea

GREECE

Crete

Lake Onega

Lake Ladoga

RUSSIA

BELARUS

UKRAINE

MOLDOVA

ROMANIA

BULGARIA

Sea of Azov

Black Sea

TURKEY

GEORGIA

Since 2014 Ukrainian territory of Crimea annexed by Russia

KAZAKHSTAN

Caspian Sea

Ural Mountains

ATLANTIC OCEAN

peace and is home to many of the world's richest countries. Access to education and standards of living are high compared to the rest of the world. The second smallest of the world's continents, Europe contains 44 countries and six "microstates". Most of Europe is Christian and almost all languages stem from Latin, Germanic, or Slavic roots. Europe is changing ethnically and religiously due to secularization and migration.

Facts and figures

LANGUAGES
The relationship between most European languages can be traced; the exception is Euskara, spoken in the Basque country of northern Spain and southwest France, which may predate the others. The most widely used language is Russian.

RELIGIONS
Most Europeans are Christian. The influence of the religion on art and culture is everywhere. Roman Catholics represent the largest branch, followed by the Orthodox church. There is a significant Muslim population of more than 25 million people.

URBAN POPULATION
Two of Europe's biggest cities are in Russia, its biggest country. Moscow has a population of 12.2 million people and St. Petersburg, 5.4 million. Istanbul is Europe's largest city with 15 million inhabitants, and London is third, with 9 million.

POPULATION BY COUNTRY
Europe's microstates have tiny populations. Only 33,600 people live in San Marino, but Vatican City has far fewer residents— around 800! Russia is the most populous country with over 143 million inhabitants, followed by Germany with almost 83 million.

CLIMATE

Europe's climate varies: toward the west it is influenced by the Atlantic Ocean and can be very changeable in countries such as Ireland. Much of Eastern Europe has cold winters and hot summers. Mediterranean countries have warm summers and mild winters, which makes them popular with tourists.

EUROPEAN FACTS

PLACES
Number of countries in Europe ....44 (incl. Turkey and Russia)
Highest point ....Mount Elbrus, Russia, 18,510 ft (5,642 m)
Lowest point........................Volga Delta, Caspian Sea, Russia, -92 ft (-28 m)
Biggest country ....Russia
6,612,000 sq miles (17,125,000 sq km)
Smallest country ....Vatican City
0.17 sq miles (0.44 sq km)

PEOPLE
Population of continent ....743 million
Proportion living in urban areas 75%

The people of Europe

THE VAST MAJORITY of Europeans enjoy a standard of good health and material comfort that is missing in many other parts of the world. High literacy rates and opportunities for different kinds of work are also present. Some people find the big-city lifestyles lonely and long for smaller communities and a less hurried way of life.

CITY LIVING

Around three-quarters of Europeans live in cities where they enjoy a high standard of living. Many are unfamiliar with the countryside, agriculture, or farming, instead buying everything they need from stores.

In the major cities, younger children are rarely allowed to go around without being accompanied by adults.

THE EUROPEAN UNION

EU flag

The euro

A UNITED EUROPE?

The EU started in 1958 when Belgium, France, Italy, Germany, Luxembourg, and the Netherlands formed the European Economic Community (EEC) to improve trade and cooperation among their countries. In 1993 it became the European Union, and it currently has 28 members, 19 of which share a currency, the euro.

CULTURAL MIX

Europe's big cities are blessed with a tremendous mix of people. Migrants, particularly from Europe, Africa, and Asia, have had a major impact on the human face of the continent. As well as adding their numbers to the workforce, immigrants have also enriched Europe with their food, music, and religious customs.

Having a good time

Most Europeans work fixed hours outside the home and all look forward to the holidays that dot their calendar. Some religious festivals, such as Christmas, have become national holidays around Europe but there are also regional and local festivals and events. Some are ancient in origin, while others, such as sports tournaments, are more recent inventions but just as popular.

SPLAT!
The tomato festival held near Valencia in Spain each year was only recently instituted. It owes its popularity to being so much fun.

FESTIVAL OF LIGHT
Celebrated in deepest midwinter in Sweden and Norway, St. Lucia's Day helps cheer people up during the darkest part of the year.

CARNIVAL
The Venice Carnival is an old tradition that allows people to disguise themselves with masks and have a wild time.

A NIGHT OUT
Most European cities have concert halls, opera houses, and theaters where formal performances of music, dance, or plays are put on. Spectators, like those at the ballet, pay to attend, and, unlike in other cultures, they do not participate.

FANTASTIC CONSTRUCTIONS
Europe has some wonderful buildings, the earliest of which are the castles and churches constructed by royalty. More recently, the emphasis has changed to buildings for government and business, and also to museums where a nation's treasures are displayed.

SPORTING PASSIONS
Soccer matches and other sporting events have, to some extent, replaced religion in arousing people's passionate involvement. Sports stadiums, especially when hosting football games, are one of the few public places where people cheer, laugh, and even cry.

Museums like the Louvre in Paris enable large numbers of people to view works of art and artifacts that they do not personally own.

ICELANDERS

A MASS OF VOLCANIC ROCK in the middle of the north Atlantic Ocean, Iceland remained uninhabited for far longer than the rest of Europe. The country was settled by Norse explorers and was later ruled by Norway, then

EUROPE'S REMOTE ISLAND NATION

Water, water everywhere

As well as being an island, Iceland has a lot of inland water, most famously hot springs, which are a major tourist attraction. The word *geyser* means a spurting, hot spring and comes from Geysir, the place in southwest Iceland where a spurt was first recorded in 1294. Geysers are caused by geothermal energy, the natural heat from Earth that also causes volcanoes to erupt. In fact, geothermal energy formed this island in the first place.

CAPITAL CITY

The first settlers came to Iceland from Norway in the ninth century. They named the city they founded Reykjavik, or "Smoky Bay" because of the steam rising from the hot springs. Over 60 percent of Iceland's population lives in or around Reykjavik, the world's most northerly capital.

GEOTHERMAL ENERGY

The Svartsengi power station takes in steam from naturally boiling seawater, heated by molten lava 6,000 ft (2,000 m) below the ground. The energy is used to heat freshwater for domestic use, or to drive turbines to create electricity. Using geothermal energy is clean and efficient, and, unlike resources such as natural gas, the water will never run out.

AN IMPORTANT SKILL

All children in Iceland learn how to swim, a skill that adults use frequently too. Iceland's outdoor swimming pools are open all year round. The weather might turn cold, but at 84°F (29°C), the naturally hot water keeps people warm.

Denmark. However, Icelanders developed their own language, and a unique, rich culture. Blessed with abundant geothermal energy, Iceland does not need to use gas, coal, or oil. This means it has almost no pollution, air quality is excellent, and food is untainted by chemicals. Being so far north, the sun is entirely absent from Iceland in winter, while during the summer weeks go by without it setting!

THE FISHING INDUSTRY

Iceland has the highest percentage of fishermen of any population. They catch over one million tons of fish every year. Cod is the most common saltwater fish but herring, redfish, and saithe are plentiful too. Freshwater trout and salmon are caught as much for sport and personal consumption as for industry.

HANGING OUT TO DRY

Fish is one of Iceland's staple foods. It is served baked, stewed, or sometimes simply dried and salted. Icelanders are proud of their fish, which swim in uncontaminated waters, and of the purity of their food, which is grown without artificial fertilizers.

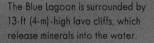

The Blue Lagoon is surrounded by 13-ft (4-m)-high lava cliffs, which release minerals into the water.

STILL HOT AFTER 30 YEARS

Heimaey island is home to a volcano that erupted very violently in 1973. Today it is still possible to bake bread by burying an unbaked loaf in the volcano's ashes and leaving it for some hours.

THE BLUE LAGOON

A by-product of the Svartsengi geothermal power station is an artificial spa known as the Blue Lagoon. After the hot seawater has been used by the station, it enters a pool where it is mixed with freshwater and cooled to a comfortable 99–102°F (37–39°C). The slightly sulfurous water is only 4 ft (1.2 m) deep, but it is brimming with blue-green algae and white silica mud, which are said to be good for the skin.

CELTIC PEOPLE

THOUSANDS OF YEARS AGO, THE BRITISH ISLES were invaded by various groups known collectively as Celts. The descendants of these people can be found throughout

CHILDREN OF ANCIENT INVADERS

Irish castles

Irish nobles from the 12th century onward protected themselves from invasion by living in castles with deep moats, thick walls, and fortified battlements. These were so well built that many are still in good condition today and have been converted into hotels.

THE HIGHLAND GAMES

With Scottish clans separated by miles of craggy hillsides, the Highland Games were a way for people to get together. Today, Highland Games are held in Scotland and elsewhere. Traditional competitions, such as caber tossing and throwing the hammer, lie at the heart of these events, but Scottish dancers, bagpipers, and drummers may feature too.

Throwing the hammer.

IRISH DANCING

Today, Irish dancing is extremely popular among people of Irish origin living outside Ireland. Its popularity is partly due to the *Conradh na Gaeilge* (Gaelic League), which was founded in 1893 to revive Irish folk culture. The organization standardized Irish dances and still issues rules governing how they are taught and judged in competitions.

SCOTTISH TARTAN

The distinctive mark of a tartan plaid is the square formed where threads of two different colors cross. Although tartan cloth had existed in Scotland for hundreds of years, its popularity grew enormously at the end of the 18th century when clans began to identify strongly with their own particular pattern.

the British Isles, particularly in Scotland, Ireland, and Wales, and many take great pride in their heritage and regional differences. There are scarcely any native speakers of Celtic languages such as Irish, Scottish, Cornish, and Manx, although their study and use are actively promoted. Welsh too is in decline, although 19 percent of Welsh people speak it, and it is taught at many schools in Wales.

PIPING IN THE HAGGIS

The Scots celebrate the birth of their greatest poet, Robert Burns, on January 25. Haggis, a traditional food made out of stuffed sheeps' stomach, is served at the meal. A great fuss is made over the haggis—it is brought in to the sound of a bagpipe, and speeches are made in its honor.

The haggis is stuffed with the heart and liver of a sheep, mixed with oatmeal and seasonings.

The caber is lifted at the thinner end, and flipped during the toss.

WHAT THE WELSH WORE

Welsh national costume is based on the clothes of Welsh peasants 200 years ago. For women and girls it consists of a striped petticoat and an open-fronted dress, called a bedgown, with an apron, shawl, and a tall hat. It is sometimes worn on Saint David's Day (March 1), Wales's national day.

TOSSING THE CABER

The caber is a long pole up to 18 ft (5.5 m) long and 150 lbs (70 kg) in weight. Competitors lift the caber and try to throw it in a straight line.

Tartan kilts (skirts) are the traditional costume of Scottish men.

SHEEP SHOW

Wales is the most important sheep farming region in Europe. There are 10 million sheep here alongside a human population of just 3 million. Sheep shows like this one allow farmers to come together to share news and information about sheep farming.

ENGLAND

A PATCHWORK NATION

THE ENGLISH PEOPLE THEMSELVES often feel uncertain about the difference between the United Kingdom, Great Britain, and England. The United Kingdom is the name of the country that consists of Great

Englishness today

English people are descended from a mixture of many groups: Romans, Normans, Danes, Vikings, and Celts. Later, waves of immigration beginning in the 19th century brought substantial numbers of people from almost all over the globe, particularly those from former colonial countries in Africa, the Indian Subcontinent, and the Caribbean.

A plush lawn, a slightly overcast sky, and a cathedral form the perfect backdrop for a cricket match.

MOST POPULAR DISH

There are more traditional contenders for the English national dish (among them roast beef, or fish and chips) but "curry"—referring to almost any Indian dish—is without doubt England's most popular meal. Indian restaurants and takeaways exist in every English city, town, and perhaps, village.

SPORTING PASSION

The game of cricket travelled around the world with British colonial administrators in the 19th and 20th centuries. While it is enjoyed throughout the United Kingdom, with games played on village greens in the summer, the English are particularly passionate about it.

MULTICULTURAL MARKET

Newcomers often maintain customs from their original culture, and seek familiar foods and clothing in shops and markets. This means that people who live in England can access a much wider variety of goods and cultural experiences than ever before.

Britain and Northern Ireland. Great Britain, then, refers to the island consisting of three somewhat independent regions: Scotland, Wales, and England. While the Irish, Scottish, and Welsh have distinctive national customs, it is harder to pick out the elements of a specific English identity. It may be fairest to say that the English people form a patchwork of identities, samples of which are explored below.

MORRIS DANCERS
Historically an important part of annual springtime festivities, Morris dancers wear bells on their feet and leap athletically to lively folk music while waving sticks or handkerchiefs.

CARNIVAL!
London's Notting Hill Carnival is a celebration of Caribbean culture. Immigrants from Trinidad organized the first Carnival in 1959 to build relationships between local English residents and the Caribbean newcomers. Now, it is Europe's largest street festival, with a parade of people in colorful costumes, as well as music and food from the West Indies.

THE WEATHER
The changeable British weather is a hot topic of conversation for the English. It is not unusual for rain, sun, and strong winds to occur at once. Britain is on the edge of the Atlantic where it bears the brunt of storms, while the Gulf Stream makes the air mild and moist. These factors add to the unpredictability and the national obsession.

The sculpture's location by the A1, a major road, means it is seen by 33 million people every year.

UNIVERSITY TOWN
World-famous (along with Oxford) for its university founded in 1209, Cambridge is still dominated by student life. There are 31 colleges where students live and socialize while at the university. Here, a punt (a flat-bottomed boat) travels along the Cam River past St. John's College.

ANGEL OF THE NORTH
Erected in Gateshead in the northeast of England in 1998, this is the largest sculpture in Britain. Designed by Antony Gormley, its wingspan is 177 ft (53 m), almost that of a jumbo jet.

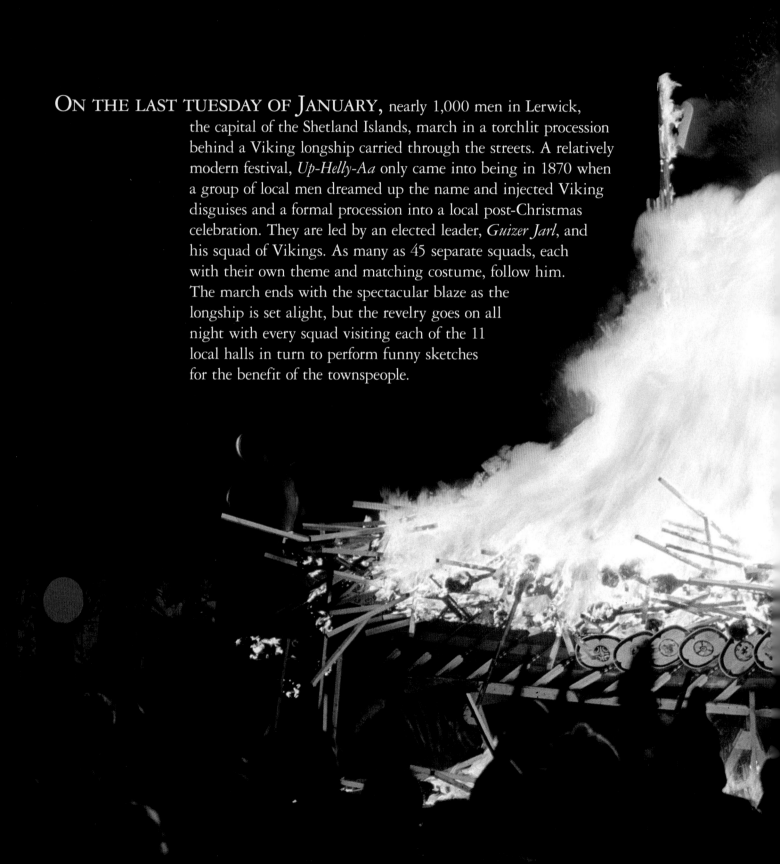

SHETLAND ISLANDERS
A VIKING FIRE FESTIVAL RECALLS A SCANDINAVIAN INVASION

ON THE LAST TUESDAY OF JANUARY, nearly 1,000 men in Lerwick, the capital of the Shetland Islands, march in a torchlit procession behind a Viking longship carried through the streets. A relatively modern festival, *Up-Helly-Aa* only came into being in 1870 when a group of local men dreamed up the name and injected Viking disguises and a formal procession into a local post-Christmas celebration. They are led by an elected leader, *Guizer Jarl*, and his squad of Vikings. As many as 45 separate squads, each with their own theme and matching costume, follow him. The march ends with the spectacular blaze as the longship is set alight, but the revelry goes on all night with every squad visiting each of the 11 local halls in turn to perform funny sketches for the benefit of the townspeople.

SCANDINAVIANS

THE NORTHERN REACHES OF EUROPE are famous for their long, cold, dark winters, and contrastingly brief summers in which the sun barely, or never, sets. People living in these regions owe tall

EUROPE'S NORTHERNERS

The Holmenkollen Ski Jump is a Norwegian insitution and home to an annual competition that first took place in 1892.

What's in a name?

The term "Scandinavia" does not have a strict definition. Geographically speaking, the Scandinavian peninsula consists of Norway, Sweden, and a bit of Finland, although the term is more commonly used to refer to Norway, Sweden, and Denmark. The broadest definition also includes Iceland and Finland.

CHURCHBOAT RACES
Church services in the Swedish village of Rattvik attracted people from across the bay, some of whom traveled by boat. A custom evolved with the villages building longboats and racing one another. Today, the races are staged for the benefit of tourists.

SANTA LUCIA
December 13 is Santa Lucia Day. Traditionally, in Sweden and Norway, a daughter of the family, dressed in a white dress, red sash, and candle headdress, brings breakfast to her parents. Lucia means "light" and the custom is observed by communities in school and town celebrations.

GETTING AROUND
Cross-country skiing was invented centuries ago in Scandinavia as a practical means of getting around in a snowy climate. It is still a popular sport today, particularly in Norway.

ICE FISHING
Even when the ice is solid enough to sit on, life continues beneath the surface. This warmly dressed Norwegian woman lying on a bearskin has drilled a hole into the thick ice covering a lake and is waiting patiently for the fish to bite.

height, blue eyes, and blonde hair to Viking ancestors. Today, the Scandinavian countries tend to be industrialized with a good standard of living. Most of the population is concentrated in the south, although plenty live within the Arctic Circle. Midsummer celebrations are second only to Christmas in Scandinavia, including dancing and singing, flowers in one's hair, and plenty of food and drink.

WELFARE STATES

Taxes in Scandinavia are set high, but in return people benefit from excellent welfare services. Scandinavian states ensure that mothers and fathers have time off to care for their new babies. Parental leave can even entail up to one year with full pay.

CELEBRATING SUMMER
Midsummer is marked across Scandinavia with lively celebrations. These people in Södermanland in southeast Sweden dance around a pole decorated with summer greenery. Some people wear traditional dress and put flowers in their hair for the occasion.

CITY OF BIKES
Bicycle travel is common in Denmark, where the government encourages people to bicycle rather than drive. The capital city, Copenhagen, is one of the most bike-friendly cities in the world. On average, Danes bicycle 1 mile (1.6 km) per day, and 49 percent of children aged 11–15 bike to school.

CONNECTING COUNTRIES
The idea for a bridge uniting Sweden and Denmark is not a new one. Suggestions date back to the 1800s. The plans finally came to fruition in 2000 with the opening of the Øresund Bridge linking Malmö in Sweden with Copenhagen in Denmark. At 5 miles (8 km), it is the longest single bridge in Europe to carry both road and railroad traffic.

SAMI

A NOMADIC LIFE IN THE CHILL

THE SAMI PEOPLE OF NORTHERN EUROPE live in the Arctic area popularly known as Lapland. Originally the Sami hunted reindeer, but by the 17th century, hunting was replaced by herding. These days few

Living and working together

In a land where the vital activities of getting food and keeping warm are the difference between life and death —temperatures can plummet to a chilly -49°F (-45°C)—the Norwegian Sami herders live remarkably in tune with the land. For centuries the Sami have formed work teams called *Sii'das*—groups of families that herd their reindeer together and share the work. Each reindeer is marked, according to the *Sii'da*, when it is born, usually by a small nick cut out of one ear.

As well as snowmobiles, the Sami people also use walkie-talkies and sometimes even helicopters to aid herding.

CLOTHING

Some Sami still wear the traditional bright red and blue costumes. Women wear dresses belted at the waist and men wear belted tunics. In the winter they wear reindeer skins with their clothes. The women use looms made of wood and antler to weave the belts and ribbons that decorate clothes.

Tall hats are sometimes stuffed with grass to help keep the head warm.

Sami people combine older traditions with the conveniences of a more modern lifestyle.

BELIEFS

Originally the Sami followed an animistic religion, believing that all objects in nature have a soul that must be respected. This has long been replaced by the Lutheran faith, and marriages take place in churches. However, they still believe that spirits inhabit the natural world and those who do not respect nature will have trouble living off the land.

The Sami people started converting to the Christian faith in the 17th century.

Sami herd and only those in the north of Norway are still seminomadic. These people migrate each spring, with their reindeer, from the tundra to the coast and islands, where the calves are born. They then return to the tundra in the fall. The Sami live in towns on the tundra and enjoy a modern standard of living much like other Norwegians. The Sami who migrate are some of Europe's last nomads.

Annual migration

In the spring instinct prompts the reindeer to start moving north on their migration to the coast or to islands off the coast where their calves will be born. A Sami group member on skis leads the herd, and teams of men with dogsleds bring up the rear to stop any of the animals from wandering off. Their long and arduous journey can sometimes take them over highlands and across rivers.

COUNTING THE HERD
Before the spring migration, the herd of up to 3,000 reindeer needs to be gathered and counted. Huge lengths of hessian are swished around the reindeer to round them up, and dogs (pointed-eared pomeranians) are used to drive the reindeer to enter into a corral. The pregnant females are sometimes taken to the coast in trucks before calving time.

Curly toed boots are strapped beneath ski straps to hold the skis in place.

GOING TO SCHOOL
In the past, the Sami's nomadic lifestyle made mainstream education difficult and from the 19th century boys were sent away to state-run boarding schools. Now community schools in Sami areas offer education in the Sami language. Some Sami, like this boy, wear traditional clothes to school.

Exhausted reindeer.

As well as snowmobiles, the Sami people also use walkie-talkies and sometimes even helicopters to aid herding.

MODERN MIGRATION
These days modern ski wear combines with traditional Sami clothing and snowmobiles are commonly used. It is however essential to let the animals walk at their own pace. If a reindeer gets tired, someone will often give it a free ride on the back of the snowmobile!

FINNS

OLD TRADITIONS AND NEW INVENTIONS

SITUATED IN THE NORTH OF EUROPE, Finland shares some unusual features with its neighbors. The most noticeable is the long, dark winter, when temperatures can drop to -49°F (-45°C). Living in the cold

An independent country

Finland belonged to Sweden from the 12th until the 19th century, and after that it belonged to Russia. It became independent in 1917 following the Russian Revolution and successfully resisted invasions from both the Soviet Union and Nazi Germany. It maintains particularly close relations with the other Nordic countries.

NATIONAL SPORTS
Naturally, the climate means that sports like cross-country skiing and snowboarding are popular in Finland, but so is *pesäpallo*, the national sport, which is rather like baseball. People also keep fit by bicycling in preference to driving cars.

HOLIDAY ON ICE
Ski holiday week, or *hiihtolomaviikko*, takes place around March and always boosts morale. Officially this is a students' vacation, but adults also take the opportunity to go cross-country skiing or snowmobiling. In the evening, people stop for a barbeque supper and set up camp overnight in the forests.

WOOD IS GOOD
Two-thirds of Finland is forest, providing land for grazing animals, for hunting, and, most importantly, wood. In the past, wood was needed for fuel, furniture, and other everyday items. Today it is used to a lesser extent, but exporting wood is still vital to the Finnish economy.

LIGHTING THE WAY
This family is making a beacon that will help their children find their way home from school in the dark. During the winter months some days will only have two hours of sunlight.

Even very young children are used to playing in the snow with sleds or skis.

and dark has created an emphasis on saunas and exercise, which help keep people feeling fit and happy. From June 21 until December 22, four minutes of daylight are lost every day. The sun might not be seen much during midwinter, but when it appears in the summer, it is celebrated. Forests cover much of Finland and up until recently, many people held jobs in forestry. Finns today still respect nature and enjoy the scenery.

MIDSUMMER BONFIRES

Midsummer, or *Juhannus*, marks the summer solstice. It became a Christian feast although it was marked even before Christianity came to Finland. Today it is a celebration of nature. People go to the countryside, or decorate their towns with lilac and birch. At night they light *kokkos* (bonfires), which symbolize purity and ward off evil spirits. *Juhannus* also provides an occasion for people to fly the national flag.

A HEALTHY SWEAT

The word "sauna' is Finnish but these steam baths are popular across all the Nordic countries. Part of Finnish culture for over 1,000 years, there are over two million saunas in Finland—that's one for every household!

1 Hot house
Almost every house has its own sauna, and mini-saunas are even inside apartments! Saunas are a great way to relax and socialize during the dark winters.

2 Heating up
In the steam room rocks are heated on a stove and then splashed with water to create steam. The point of a sauna is to induce sweat and thereby open the skin's pores.

3 Cooling down
From the steam room, bathers plunge into a pool of icy water or else roll in the snow. The sudden contrast is invigorating and refreshes both body and mind.

LAST DAY OF SCHOOL

Graduating from school in Finland calls for a big celebration. Those graduating are presented with their college entrance exam certificates, red roses, and a distinctive white cap. After the formal ceremony in school, families host parties for their graduating son or daughter.

DUTCH

TULIP FIELDS IN FULL BLOOM

ALTHOUGH THEY ORIGINATE IN THE MOUNTAINS OF CENTRAL ASIA, tulips first arrived in Europe more than 400 years ago as a result of trade with the Ottoman Empire. They became such a desirable status symbol that in the 17th century "Tulipomania" broke out and people began trading bulbs for enormous sums—one buyer exchanged his canal-side house in Amsterdam for a single rare bulb! Even though this sort of exchange was unsustainable, the Dutch created a strong tulip industry that continues to dominate the world market. The Netherlands grows around three billion bulbs each year, of which two billion are exported.

SPANISH

THE KINGDOM OF SPAIN was formed in 1492, when King Ferdinand and Queen Isabella united the kingdoms of Castilla and Aragón and made Roman Catholicism the national religion. Today, Spain has 17 regions

Old traditions, current passions

Many aspects of Spanish culture have evolved out of traditional folk customs, yet it is Roman Catholicism that has had the greatest impact on Spanish culture. Over 3,000 religious festivals—ancient and modern, local and national—are celebrated throughout the country.

CAPITAL CITY

Madrid sits in the very center of the country. Of the many modern buildings in the city, none is more immediately striking than these leaning office blocks in the Plaza de Castilla.

FERIA DE ABRIL

Men dressed as Andalucian peasants ride horses and carts through the streets during Seville's annual fair. Hundreds of tents house temporary dance halls during the week-long festival that attracts one million people.

SPANISH SNACKS

Every bar in Spain serves *tapas*, small plates of snacks to go with drinks. Originally free, these days they must be paid for. Typical *tapas* might be Spanish omelette, cured ham, squid, shrimp, olives, potatoes, or anchovies. Spanish people sometimes spend an evening going from bar to bar sampling each one's speciality dish.

and there are four official ethnic groups with their own languages—Castilian, Catalan, Galician, and Basque. Regions are self-governing and relatively independent but connected by their national government. For much of its history, Spain was ruled by other civilizations ranging from the Romans to the Moors. Each group has left its influence on the culture, arts, and landscape of today.

CASTELLS IN THE SKY

These men making a human castle (*castell*, in *Catalan*) at a festival in Tarragona are called *castellers*. Castellers attend every festival in the region and are also a popular sight on television. Tradition says that the *castell* must be at least eight tiers tall.

BAGPIPES

The music of Galicia in northwest Spain is nothing like the *flamenco* music of Andalucia in the south. *Gaita* (bagpipes) feature strongly because Galicia was once occupied by Celtic people like those who settled in Scotland and Ireland.

FALLAS DE VALENCIA

Spectacular explosions mark the end of Valencia's week-long fire festival. In early March ninots—satirical statues made of cardboard, wood, and plaster—are erected all around the town to be admired and judged. At midnight on March 19, they are blown up with only the winning ninot spared for permanent display in the city's museum.

THE GUGGENHEIM MUSEUM, BILBAO

Opened in 1997, the Guggenheim Museum in Bilbao is one of the most spectacular buildings in the world and a major tourist attraction. This extraordinary collection of sweeping curves covered in thin titanium tiles is 160 ft (50 m) high and spans the area from the city center to the edge of the Nervión River.

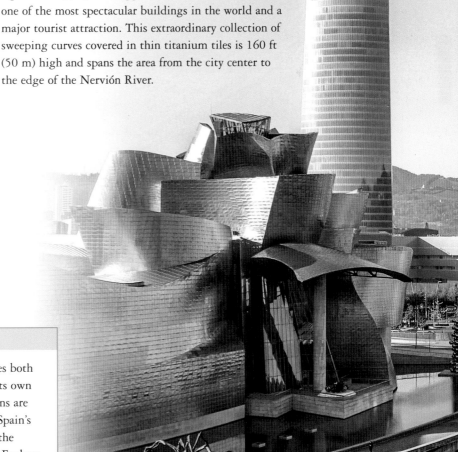

BASQUE REGION

The Basque region straddles both France and Spain and has its own distinct identity. Street signs are written in both Castilian (Spain's main Spanish dialect) and the Basque language, Euskara. Euskara is a source of intrigue to scholars because it bears no relationship to any other European language.

PORTUGUESE

HOPING FOR A GOOD CATCH

PUSHING THEIR COLORFUL *DÓRI* (FISHING BOAT) OUT TO SEA these fishermen hope they won't need to travel too far from the coastal village of Praia de Mira to find fish such as sardines, anchovies, and tuna. Their ancestors were a hardy breed, many of whom were prepared to venture a great deal farther. From the 15th to the mid-20th century, Portuguese fishermen spent long months from April to September in the hazardous, freezing waters of the North Atlantic. They traveled as far as the coasts of Norway, Iceland, and Labrador in search of cod. Sometimes fog or storms would suddenly descend and a boat would disappear, making widows and orphans of entire communities back home.

FRENCH

THE FRENCH ARE VERY PROUD OF THEIR COUNTRY, believing its intellectual and cultural life, cuisine, and wine to be among the best in the world. They are known for their style, which is reflected in their fashion,

AN APPRECIATION OF THE GOOD LIFE

SINGING CHANSON

France has a rich musical heritage and the tradition of *chanson*, songs sung in French with poetic lyrics, dates back centuries. Today singers of *chanson* take care to respect the rhythms of the French language when writing lyrics, resisting the influence of English pop music. Artists include Zaz, pictured here.

WINE PRODUCTION

The French have been producing wine since at least Roman times. Wines from each region taste different thanks to a variety of factors including the type of grape, climate, soil, and the way the wine is fermented.

Free time

Quality of life and leisure time are very important to the people of France. All French workers are entitled to five weeks of paid annual leave, and many take off the entire month of August. They decamp to the countryside to vacation homes or hotels, leaving the cities virtual ghost towns.

TRADITIONAL PASTIME

Boules, or *pétanque* is a popular French game played with metal balls. The aim of the game is to get your ball as close as possible to the target ball known as the *cochonnet*. Players are also allowed to throw their balls at the *cochonnet* so as to nudge it further from their opponents' balls and closer to their own.

Grapes are delicate and are still picked by hand for high-quality wines.

store window displays, and in the presentation of food. There is a strong movement to protect French language and culture from the global influence of English. France has indigenous minorities, Bretons in the west and Occitans in the south, but also many immigrants from former colonial countries such as Algeria and Morocco, as well as a significant Jewish population.

BASTILLE DAY

On July 14, 1789, the French people stormed the Bastille Prison, beginning the revolution that freed them from the monarchy and made the country a republic. The day is celebrated every year as a national holiday.

ENDURANCE TEST

The *Tour de France* is a world-famous bicycle race that lasts for three weeks. Its 2,100 miles (3,400 km) are broken into 20 stages covering many of the different terrains that make up the French countryside. The leader from the day before wears a yellow jersey.

The Eiffel Tower.

BRETONS

This Celtic people are native to Brittany in the west of France. Over 200,000 people speak the Breton language. The Fest-Noz, a traditional festival, includes dances dating to the Middle Ages.

CAFÉ CULTURE

The Champs Elysées is the most famous street in Paris. Wide, tree-lined sidewalks allow people to sit outdoors at its cafés and restaurants and watch the world go by. Dining or just drinking coffee at an outdoor café is an everyday pleasure greatly valued by the French people.

Big country

FRANCE IS THE LARGEST COUNTRY in Western Europe. It mostly consists of flat plains but there are some mountainous areas including the Pyrenees in the south, the Massif Central in the centre, and the Alps in the east. France also administers some overseas territories left over from colonial times.

MODERN MONUMENT

The *Grande Arche* is a striking 35-story office building. It was one of a number of buildings commissioned at the end of the 20th century to symbolize France's role in art, politics, and the world economy. It is situated in Paris's La Defense district, and is home to more than 70 French and foreign companies.

At the top of the building is a public gallery that looks out onto spectacular views of Paris.

APPRECIATING THE ARTS

France has a long tradition of distinguished artists and an appreciation for the arts is instilled in French children from an early age. Art education is a compulsory part of the French school curriculum for children aged 5–15. They are taught how to enjoy and understand art, and how to produce artworks of their own.

FILM FESTIVAL

Cannes' population is just under 80,000 but swells to almost three times that number during the annual international film festival every May. The town is situated on the French Riviera in the south of France and is also a popular destination during the summer months for both French and foreign travelers, drawn to its mild climate and beautiful beaches.

Away from the cities

France enjoys great geographical diversity and each region has its own distinct character and food. Particular areas of natural beauty include Brittany with its rugged coast, the mountain ranges of the Alps and the Pyrenees, the Mediterranean coast around the Cote d'Azur, and the glorious vineyards and lavender fields of Provence.

WEEKLY MARKETS
Many French towns host weekly markets where farmers sell their own produce ranging from fruit and vegetables to wine, sausages, and cheeses. The foods vary according to the region and season.

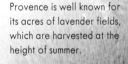

Provence is well known for its acres of lavender fields, which are harvested at the height of summer.

SKIING

There is plenty of choice when it comes to winter sports in France. There are many well-established ski resorts in the mountains of the Alps and the Pyrenees, and cross-country skiing is becoming more popular in the Jura and Massif Central.

FRAGRANT FIELDS
The lavender plant needs little water and grows well in the hot, dry climate of southern France. Its sweet fragrance makes it a popular ingredient in soaps and perfumes. It has one additional quality—it is a strong natural insect repellant.

GERMANS

TODAY, GERMANY HAS THE FOURTH LARGEST ECONOMY in the

NO LONGER DIVIDED INTO TWO NATIONS

world. With its powerful car manufacturing and engineering industries, it has high and steady employment and is among the

FRIESIAN FOLK
Both the Netherlands and Germany have Friesian populations who traditionally live a rural life and keep animals. Windmills and cottages (often thatched) dot the region.

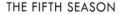

THE FIFTH SEASON
During the carnival in the village of Bad Waldsee, revelers wear fancy dress or traditional handcrafted wooden masks to parade through the streets. It only lasts a few days but the carnival is so important that it is referred to as the "fifth season" of the year.

A unified country

Germany's 16 states each have their own capital and regional government. Prior to reunification, East Germany was one of the richest of the communist countries, yet its citizens experienced a considerable degree of material hardship and cultural repression compared to the people of West Germany. Today, the gap in prosperity between these two groups still persists, although it is slowly closing.

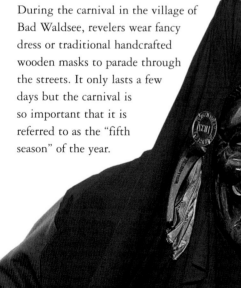

CENTER OF LEARNING
Heidelberg University is one of the world's oldest surviving universities. It was founded in 1386, at the time of the Holy Roman Empire. Today, it welcomes students from around the world who can choose from over 160 subjects of study.

world's top exporters of goods. In 1945, after the Second World War, the country was divided—the Federal Republic in the west and the German Democratic Republic in the east, dominated by the communist Soviet Union. The GDR erected a wall to prevent its citizens from defecting to the west but the Berlin Wall came down in 1989 amid great rejoicing and emotional reunions. Berlin is now the capital of unified Germany.

THE BRANDENBURG GATE

Berlin's Brandenburg Gate is an important landmark. It was modeled on the entrance to Athens' Acropolis and was completed in 1791. Ironically, although intended to symbolize peace, the gate was incorporated into the Berlin Wall and its meaning only restored in 1989 when the wall came down.

The Gate is a major tourist attraction. Only taxis, buses, and officials are allowed to drive through it now.

GERMAN SAUSAGES

There are thousands of different types of *wurst* (German sausages); some are cooked and eaten hot while others are sliced or spread. The meat—mostly pork, sometimes beef or veal—is combined with peppercorns, spices, and other ingredients.

WOOD-CARVING WORKSHOP

A clockmaker carves the face for a cuckoo clock in his Black Forest workshop. Cuckoo clocks were first made in the 18th century when peddling "clock carriers" found customers for them by literally carrying the clocks around in knapsacks to prospective buyers. Demand still remains high for the handmade clocks today.

CAR INDUSTRY

Germany was producing 900 cars a year in 1901. Today the number is more than 6 million, and firms such as Audi, Daimler, Mercedes, BMW, Volkswagen, and Porsche employ more than 800,000 people.

Bavarians

THE LARGEST REGION IN GERMANY is called Bavaria, but Bavarian dialects and architecture can be found in other parts of Germany, the Austrian Tyrol, and even South Tyrol in Italy. The folk customs of this area are particularly rich—yodeling, the alpenhorn, many different kinds of dance, and a variety of national costumes all originate in this region.

A rich heritage

Local governments support cultural organizations in their efforts to keep Bavarian traditions alive. No subsidies are necessary, however, to promote Bavarian foods: beer, meatballs, and sausages are still as popular as ever.

TOWN SQUARE
The town of Lindau nestles on an island on the shores of Lake Constance, Germany's biggest lake. During the Middle Ages prosperous merchants lived here. Their brightly painted, half-timbered houses overlooking picturesque town squares are very popular with tourists.

OKTOBERFEST
The Oktoberfest has been held in Munich every year since 1810 when it was instituted to celebrate a royal wedding. It is an enormous festival with over six million visitors annually. The mayor opens the event by tapping a keg of beer and declaring "O'zapft is" which means "it's been tapped."

BRASS BAND
Jolly Bavarian "oom-pah" music is traditionally played outdoors by a brass band. It is featured at celebrations—most famously at Munich's boisterous Oktoberfest.

SCHUHPLATTLING

The *Schuhplattling* (shoe-slapping) dance which goes back to the 11th–14th centuries is the most well-known Bavarian dance. The man's slapping movement is said to mimic a species of bird which flaps its wings to attract a mate.

CHURCH IN THE HILLS

The town of Berchtesgaden nestles among valleys and lakes with the magnificent Bavarian Alps as its backdrop. This region was once a separate little country, one of the smallest states in the Holy Roman Empire.

SAINT NICHOLAS NIGHT

On December 5 at 8 pm black hooded figures with long straw beards and bells attached to their stomachs meet in Berghofen. Until midnight they run through the town, bells clanging deafeningly, visiting the local farms to banish evil spirits.

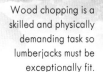

Wood chopping is a skilled and physically demanding task so lumberjacks must be exceptionally fit.

WOOD PULLING

Traditionally, during the autumn lumberjacks chop wood in the forests of the Allgau. The logs are stored high in the mountains and brought down to the valley when needed. The wood is transported by helicopter or by horse-drawn carriage, which is cheap, efficient, and much better for the environment!

CZECHS

IN THE CITY OF A HUNDRED SPIRES

THE CAPITAL CITY OF THE CZECH REPUBLIC, or Czechia, is Prague. It is known as the City of a Hundred Spires thanks to the many churches in its beautiful and architecturally diverse Old Town. Running through the city, the Vltava River is spanned by numerous bridges, including the statue-lined Charles Bridge, below. The Czech Republic has a population of nearly 11 million people, more than 1 million of whom live in Prague. Formerly part of Czechoslovakia, the Republic was formed in 1989 after the Velvet Revolution, which saw the fall of the communist regime. The majority of the population is ethnically Czech but, with its growing economy, the country attracts many immigrants—around 500,000, from countries including Ukraine, Slovakia, and Vietnam.

ALPINE PEOPLE

RUNNING ACROSS EIGHT DIFFERENT COUNTRIES and approximately 750 miles (1,200 km), the Alps divide the northern and southern parts of mainland Europe. This mountain range

EUROPE'S MOUNTAIN PEOPLE

Outnumbered by skiers

Winter was once the quiet season, but is now the busiest and most profitable time of year for many Alpine towns and villages. In some towns, during the skiing season, tourists outnumber locals by 40 to one. Hotels, restaurants, cable cars, and ski lifts as well as new roads have all been built to support the booming tourist industry.

Tourists also visit the Alps during the summer to hike and enjoy the warmer weather.

Cheese is made by mixing fresh milk with rennet, an enzyme found in the stomach lining of calves reared solely on milk.

DELICIOUS CHEESE

The fresh, sweet grass and wildflowers eaten by Alpine cows result in wonderfully tasty milk and cheese. The best cheeses are made by hand and then left to mature for weeks or months in a special cheese cave, where they must be turned over and rubbed with salt on alternate days.

POTATO FARMING

Some Alpine regions provide the right conditions for growing potatoes. Seeds are planted between February and April and the crop is harvested between May and September. Potatoes were brought to Europe by explorers returning from travels in the New World in the late 1500s.

stretches from southeastern France through Monaco, Italy, Switzerland, Liechtenstein, Germany, Austria, and Slovenia. The Alps can be divided into four climatic regions, although in fact virtually every valley has a different climate. Until recently, the mountains were considerable barriers to travel, so people developed in separate clusters resulting in different traditions, languages, and dialects.

HEADING FOR THE HILLS
During the winter, the cows must be kept away from the snowy slopes and eat hay in the valley. In the middle of June, they are herded back up the mountains. A whole day is dedicated to the task. People armed with sticks keep the cows moving if they get distracted by the juicy grass.

MAKING HAY
June and July are a particularly busy time for Alpine farmers. While their cows are enjoying the grass high above the treeline, the farmers gather the grass growing on the lower slopes to make hay. It is heaped into nets and hauled away to be stored in haylofts. This hay will provide the cattle with food during the long winter to come.

RUSSIANS

RUSSIANS ARE DESCENDED FROM THE SLAVIC PEOPLE living north of the Black Sea. The country is home to many different ethnic groups including Tartars, Ingush, and Chechens, as well as immigrants from

EUROPE'S LARGEST ETHNIC GROUP

City life

About three-quarters of Russians live in cities. A shortage of housing means that most families have small flats inside enormous apartment blocks. During the communist era, flats were owned and allocated by the government. These days property is privately owned or rented. The high costs, in cities such as Moscow, mean it is quite common for grandparents, parents, and children all to live together.

CONSUMER CULTURE

Until communism ended in Russia in 1991, the state looked after many aspects of peoples lives. Food, clothing, and various other items were rationed. These days, big Russian cities boast boutiques, smart restaurants, and well-stocked department stores, but the goods are too costly for many people.

St. Basil's Cathedral in Moscow features striking onion-shaped domes and spires.

PEOPLE'S PALACES

The Moscow Metro is famous for its beautiful stations, lavishly decorated with marble columns, ornate chandeliers, and frescoes. The metro opened in 1935 and now has over 200 stations. One of the most opulent is Komsomolskaya station, pictured here.

outside Russia. Most Russians were rural peasants working for aristocratic landlords until the Communist Revolution. In 1917–1991, under communism, the central government managed land in large state farms and was responsible for allocating housing. Industry was also centralized and the state controlled the media and press. Literature and all the arts were highly valued and well supported by the government.

ICE SCULPTURES

Every February, Moscow's Gorky Park hosts an ice-sculpture festival featuring the work of both local and international artists. It takes hours of work in the freezing cold to create a sculpture like this cat.

A PLACE IN THE COUNTRY

Many urban Russians own a home in the country, called a *dacha*, where they spend the weekends and summer vacations. Under communism, food came from collective farms, which were controlled by the government. People would supplement this food with vegetables that they grew on plots of land next to their *dachas*. These small allotments are still an important part of the *dacha experience*.

TIME FOR TEA

The *samovar* symbolizes home for Russians. Its function is to keep tea—drunk at all times of day—and the water used to dilute it hot. A central cylinder containing smoldering charcoal keeps the brew hot in a traditional *samovar*. Newer models sit on the gas stove or use electricity instead.

TEMPERING

Russians traditionally believe that the body should be "tempered" in order to enable it to withstand diseases in the cold climate. This process, which is still performed on children today, is called *zakalivanie*. It involves briefly plunging all or part of the body into snow or freezing cold water.

MASLENITSA

Maslenitsa is a festival that dates back to pre-Christian times. Its counterparts exist in many festivals in the Northern Hemisphere that commemorate the rebirth of nature at the end of a long, dark winter. Different activities are assigned to each day of the weeklong celebration including parties, sleigh rides, and snowball fights in city parks.

POLES

LIKE OTHER COUNTRIES IN EASTERN EUROPE, Poland was badly damaged by the Second World War (1939–1945), and shortly afterward adopted communism. Unfortunately, the country also suffered

A DEVOUTLY RELIGIOUS PEOPLE

Ethnically and religiously unified

The borders of the country that is modern Poland have changed significantly since the 10th century. Despite this, nearly all of its population today is ethnically Polish and almost all Roman Catholic, with three-quarters actively practicing their religion. Polish people were proud that John Paul II, Pope from 1978 to 2005, was a Pole. The population of Poland is some 38 million people but many more Poles live outside the country, for example in Russia and Germany.

SOCIALIST HOUSING
During the communist era enormous, identical apartment buildings were built in Poland and other communist countries. It was believed that identical homes would make people feel equal.

FIRST COMMUNION
By the time they are eight or nine, Polish children will have experienced their First Communion. On this day girls in white dresses and veils, and boys in dark suits participate fully in the Catholic Mass for the first time.

MUSHROOM PICKING
Historically, mushrooms were the great equalizer in the Polish diet; growing wild, they were available to rich and poor alike. To this day, mushroom picking is a favorite Polish pastime.

for many years under communist rule. The Polish solidarity movement led the way throughout Eastern Europe for the rapid yet peaceful decline of communism in the late 1980s and early 1990s. Poland enjoys fertile farmland, and even though the country has recently transformed itself into a capitalist democracy, nearly a third of its citizens maintain a rural lifestyle, living and working on small, family-run farms.

FARM LIFE

In Poland, farms remained the property of private owners and were not taken over by the state during the years of communism. Today there are over two million farms, many of them small-scale. Agriculture is a growing part of the economy with support from the European Union, and organic farming is becoming more popular and profitable.

Small, family-run farms in Poland often rely on human and animal power.

COLORFUL COSTUMES

About 60 distinct ethnic regions exist in Poland. In some highland areas, traditional dress is still made and worn on holidays and at festivals. In other areas, folk costumes are made mostly for dance groups or choirs.

FOLK ART

For centuries, traditional art has thrived in rural Poland. The paintings on the walls of this cottage are a good example of folk art—the creation and decoration of functional objects.

COMMONLY CALLED GYPSIES, Roma were persecuted because their

ROMA

nomadic lifestyle meant they were perceived as outsiders with foreign customs and their own language. There are more than 12 million Roma

A TRADITION OF TRAVELING

Mobile home

Roma living in mobile homes value their freedom, but they also live this way because many European peoples have refused to let them set up permanent homes. Roma like to do many household activities, such as eating and cooking, out of doors. This is true even of those who today live in houses.

TRAVELING HOME
Throughout Europe, Roma were well known for their beautifully decorated *vardos* or caravans. This one belongs to a Roma family visiting the French village of St. Maries de la Mer. Roma gather there every May to celebrate Sarah, their patron saint. *Vardos* used to be drawn by horses, which not only provided a means of transportation but were also at one stage a commodity that Roma bought and sold.

MARIMÉ LAWS
Roma have complex laws so they do not come into contact with anything *marimé*, or impure. Food cooked by non-Roma is *marimé*. Cooking and eating utensils must be washed in a basin used only for this purpose. It would become *marimé* if anyone were to wash their hands or launder clothes in it. Roma would prefer to eat with their hands rather than use *marimé* implements.

FUNERAL CUSTOMS
Roma funerals are big events. Dead people are buried in their best clothes and tools, food, jewelry, and money may be buried with them. After the funeral, their remaining belongings are destroyed.

worldwide today. The largest communities are in Romania, Bulgaria, and Hungary, but there are Roma throughout Europe as well as North America and Australia. The Roma people originated in northern India. They left India in the 11th century in search of a better life, reaching Europe a couple of centuries later. Prejudice against them persists, although most are now settled.

A LOVE OF MUSIC

Because they valued the freedom to travel, Roma chose professions that they could practice wherever they found themselves. They became famous for their music. Roma musicians have contributed to Hungarian and Spanish music, particularly the Spanish *flamenco* style.

A ROMA CELEBRATION

An international Gypsy Festival is held every May in the Czech Republic. Roma dancers and musicians from as far as Brazil, Russia, and Egypt attend the festival, which features concerts, performances, discussions, and a parade through the city's streets. The festival shows how Roma performers have contributed to the cultural life of the countries they live in.

GETTING MARRIED

Family is important for the Roma and everyone is expected to marry. Families usually help young people find a partner but today many young women and men voice their preferences. Weddings are elaborate and women wear their finest clothes.

Many of the would-be brides are still in their teens.

ALBANIANS

THERE ARE ALMOST THREE MILLION ALBANIANS living in Albania itself and more than twice that many living in the areas nearby and around the Adriatic Sea. Albanians form the majority in Kosovo and large numbers

PREPARING FOR A BRIGHT FUTURE

Many religions, one nationality

Religion never divided the Albanian people. In fact, Albania was the only country during the Second World War that managed not only to save their own Jews from the Nazis but also to save the Jews from neighboring countries who fled to Albania. Since communist rule ended, Albania has been trying to find a way to accommodate religious practices within a secular state.

YOUNG PEOPLE
Education in Albania is compulsory between the ages of six and 14. Albania is still a very poor country, so conditions in schools are often very basic, with many even lacking adequate toilets. Polls suggest that many young Albanians would like to emigrate, but confidence in the future of the country is growing as conditions get better.

RELIGIOUS MIX
More than half of Albanians are Muslim. Christianity is the next most popular religion, both Orthodox and Roman Catholic. All mosques and churches were closed and religious observances forbidden under communism from 1967 to 1990. They are undergoing a cautious revival now.

ANCIENT ROOTS
Christianity came early to Albania. Saint Paul, one of the religion's founders, came to preach in the area in the first century CE.

THE ADRIATIC COAST
At their closest point, Albania and Italy are separated by less than 30 miles (50 km) of sea. Apart from its coastline, Albania is largely a rocky and mountainous place. This may explain why 19th-century European explorers regarded it as a mysterious, impenetrable country.

also live in Macedonia, Greece, and Italy. The Albanian language contains many Latin and Greek words but it does not really resemble any of the Slavonic languages. Albanians are proud that for centuries their shared ethnicity has united them above their religious differences. Albania was isolated and relatively poor under communist rule, but with communism's demise in the 1990s, its standard of living started steadily improving.

TRADITIONAL MUSIC

Albanian folk music shows Persian and Turkish influences. One popular instrument is the *šargija*, with a long neck and multiple strings to pluck, shown here.

GETTING AROUND

Many people use the furgon or minibus to get around in Albania but private car use is growing quickly. There are still horses and carts seen in the rural areas where about a third of Albanians live. In recent years, cell phone use has become very popular although access is still difficult in some areas.

RURAL LIFE

Agriculture brings in about twenty percent of the money made in Albania, yet many farms still consist of small, family-owned plots of land where traditional methods are used and people and animals do the work that, elsewhere in Europe, would be done by machine.

ITALIANS

THE COUNTRY WE KNOW AS ITALY only came into existence in 1861,

CUSTODIANS OF AN ANCIENT LEGACY

around the same time as a widespread knowledge of the national language, Tuscan Italian, began to take root. Even today people still feel a strong

Rome wasn't built in a day

Italy's capital, Rome, is known as the Eternal City due to its long history. Legend has it that Rome was founded by twin brothers named Romulus and Remus around 753 BCE. Many civilizations have left their mark on the city, which is said to have more spectacular buildings than any other in the world.

CITY WITHIN A CITY
Vatican City has the status of a country, but it lies entirely within Rome. It is officially governed by the Pope, who is also the religious leader of one billion Catholics worldwide.

The Spanish Steps lead down to the Spanish embassy.

BUZZING AROUND
Mopeds became popular in Italy after the Second World War with the creation of the curvy yet robust *vespa* ("wasp"). They were easier to drive than cars on bomb-damaged roads.

Mopeds are slower and less powerful than motorcycles.

SMART TAILORING
Stylish clothes are a matter of honor for most Italians. The fashion industry is a vital part of Italy's economy as well as a symbol of the country. It employs more than half a million people.

MOTOR INDUSTRY
Turin is the center of the Italian motor industry. Giovanni Agnelli founded a car factory here in 1899, which later became the Fiat factory. Other companies that designed and manufactured car components sprang up alongside it.

loyalty to their region, its customs, and language. Nevertheless, there is much that Italians share despite their regional variations—among these are strong family ties, the Roman Catholic faith, and an utter obsession with soccer. Traditional features of the daily routine, although less common now, include a midday nap, and the *passeggiata*—an evening stroll instituted more to satisfy the need to see and be seen than for exercise.

CHESS GAME

Every two years a life-size game of chess is played on an enormous board in the public square of Marostica. About 700 performers in old-fashioned costumes take part while an audience of 3,600 watch the game.

Eating well

Italians are proud of their healthy Mediterranean diet of pasta, beans, fruit, vegetables, and small amounts of meat, fish, and seafood. A leisurely lunch of three or more courses used to be the main meal of the day but this is changing as more women work outside the home.

As with wine, many factors influence the taste of olive oil—the type of olives used, when they are harvested and pressed, the climate, and the soil where they are grown.

PASTA CHEFS

The Italians did not invent pasta, their national food. However, Italy is the leading producer of durum wheat, which, in the form of semolina, is the main ingredient. On average, every Italian consumes 51 lb (30 kg) of pasta annually.

STREET FESTIVAL

Italians love their festivals. As well as national holidays, every town and village has its own holidays, often involving communal eating and drinking. Here, tables and chairs have been laid out in the town of San Casciano in Tuscany so that all the locals can join in the feasting.

SICILIANS

LIFE NEAR EUROPE'S BIGGEST VOLCANO

THE ISLAND OF SICILY lies just west of the southern tip of Italy. It is the largest island in the Mediterranean and has a very rich historical and artistic heritage. Archaeological evidence shows that people were

Fruits of the land and the sea

Sicily's mild climate is perfect for farming. In fact, centuries ago, the island was one of the main suppliers of food to the entire Roman Empire. Fishing is important too, and enormous tuna, which can be 10 ft (3 m) in length and weigh up to 1,400 lbs (650 kg), are still caught in the traditional way.

TUNA FISHING

Traditionally, mass catches of tuna called *Mattanzas* occur each year when the fish return to the region to mate. A series of nets are used, and the catch starts with a prayer led by the head fisherman, or *rais*. Recently, lower tuna stocks and high demand has led to legal restrictions on the catch.

SALT FROM THE SEA

Salt marshes lie between Trapani and Marsala on the west coast of the island. Salt extraction for human use here dates back to Roman times. In the 19th century salt was obtained from the water with the help of windmills.

CITRUS ORCHARDS

Oranges and lemons were first planted in Italy during the Arab conquest of neighboring Spain. Today, orchards of citrus trees are a common sight and Sicily is famous for its oranges, particularly the ruby-red blood orange with its sour taste.

already living in Sicily 12,000 years ago. Its location has been responsible for a culture that contains Arabic, Greek, and Spanish, as well as Italian influences. The soil of Sicily's coastal regions and the Mediterranean climate lend themselves to farming, and the region is famous for its grapes and citrus fruits. Fishing is also extremely important to the local economy, although overfishing is a growing problem.

Every day is a festa

Sicilians love their festivals and many are held in the course of a year. As well as Christian holidays such as Christmas and Easter, many people celebrate St. Joseph's Day in March, which commemorates the time when the saint saved people from famine. Every town and village holds celebrations to honor the local patron saint.

PALERMO'S SAINT

The festival of St. Rosalia is the occasion for a spectacular parade every July in Palermo. Rosalia was born in Palermo and became a hermit. The discovery of her remains 450 years after her death was said to have halted a plague devastating the city.

VILLAGE LIFE

Life on Sicily and the tiny islands associated with it runs at a peaceful pace. Stores open early and shut late, but they close for a rest during the hottest part of the afternoon, from 1 to 4 o'clock.

DEVIL MASKS

San Fratello hosts a Parade of Devils during the Good Friday Festival just before Easter. The parade began life as a religious ritual, but bright costumes and large crowds have given it the air of a carnival.

LIVING NEAR A VOLCANO

Mount Etna, Europe's most active volcano, is still erupting regularly today. The town of Catania, which lies at the foot of the mountain, is used to the disruption, and local farmers even use ash from the volcano as fertilizer.

CYPRUS

AN ISLAND DIVIDED BY A GREEN LINE

NICOSIA, THE CAPITAL OF CYPRUS, is the only remaining divided city in Europe. The center is surrounded by a beautiful stone wall built by the Venetians in 1567 before they lost Cyprus to the Ottoman Empire. The British later made Cyprus their colony until 1960 when it gained independence. Today a "Green Line", creating a buffer zone, snakes across the city, dividing it between Greek and Turkish Cypriots. The division of the island followed some ten years of conflicts, ending with Turkish forces taking over the northern third of the island. Since then, the United Nations Peacekeepers patrol an empty zone stretching across the island and Turkish and Greek Cypriots live apart with few exceptions. Nicosia symbolizes the difficult transition from colonial times to sharing a new state with neighbors of different backgrounds. Since 2003, there are openings in the Green Line where Cypriots and tourists can cross, enjoying the hospitality, historical sites, and work opportunities each side offers. Memories of the conflicts are strong but the openings now provide opportunities to get to know each other and give hope for a future of sharing the beautiful island again some day.

CRETANS

A HIGH REGARD FOR TRADITION

THE ISLAND OF CRETE is part of Greece, and home to more than 600,000 people. Every year, at least five times that many visit Crete on vacation, making tourism the island's biggest industry. The Mediterranean climate

Christian calendar

Almost all Cretans belong to the Greek Orthodox church. Many people on Crete still celebrate saints days according to the Julian calendar, which was dropped by most of Europe in the 16th century in favor of the Gregorian calendar. They are known as "Old Calendrists."

ANCIENT SITE
The legendary King Minos is believed to have lived at the Palace of Knossos. In the vast palace grounds is a huge courtyard that was used for "Bull-Leaping" where people would run toward a bull and somersault over it by grabbing its horns!

NAME DAYS
People in Crete celebrate "name days" more than their birthdays. Everyone is named after a saint and on your saint's day you throw a party for your family and friends. Churches and villages also celebrate name days, like these people dancing on St. Mary's day.

ROADSIDE SHRINES

There are thousands of small shrines by the roadside in Crete. Some commemorate traffic accidents, but many are simply dedicated to a particular saint. When people pass by they light a candle and say a short prayer.

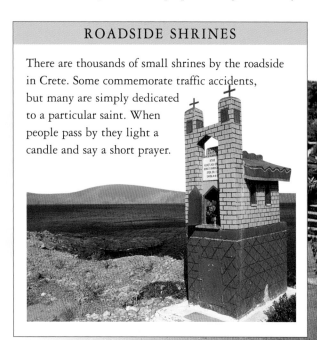

is perfect for cultivating olives, grapes, and other fruit. Cretan olive trees represent more than 30 percent of the Greek crop. Farmers keep flocks of sheep and goats for their milk, wool, and meat. From 1645 to 1898 Crete was under the control of the Ottoman Empire but prior to that it was ruled by the Venetians. The Greek spoken on the island differs from that of the mainland, retaining traces of these conquests.

PLACE OF WORSHIP
This modern church can be found in Neapoli, eastern Crete. Its tiled dome looks quite plain, but belies its more ornate interior. Cretan churches are famous for their medieval frescoes (wall-paintings), which depict Biblical scenes.

Churches are among the top Cretan tourist attractions.

COFFEE AND COMPANIONSHIP
The local *kafenion* is the center of village life in rural Crete. Men, particularly, spend hours drinking coffee or raki, snacking, gossiping, discussing politics, and playing tavli (backgammon) at the local coffeehouse.

THE LOCAL BREW
Cretan *tsikoudia* or *raki* is an alcoholic drink made from the residue left after grapes have been crushed to make wine. The traditional time for making the drink is October.

ISLAND FOOD
Because Crete is an island, seafood features largely on its menu, with octopus a common appetizer. Fish, beef, and rabbit are also staple foods, and salads are served at every meal.

ISTANBUL

LIFE BRIDGING TWO CONTINENTS

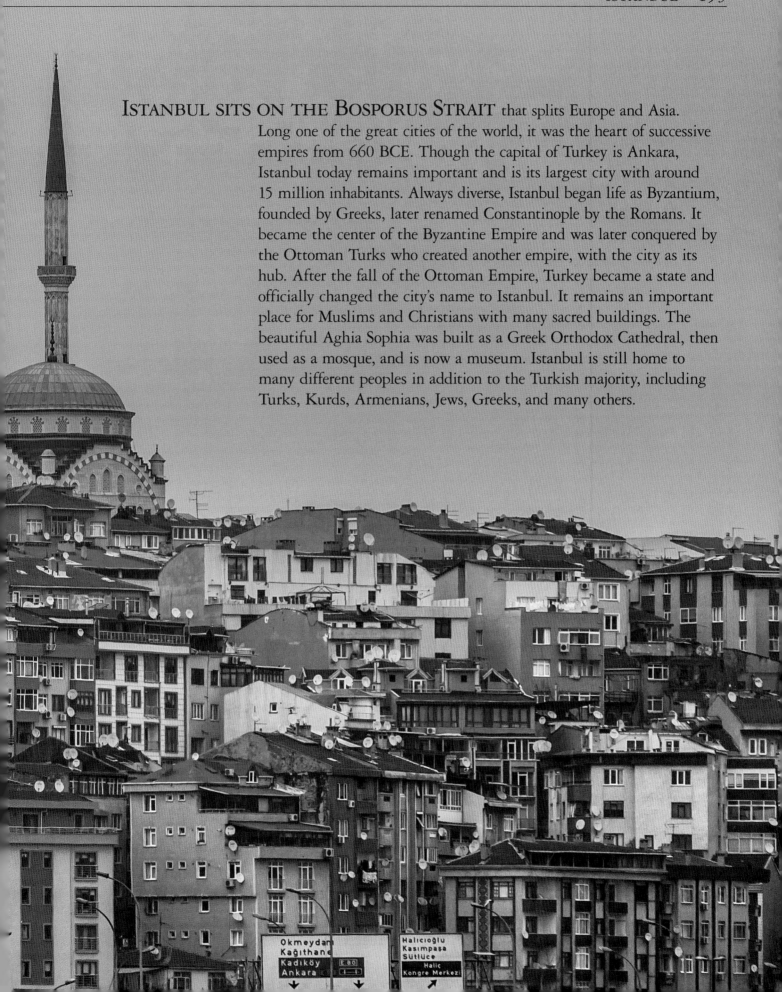

ISTANBUL SITS ON THE BOSPORUS STRAIT that splits Europe and Asia. Long one of the great cities of the world, it was the heart of successive empires from 660 BCE. Though the capital of Turkey is Ankara, Istanbul today remains important and is its largest city with around 15 million inhabitants. Always diverse, Istanbul began life as Byzantium, founded by Greeks, later renamed Constantinople by the Romans. It became the center of the Byzantine Empire and was later conquered by the Ottoman Turks who created another empire, with the city as its hub. After the fall of the Ottoman Empire, Turkey became a state and officially changed the city's name to Istanbul. It remains an important place for Muslims and Christians with many sacred buildings. The beautiful Aghia Sophia was built as a Greek Orthodox Cathedral, then used as a mosque, and is now a museum. Istanbul is still home to many different peoples in addition to the Turkish majority, including Turks, Kurds, Armenians, Jews, Greeks, and many others.

THE PEOPLE OF
Asia

ASIA

AS WELL AS BEING THE LARGEST and most populous continent, Asia is remarkable for the enormous range of climates and geographic terrains it encompasses. North to south it extends from the Arctic Sea to the

ONE-THIRD OF THE WORLD'S SURFACE

Big countries

The world's biggest continent is home to some very large countries. The vast Russia, which straddles both Europe and Asia, is the biggest country in the world; China, India, and Kazakhstan also feature in the top ten.

0 km 400 800
0 miles 400 800

Japan is prone to earthquakes because it lies on the overlap between a number of the plates that form the Earth's surface.

Indonesia The largest archipelago in the world consists of almost 18,000 islands.

Indian subcontinent
India takes up three-quarters of this land mass. The rest is made up of Pakistan, Nepal, Bhutan, and Bangladesh.

tropical islands of the East Indies; while east to west it ranges through the desert countries of the Middle East—a distinct region bordering both Europe and Africa—across the majestic Himalayan mountain range, and along to the volcanic islands of Japan and the Philippines. The people themselves are also very diverse, with different world views as well as local religions, languages, and lifestyles.

Facts and figures

LANGUAGES
Almost three times as many people use Mandarin Chinese as use English, the next most popular of the world's languages. The number of Mandarin speakers is around 1 billion. On the Indian subcontinent Bengali and Hindi are the most spoken.

RELIGIONS
Religions in Asia include most of the major world beliefs. Islam is most prevalent with more than 1 billion followers in Asia. China is officially an atheist country though many Chinese practise Buddhism, Taosim, or Confucianism.

URBAN POPULATION
Asia is home to some highly populated cities. The most populous is Shanghai with 25 million inhabitants. Delhi is the most populous city in India with 22 million. Tokyo has 13 million inhabitants in the city and many more in its suburbs.

POPULATION BY COUNTRY
Around 60 percent of the world's population live in Asia, that is around 4.6 billion people. China and India have the most people, not just in Asia, but in the world. Both countries have around 1.4 billion inhabitants.

CLIMATE

The Asian climate varies more than that of other continents. Siberia, part of Russia, experiences cold, Arctic conditions, while Southeast Asia has a hot, tropical climate. The monsoon, a seasonal wind system, brings warm, wet weather to parts of the region, such as Vietnam, in the summer.

ASIAN FACTS

PLACES
Number of countries 48
Highest point ....Mount Everest, China-Nepal, 29,035 ft (8,850 m)
Lowest point ....Dead Sea, Israel-Jordan, -1,293 ft (-394 m)
Biggest country ....Russia 6,612,000 sq miles (17,125,000 sq km)
Smallest country ....Maldives 115 sq miles (298 sq km)

PEOPLE
Population of continent ....4,573 million
Proportion living in urban areas 50%

The People of West Asia

RELIGION EXERTS A STRONG influence in this part of the world. Islam, which originated in the Middle East and spread rapidly to both North Africa and western and central Asia, is an important force. Hinduism and Buddhism developed farther east in India and Nepal and are very much alive around the Asian continent.

MECCA

One of the Five Pillars of Islam is the hajj (pilgrimage to Mecca). Devout Muslims, like those surrounding the Kabaa Stone below, dream of making this journey at least once in their lives. Mecca was the birthplace of Islam's founding prophet, Mohammed, and the place where he first preached his faith.

TRADITION AND MODERNITY

This bride preparing for her wedding wears a white bridal gown similar to those worn in the West. People worldwide are being exposed to foreign practices, some of which they take on, adapt, and even incorporate into their own traditions.

DUBAI

One of the Gulf States, the United Arab Emirates has enjoyed great prosperity thanks to its precious natural resource—oil. Dubai, one of its main cities, is a wonder of both traditional Arab and ultramodern architecture.

Many Muslim girls and women cover their head.

Art and culture

Where people have lived nomadic lives, their arts tend to be portable, so textiles, jewelry, music, and dance are the most notable art forms in the more mountainous reaches of central Asia. Wonderful examples of literature and architecture have been and continue to be produced in the region too.

Cricket came to India with the British in the 19th century and became an absolute and lasting passion.

A MONUMENT TO LOVE

India's most famous building, and perhaps one of the most beautiful in the world, is the Taj Mahal. It was built by Emperor Shah Jahan in memory of his second wife. The structure was finally completed in 1648, having taken 20,000 craftsmen and builders over twenty years to build.

ARABIC ARTS

Islam forbids the depiction of God or of the human form, but Arabic buildings and artifacts are far from plain. They are decorated, instead, with geometric shapes or with curvacious Arabic script—an exquisite art form in itself.

MAGIC CARPETS

Wonderful rugs and carpets are produced, often by hand, throughout west Asia. Beautiful as well as durable, they often function as family heirlooms or substitute for savings accounts, in the way that jewelry sometimes does in the West.

BOLLYWOOD

The Bollywood film industry is based in Mumbai (Bombay). India produces more than 1,500 films each year.

MIND AND BODY

The discipline of yoga, which consists of exercises good for both physical and mental well-being, originated in India centuries ago.

DRUZE

GUARDIANS OF A SECRET RELIGION

THESE ARABIC-SPEAKING PEOPLE TRACE THEIR ORIGINS to 11th century Cairo, where they began as a reform movement within Islam. Because they do not adhere to the five pillars of Islam they are not recognized

Inside and outside knowledge

Druze society is comprised of two groups. Everyone attends the *khalwa* (place of worship) on Thursdays. The "ignorant" majority—the *juhaall*—leave after the first part of the service, while a select "knowledgeable" few—the *uqqal* (the initiated)—stay for the recitation of religious texts.

THE STATUS OF WOMEN

Women are considered to be more spiritual than men because it is assumed that they have less contact with secular society. They may be initiated alongside men into the *uqqal* and are entitled to equal rights under Druze religious law.

THE *UQQAL*

Only the most pious and wise men and women belong to the *uqqal*, and even then only after a lengthy period of candidacy. Within the *uqqal*, the most honored group are the *ajaweed* (the good), who possess religious and legal authority.

While Druze women used to work mostly at home and in the fields nearby, in recent times girls and young women have been encouraged to be well educated and are often high achieving outside the home.

WHAT THE WISE WEAR

Uqqal men wear a distinctive white hat and a long dark robe. Weaving is an important craft in Druze villages because some very devout Druze only wear clothes made of hand-woven fabric. One Druze sect is known as "the blues" because they wear only hand-dyed and hand-woven blue garments.

by Muslims. They believe strictly in one god and in reincarnation, and do not accept converts into their religion. Men are forbidden from having more than one wife. There may be as many as one million Druze people alive today but it is hard to know the exact number because many practice their faith privately while outwardly conforming to the local religion. Most live in the mountain regions of Syria, Lebanon, Israel, and Jordan.

A PLACE OF PILGRIMAGE

Druze believe in seven prophets—Adam, Noah, Abraham, Moses, Jesus, Muhammad, and Muhammad ibn Ismail al-Darazi. They also revere Jethro, Moses' father-in-law. He is said to be buried at Nebe Shu'eib in northern Israel. Every April Druze make a pilgrimage to this site.

ALL DRESSED UP

Druze schoolchildren in Israel are taught in Arabic and Hebrew, which is the official language of Israel and is spoken by many Jewish people around the world. Many Druze children belong to the Druze wing of the Israeli Scout Organization. Here, Druze schoolgirls wear their best dresses to attend a dance party.

MOUNT HERMON

The Druze town of Majdal Shams is built on the lower slopes of Mount Hermon, Israel's highest mountain. There are four other Druze villages in the area, which was captured by Israel from Syria during a war in 1967. Many Druze have relatives living just across the border in Syria.

ARMENIANS

ARMENIA, ALONG WITH AZERBAIJAN AND GEORGIA, lies close to the Caucasus Mountains. Armenians are proud to be one of the world's ancient civilizations. They call themselves Hai because they believe

THE FIRST CHRISTIAN NATION

A new republic

Armenia is the smallest of the independent states of the former Soviet Union. It regained independence in 1991 with the fall of the Soviet state. Now, religion is thriving and traditions are being revived in new forms. Many Syrian Armenians sought shelter in Armenia with the war in Syria and they are part of the cultural changes taking place.

An elderly Armenian with his worry beads. Men gather with their beads in the evening to chat.

This Armenian is preparing for the cold weather by collecting firewood on his cart.

IN THE COUNTRYSIDE

There are over 900 small, rural communities in Armenia. After independence, previously state-owned farms became private. New food and beverage products are being developed or improved for export, including wines, teas, dried fruits, and jams.

GROWING ECONOMY

Armenia's economy relies on agriculture, with nearly half the population working on small, family-run farms. Stalls of home-grown produce, such as apples, grapes, and apricots, are a common sight in markets and along the roadside.

ARMENIAN APOSTOLIC CHURCH

In 301 CE, Armenia became the first nation to accept Christianity as its state religion. The independent Armenian Church (along with the Russian and Greek Orthodox Churches) is part of the Eastern Church. These worshippers are lighting candles during a morning service in a cathedral.

they are descended from Haik, great-grandson of the Biblical Noah, whose ark many think settled on Mount Ararat, now an important symbol for Armenians. Yerevan, Armenia's capital city, is one of the oldest continuously inhabited places on Earth. Archaeological evidence demonstrates that a city existed in this region as long as 5,000 years ago. Today, just over 1 million people live in Yerevan.

CITY LIFE

Two-thirds of Armenians live in cities or towns, half of them in Yerevan. Some live in apartment buildings built in the Soviet era. The capital is also home to the Armenian National Opera and Ballet Theater based at the Opera House, which opened in 1933.

MOUNT ARARAT

In the past this mountain was part of Armenia, but today it lies inside Turkey's borders. However, it is still a symbol of Armenian national identity. Although it is across the border, Armenians love to look at the beautiful mountain; for those living far away, it represents their homeland.

LOVE OF DANCE

Armenia has a strong tradition of both folk dance and ballet. As part of the Soviet Union, the arts were heavily subsidized but less money is available for music and dance today.

VOSKI ASHUN

Every October in the town of Hrazdan, people from all over Armenia gather in traditional dress to celebrate the changing seasons in the festival of *Voski Ashun*, or "Golden Fall."

VARDAVAR

Held on the Christian Feast of the Transfiguration, this festival shares the date with an ancient one linked to Astghik, goddess of love and water. Across Armenia, people throw water over each other, friends and strangers alike. Celebrated 14 weeks after Easter, it is usually hot so people don't mind getting wet!

There's nowhere to hide from *Vardavar*—even drivers keep their windows shut to avoid a drenching.

MARSH ARABS

MAKING THE MOST OF THE ENVIRONMENT

IN A REGION KNOWN FOR its deserts,
artificial islands scattered
throughout the marshlands of
Iraq are home to the Ma'dan, or
Marsh Arabs. The Ma'dan are accomplished canoeists and
experts at utilizing this environment, which they have inhabited
for over 5,000 years. They build islands and homes from marsh
reeds, grow rice in the marsh water, and catch fish for
food and trade. Perhaps most importantly, the marsh
provides ideal grazing for the buffalo, a family's
most prized possession. A
buffalo supplies dung for fuel
and milk for dairy
produce, which is eaten or
traded for wheat to make bread.
Buffalos are rarely eaten, and are so
cherished that an owner
will even sing to soothe
a sick animal.

ZOROASTRIANS

AN ANCIENT RELIGION AND CULTURE

THE ORIGINAL RELIGION OF THE PERSIAN EMPIRE and one of the oldest monotheistic religions still alive today is Zoroastrianism, which flourished until it was overtaken by Islam in the 7th century. Parsis,

Celebration of spring

Millions of people from Asia to the Middle East celebrate the main Zoroastrian festival, *Nowruz*. In recent years *Nowruz* has enjoyed renewed popularity in some Central Asian republics that were previously part of the Soviet Union, where religion was not encouraged, and also in Afghanistan, where non-Muslim traditions used to be forbidden.

THE *AVESTA*

The Zoroastrian holy book is called the Avesta. It contains a range of different writings, but the oldest sections are thought to be written by Zoroaster (also known as Zarathustra), the prophet who founded the religion sometime between 1500 and 1000 BCE.

Girls dancing to celebrate Nowruz in Afghanistan.

PERSIAN RUGS

Persians regard their rugs as some other cultures regard jewelry—a luxurious display of wealth and skill and a thing of beauty. They also function as a form of savings account, which can be sold off at any time for cash if needed.

meaning "Persian," are also followers of the prophet Zororaster. Today Zoroastrians and Parsis are religious minorities in Iran, India, and elsewhere, descendents of a truly ancient religion. They believe in one god, *Ahura Mazda*, who created the world and whose sacred symbol is fire, representing the triumph of light over darkness. *Ahura Mazda* is in perpetual conflict with the force of evil, called *Angra Mainyu*.

ENJOYING THE SPRING WEATHER

On *Sizdah Bedar*—the 13th and final day of *Nowruz*—it is considered bad luck to stay indoors so people go for a festive picnic in the countryside. Some people take a small pot of sprouting grain, planted some weeks earlier, and toss it into running water or plant it to signify the start of a new agricultural year.

GOLDFISH FOR THE NEW YEAR

Seven items—the *haft sin* (see below)—are displayed in honor of *Nowruz* in Persian homes. Other objects such as candles, a mirror, a copy of the *Avesta*, and goldfish in a bowl may also be laid out.

A HOLY PLACE

More than half of the world's 200,000 Zoroastrians live in Iran. Every year, pilgrims gather for a five-day pilgrimage to one of Zoroastrianism's most sacred sites, the mountain temple at Chakchak in southern Iran. The entrance to the temple displays the cardinal principles of their faith—"Good Thoughts, Good Words, Good Deeds."

OUT WITH THE OLD

Chaharshanbeh Souri is the first day of *Nowruz*, the holiday that celebrates the new solar year in March. It is believed to date back to 1725 BCE. Bonfires are lit and people jump over them to bring good luck for the coming year.

THE SEVEN Ss

A festive table of items called the *haft sin* might consist of *seer* (garlic), *seeb* (apple), *serkeh* (vinegar), *samanu* (a sweet made of wheat shoots), *sombol* (hyacinth), *sekeh* (a gold coin), and *somagh* (sumac).

BEDOUINS

ORIGINALLY THERE WERE TWO DISTINCT ARABIC CULTURES—

ARAB WANDERERS OF THE MIDDLE EAST

settled and nomadic. Settled Arabs found fertile land and cultivated it, while nomadic herdsmen— Bedouins—traveled between oases,

The Bedouin way

The detailed knowledge the Bedouins have of the deserts allowed them in the past to control trade routes, acting as guides and charging taxes to those who wanted to cross the desert. Although many Arab countries romanticize the Bedouin lifestyle, they are frequently less enthusiastic about actual Bedouin groups who make use of the desert's precious resources despite not owning the land. Some have tried to make the Bedouin abandon their nomadic ways and settle in one place.

HOSPITALITY
In the vast, inhospitable deserts, meeting a stranger is an unusual event and a welcome surprise. *Diyafa*—or honoring guests—is part of the Bedouin code of behavior, so guests will always be welcomed and plied generously with sweet tea, strong coffee, and the best food available.

AT THE BACK OF THE TENT
These women are spinning wool and milling grain. Bedouin women tend the flocks, do the housework and cooking, and are responsible for pitching and dismantling the tents. They are protected by a strict code of honor and many live less restricted lives than their non-Bedouin counterparts. Bedouin tents are divided into two sections. The front is reserved for men, and the back for women.

DESERT CLOTHING
All women cover their heads and some also wear a veil. The coins on this woman's veil show how wealthy her family is. Their long dresses are often dyed or beautifully embroidered. The traditional dress for a man is a roomy robe worn with a checked or plain headscarf. The scarf is secured with a doubled black cord called the *agal*.

extracting what they could from the harsh environment before moving on. Bedouins originated in Saudi Arabia and other countries of the Arabian Peninsula. Today they also live in Jordan, Egypt, and Israel. They travel in family groups and trace their descent through the male line back to a particular clan, and beyond that to a tribe. They have a strict code of honor and even those who are no longer nomads are proud of their heritage.

Bedouins belong to the Muslim religion, although they sometimes maintain pre-Islamic beliefs and customs too.

GOD'S GIFT

Camel breeding is traditionally the most noble Bedouin profession. Camels are known as "God's gift" because they are so well adapted for the desert. Camel breeders travel huge distances in large groups, sometimes surviving for months on camel milk alone.

AN ORAL TRADITION

Bedouin are excellent poets and record their history through poems that are passed down from one generation to the next. These may be accompanied by instruments such as a drum or a harp like the one shown here.

KAZAKHS

A FORMER SOVIET REPUBLIC, Kazakhstan is named after its majority population, the Kazakhs, a Turkic people (an ethnic group including Turkish and Azerbaijani people).

ROAMING THE STEPPES OF CENTRAL ASIA Russians, Ukrainians, Uzbeks, and

A round house

A domed wooden frame covered with felt forms the basis for a *yurt*. At the entrance to the *yurt* is a carved wooden door of birch or pine, often decorated with traditional motifs. Inside there is a gap in the *yurt's* roof where smoke from cooking can escape. Scattered everywhere are brightly colored rugs made of wool and felt.

FELT

The *yurt* is covered in one or two layers of felt. Kazakh women are famous for their felt, which they make by pounding wool in hot water, then rolling and compressing it until durable and waterproof.

Yurt-dwellers love having guests. A Kazakh saying claims "Kazaks' hearts are like the steppes – wide, kind and generous."

others also live there. The traditional occupation of Kazakhs was herding animals but few today live as nomadic shepherds, traveling with their animals around the grasslands of the steppes. More than 60 percent of people in Kazakhstan today live in cities but modern Kazakhs recall their nomadic life fondly and with pride, even building yurts (traditional tents) for use on special occasions.

COOKING AND EATING

At the very center of the yurt is the hearth, with a cauldron called a *kazan* suspended above it. On the steppes, Kazakhs rely on meat such as mutton or horse, dairy products, and bread. Vegetables are very rarely available. Meals traditionally start with *chai* (tea), which may be accompanied by bread, nuts, and sweets as appetizers.

Bundled up snugly, this baby will be warm and cozy while the family is travelling.

SHINING CITY

Kazakhstan is one of the most urbanized countries in the region. Its capital city, Astana, rises from the flat plains and is home to more than 1 million people. Astana houses many strikingly futuristic buildings, including the golden towers that flank Nurzhol Boulevard at its center.

A LOVE OF HORSES

Some archaeologists believe that human beings first learned to ride horses on the steppes of Central Asia as long as 6,000 years ago. Nomadic Kazakhs—heirs to this tradition—are accomplished riders and some are capable of shooting arrows accurately from the back of a moving horse. In the past, it is said, children often learned to ride before they could walk.

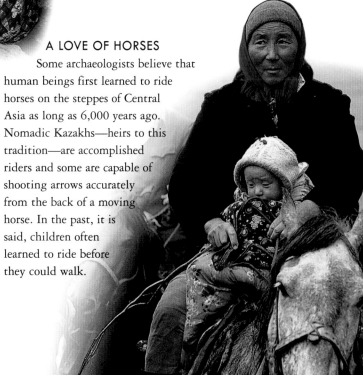

THE BIG MATCH

The people of the steppes invented a number of games that were played on horseback. *Kokpar* is a bit like polo and is played with a headless sheep's or goat's carcass. Two teams line up at either end of a large meadow and charge forward. In this exciting game the players have to grab the carcass and drop it into their goal.

WESTERN SIBERIA IS A COLD, WILD PLACE with few habitable areas.

NENETS

LIFE AT THE END OF THE EARTH

One group of people who live in this vast area of Russia are the Nenets. Certain Nenet groups are entirely nomadic, traveling with the reindeer

The reindeer

The Nenets people's lives revolve around reindeer. They could not live without the animal—the fur is used for clothing and houses, ropes are made from the hide, the reindeer are used as transportation and, of course, as food. For this reason they take great care of these hardy animals, watching over them each night and looking after the ill ones. They maintain a close relationship with one another.

ADAPTING TO MODERN TIMES

Some Nenets are completely nomadic, setting up their camp where the reindeer migrate. For this reason, children are sent these days to boarding schools in order to gain an education. The Nenets are keen that they return to carry on the traditional way of life.

CROSSING RIVERS

To help them walk over snow, reindeer have large, splayed feet, which make very efficient paddles as well. They can swim at 10 mph (15 kph) and at this speed the sleds they pull through the water remain dry and above the waterline.

STAPLE DIET

The Nenets eat mainly meat, fish, and some bread but reindeer meat is the staple diet. The meat is sometimes cooked, but often eaten raw. When a reindeer is killed, everyone gathers around to drink the warm blood, which is rich in vitamins and minerals.

ARCTIC CLOTHING

Everything that the Nenets wear is made from reindeer skin—from coats to boots. *Yagushka* are women's double-layered reindeer coats that have the fur facing both inside and out. The skins are incredibly warm and windproof. Baby reindeer skins are used for baby clothes, and woodshavings are used as filters in baby diapers.

on their migrations twice a year, with no permanent living area. The Yamal Peninsula (Yamal means "the end of the Earth") is home to some groups of Nenets who travel across it seasonally. This peninsula stretches into the Arctic Ocean and in the winter temperatures can sink to -58°F (-50°C). It is a difficult place to live, but these Nenets have survived the harsh conditions for over 1,000 years.

Ancient beliefs

The Nenets practise an animistic religion and worship their own God *Num*. A lot of Arctic people converted to Christianity as missionaries spread their word, but in Siberia, when it was part of the Soviet Union, it was impossible for missionaries to reach the Nenets people. This means that in most instances their ways of life and beliefs are as they were hundreds of years ago.

THE SACRED SLEIGH

At times of sacrifice or on special occasions, the sacred sleigh will be unpacked by a respected elder. The sleigh carries religious idols, bear skins, coins, and anything special that has been collected in a lifetime. A sacred drum is sometimes carried, which is given in difficult times to a shamen (a religious man), who uses it to appeal to the gods.

White reindeer are viewed as special and prestigious and are often chosen to pull the sacred sleigh.

GAS AND OIL

The Yamal Peninsula holds valuable reserves of natural gas and oil, which companies have been exploring since 2008. Building roads, railroads, and pipelines damages the tundra, disrupts reindeer migration routes, and threatens the Nenets' way of life.

HONORED ANCESTORS

If a respected member of a family dies, a doll is made with reindeer skin to represent them. The person's artifacts, such as jewelry, are attached. They are kept to protect the family and ward off evil.

SUPERSTITION

The Nenets have many superstitions. For example, women can never step over a lasso, and household contents have to be laid out in such a way so as not to bring bad luck. They have a number of religious artifacts that are carried on the sacred sleigh, which is very rarely unpacked.

As Arctic people evolved they had less facial hair as it is not practical in cold climates.

KYRGYZSTAN
UNITING NOMADIC CULTURES IN STRENGTH AND SPIRIT

MOUNTED ON HORSEBACK, AN EAGLE HUNTER from Kyrgyzstan, known as a *berkutchi*, readies his bird. He is a competitor in the World Nomad Games, which were first held in 2014 at Kyrchyn Gorge and have taken place there every two years since. The first games attracted athletes from 19 countries competing in ten ethnic sports that included horseback riding, wrestling, martial arts, traditional mind games, archery, and hunting. Teams of athletes came from countries including Azerbaijan, Belarus, and Mongolia to take part. The event was televised and attracted a huge audience of 230 million people. By 2018, athlete numbers had risen to around 3,000 from 77 countries competing in 37 sports. One such event is *Burkut Saluu*, hunting with golden eagles from Kyrgyzstan. A cultural program runs alongside the contests and the aim of the Games is to revive, develop, and preserve the culture of nomadic civilization. Reflecting nomadic cultures' concern for ecology, the mascot of the Games is the snow leopard. Organizers aim to highlight the endangered species and its habitat, which like many traditional, nomadic ways of life, is under threat in the modern world.

SHERPAS

THE WORD "SHERPA" is a combination of two words from the Tibetan language—*shyar* (east) and *pa* (people) to give "People of the East." The Sherpas are a distinct group of people who

PEOPLE OF THE EAST

The high life

Sherpas are famous for guiding mountaineers up Mount Everest. Living at high altitudes between 8,500 and 14,000 ft (2,600 and 4,300 m), Sherpas are used to the mountainous terrain and thin air. Only certain animals and plants, such as yaks and potatoes, survive in this environment. Sherpas use them as much as possible, because everything else has to be brought in, even essentials like food and paper.

By law, no load should weigh more than 66 lb (30 kg).

A LOAD TO BEAR

Portering is a common occupation for men and women. 70 percent of Nepal is so mountainous, it has no roads. All goods must be carried in, including cooking pots and oil.

POTATO HARVEST

Sherpa women and men have equal status. They share the work, from raising children to heavy farming. These women are hoeing potatoes, a staple food that is able to grow at high altitudes.

MORE THAN A PET

Looking after the yaks in the highlands is an important job. They provide almost everything the Sherpas need. Wool is turned into clothes, and leather into shoes. Dung is used as fuel and fertilizer. Yaks also transport heavy goods over long distances.

MAKING CHEESE

Yak's milk is an important commodity. It can be drunk in tea, or turned into butter or cheese. This boy is stirring cheese curds for his family. Cheese making is a growing industry, with cheese sold mainly to tourists.

come from Tibet. There are 18 Sherpa clans, and each person takes the name of their clan as their surname. Over 40,000 Sherpas live in West Asia. High in the Himalayas, eastern Nepal has the largest Sherpa population, with over 100,000 people. Sherpas also live in Tibet, Bhutan, and India. In Nepal, the biggest community is in the Khumbu valley, "the gateway to Mount Everest," where there is plenty of work in the tourist industry.

SERVING THE TOURISTS

This village store caters to tourists, many of whom come to Nepal to see the Himalayas. The store sells souvenirs such as Sherpa-style teapots, and practical goods like backpacks used in mountaineering. Sherpas also act as guides for mountaineers, especially on major expeditions up Mount Everest. Before climbing Everest, Sherpas perform *puja*, a ceremony honoring the mountain deities, asking for a safe return.

BUDDHISM

Sherpas are Buddhists. A small minority become monks and dedicate themselves entirely to their faith. They live in the monastery all year round, studying scriptures and praying.

These houses are built into the mountainside at a height of around 13,000 ft (4,000 m) above sea level.

UZBEKS

MERCHANTS OF THE SILK ROAD

AMONG THE ANCESTORS OF TODAY'S UZBEKS were merchants who traded along the Silk Road centuries ago. Persian influence was replaced in the seventh century by an Arab conquest, ushering in a new golden

The importance of Islam

The vast majority of Uzbekstanis are Muslims. Islamic religion and culture have been a major influence in Central Asia since the arrival of the Arab conquerors in the seventh century. Informal Muslim groups managed to meet during the official atheism of the Soviet period but since independence they enjoy freedom of religion.

JEWS OF BUKHARA

A Jewish community has lived in Bukhara since the 5th century. With the spread of Islam, the Jews here were given protected status. A small Jewish Quarter still exists today. Among its winding streets stands the main synagogue, which dates back to the 16th century.

PERSIAN INFLUENCE

People have lived in Bukhara for over two and a half thousand years. The Persian Empire was an important influence until the area was conquered by an Arab dynasty, which introduced Islam. Persians took back the area two centuries later and Islamic architecture continued to develop. Among its many beautiful buildings is the Kalyan Mosque.

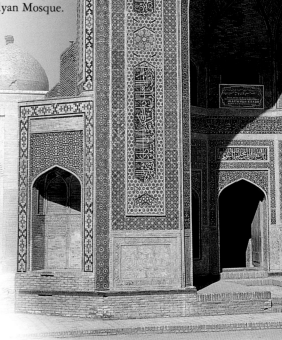

BEAUTIFUL BREAD

Round Uzbek loaves known as *nan* (as in India) are subject to many traditions. It is considered disrespectful to place bread upside down on the table; and bread is never cut with a knife but torn into pieces and given to those present.

CARPET SUPERSTORE

Merchants and traders have plied their wares along the cities of the Silk Road for hundreds of years. Even today Tashkent, the capital of Uzbekistan, is famed for its lively bazaars. This is the carpet department of the main market.

age. Bukhara became one of the world's great cities, ruled again by Persians, then Turkic tribes settled in the region. A national Uzbek identity emerged in the 20th century with the creation of Uzbekistan by the Soviet Union.

The country became independent in 1991. Its population of 32 million, of whom 75 percent are ethnically Uzbek, is the largest in Central Asia. Uzbek communities also exist in Afghanistan, China, and Kazakhstan.

TEA GARDENS

Uzbeks drink green tea, served with *nan* (bread). Men gather at a *chai khana* (tea house) or tea garden, where they sit on flat wooden beds covered with a thin mattress of colorful fabric. A plastic tablecloth is spread in the middle on which the tea and food is served.

SILK WEAVING

Silk thread is produced from the cocoons spun by a type of moth larva. Each cocoon is made of one continuous thread 1,000–3,000 ft (300–900 m) long that is unraveled, dyed, and then woven in a labor-intensive process. Uzbek silk production is particularly centered around the city of Margilan.

Islam forbids the depiction of God or the human form, so buildings are decorated with geometric patterns and verses from the Koran.

GUESTS OF THE GROOM

The traditional Uzbek wedding consists of three parts: the *erkak ash*, a morning ceremony open only to men (pictured below); the afternoon ceremony known as *khotin ash*, which is just for women; and the *toy*, an evening celebration for all the guests. Professional musicians and dancers often perform at these lively events, which are always attended by hundreds of guests.

THREADS OF GOLD

Embroidery is one of the most popular of the applied arts in Uzbekistan. State-sponsored handicraft schools make sure that the skills are taught to a new generation of artisans. Here a student at one school models a wedding gown richly encrusted with gold thread.

KALASH

DESCENDANTS OF THE ANCIENT GREEKS

AROUND 4,000 KALASH PEOPLE LIVE IN CHITRAL, northwest Pakistan. An indigenous people, they believe they are descended from the ancient Macedonian ruler, Alexander the Great, who passed

Valley people

As well as cultivating corn, wheat, and millet on the mountain terraces, and tending to their fruit trees, the Kalash also keep sheep and goats. While the milk is a valuable part of their diet, goats are important for another reason—they are sacrificed, sometimes in large numbers, on many of the festivals that punctuate the Kalash year.

HOME SWEET HOME
Houses are built out of local wood and stone and normally have two floors and a balcony. The ground floor is used to store grain or to shelter cattle, while people live on the upper floor. A fireplace in this room provides heat and somewhere to cook. During the summer, people cook and sleep on the balcony.

GOING TO SCHOOL
Kalash children in the remote valleys travel quite far to get to school. Because government schools are Muslim, they are taught about Islam, and many have subsequently converted.

through the area around 400 BCE. Although some Kalash have now converted to Islam, traditionally most Kalash are not Muslims—unlike more of Pakistan's population. At least half continue to follow their own nature-based religion, which bears some similarities to ancient Hinduism and pre-Zororastrian traditions. They speak Kalasha, a unique language, part of the Dardic group spoken in the region.

SACRIFICIAL ALTAR

The most important Kalash festival is *Chaumos*, which lasts for two weeks around the time of the winter solstice. On the final day of *Chaumos* large numbers of male goats are ritually slaughtered in front of an altar dedicated to the god *Balimain*. The altar is decorated with four horses heads carved in wood because the god is said to appear on a horse.

OLD AND NEW

The Kalash adopt aspects of modern life, such as modes of transportation, but some traditions are protected. *Suri Jagek*, or "observing the sun," is a Kalash meteorological and astronomical system used to judge the best time to sow crops and predict natural disasters.

WOMEN'S CLOTHING

A plain black dress, called a *piran*, provides the basis of the clothing worn by Kalash women. It is decorated with an embroidered sash and elaborate embroidery on the chest and cuffs. Strands of colored beads and a headdress complete the outfit. On special occasions a different headdress is worn, which features an enormous pompom on the top.

Unlike elsewhere in Pakistan, Kalash women do not wear veils or cover their hair.

CROWNING GLORY

Traditionally, Kalash women wear their hair divided into five braids, with the middle braid emerging from the front of the head. Over this sits a headband decorated with shells and beads running down the back of the head to the waist. They comb their hair outside near a river because they believe it brings bad luck to do this indoors.

Headdresses are studded with buttons and cowrie shells.

THE NAME OF THE INDIAN STATE OF RAJASTHAN derives from

RAJASTHANIS

INDIA'S MOST COLORFUL RESIDENTS

the *rajputs*, a high-caste people who commonly married Mughal royalty and nobility. But Rajasthanis are descended from other tribes too. The

Colorful culture

Rajasthan is famed for its three colored cities; the pink city of Jaipur; the golden city of Jaisalmer; and the blue city of Jodhpur—all of which are filled with colorful buildings. In Jodhpur, high-caste Brahmin people traditionally painted their houses blue but today the neighborhoods are mixed.

HENNA

Women throughout much of Asia use henna or *mehndi* to decorate their skin on special occasions. The custom originated in Rajasthan, which is still a center for the manufacture of henna.

CITY LIFE
Buzzing with noise and full of vivid sights, city streets can be a sensory overload. In this Udaipur street, women in brightly colored dresses pass lines of mopeds.

HILLTOP FORT
Towering 400 ft (120 m) over Jodhpur, Mehrangarh Fort was built from around 1459 by Rao Jodha of the Rathore clan, who ruled the region. The imposing red sandstone edifice stands in striking contrast to the teeming blue houses of Jodhpur at the bottom of the cliff.

desert state is renowned for its temples, forts, and mosques, and also for the arts and crafts produced here, with each principality having its own specialization. Most striking, however, are the colors of Rajasthan. Women wear dazzlingly bright fabrics studded with embroidery or mirror work and accessorized with quantities of silver jewelry. Men wear colorful turbans, and even working animals and their carts are often vibrantly painted.

POPULATION EXPLOSION

While over 21,000 people live in Pushkar, during the fair a further 400,000 descend on the town, bringing with them 50,000 camels, horses, and cattle. Most stay in tents, turning the sand dunes just outside this tiny town into an enormous campsite.

SWIRLING SKIRTS

Rajasthani women are famous for their vibrant clothes. During the *ghoomer* dance they twirl gracefully, allowing their skirts to flare out. Most folk dances are performed by groups of men or women, but rarely by both together.

SALVATION

Pushkar has a temple dedicated to the god Brahma, which attracts pilgrims who bathe in its sacred lake. Devout Hindus believe that bathing in the water can put an end to further reincarnation and guarantee instead that they will go straight to heaven when they die.

Pushkar fair

During the annual five-day festival every November thousands of people, including both Indian and foreign tourists, visit the city. Another tradition has grown up around this event—cattle and camel trading. At least 25,000 camels are brought here to be groomed, admired, raced, and, with luck, sold.

BENGALIS

THE PEOPLE OF BANGLADESH—which got its independence in 1971— and those of the Indian province of West Bengal speak the same language, share a rich literary heritage, and come from the same ethnic stock. However,

PEOPLE OF THE GANGES RIVER DELTA

Kolkata

Formerly called Calcutta when a British colony, Kolkata is India's third most populous city with 4.6 million people, and millions more living around it. The name is from the old Bengali language, perhaps meaning "field of the goddess Kali." Now modern buildings, old palaces, and slums exist side-by-side here.

Garlands of flowers for Hindu worship on sale at Howrah flower market.

HINDU WORSHIP

Having ritually bathed in the Ganges River these women offer gifts of flowers, incense, and holy water to the god Shiva. Shiva represents destruction and is identified with the Ganges, whose waters bring both prosperity and death. There are many gods in the Hindu religion, each representing a different aspect of the one ultimate god, Brahman, and the workings of the universe.

GETTING AROUND

Kolkata has buses, trams, taxis, a metro, and autos, bicycles, and human-drawn rickshaws. The latter are the only ones that function during the floods when water can reach waist height.

ON THE STREETS

Many homeless people live on the streets of Kolkata. This small shelter is home to a family of seven. Their father can afford to send only one of his five children to school.

the majority of Bengalis in Bangladesh are Muslims, while most of those in West Bengal are Hindus. Some live in densely populated cities such as Kolkata in India and Dhaka in Bangladesh, but millions more live in rural areas. Bengali fishermen and farmers rely on the annual flooding of the Ganges and Brahmaputra Rivers for their livelihoods. Often though, these very same floods cause devastation and huge loss of life.

GROWING METROPOLIS

Straddling the Buriganga River, Dhaka is the capital of Bangladesh. It is one of the fastest-growing cities in southern Asia and is home to nearly 9 million people. The old city dates to the 17th century and has many palaces and mosques.

Farming in Bangladesh

Almost half of Bangladeshis work in agriculture, growing rice, jute, tea, and wheat as their main crops. Many live on and cultivate land that is prone to flooding—they have little choice when about a third of the country floods regularly during the monsoon season. The climate coupled with widespread poverty has resulted in numerous environmental problems.

AN IMPORTANT CROP

Jute, used to make sacks and carpet backing, used to be Bangladesh's biggest export. Until recently almost a quarter of the population made a living from growing or processing the crop. It is still a vital part of the economy.

1 Harvesting
Jute grows in hot, humid conditions. Plants are harvested when they are 8–12 ft (2.5–3.5 m) tall. The stalks are bundled up and soaked so the fibre can be extracted.

2 Processing
The fibers are passed through a series of machines to soften them and remove any bits of bark. Eventually they are turned into a strong yarn.

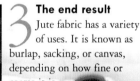

3 The end result
Jute fabric has a variety of uses. It is known as burlap, sacking, or canvas, depending on how fine or coarse it is.

Women extract the golden fibers from jute plants that have been left to soak.

HINDUS

BATHING IN THE HOLY RIVER

EVERY YEAR THOUSANDS OF HINDUS make the journey to Varanasi on the banks of the Ganges River in India. Many plan to live out their final days and die in this holy city. They believe that when, after death, they are cremated and their ashes scattered on the river they will finally escape the cycle of death and rebirth and attain eternal peace. At dawn, the faithful descend to the waterfront down flights of stone steps known as *ghats*. They practice meditation and yoga, make offerings, and bathe in the holy waters.

SRI LANKANS

A PEARL-SHAPED ISLAND JUST TO THE SOUTH OF INDIA, Sri Lanka is home to two distinct ethnic groups. Sinhalese account for three-quarters of the population, while the remainder are mostly Tamil.

A NATION OF TWO PEOPLES

The changing face of work

Almost half of Sri Lanka's population works in the service industry, including tourism. Agriculture and manufacturing, such as clothing and textiles, are also an important part of the economy. Unemployment rates and poverty have decreased since the end of the war and income is rising.

HARVEST FESTIVAL

Tamil people give thanks for a good harvest during the festival of Thai Pongal. Here, people leave offerings of rice, milk, and fruit at a temple.

TEA PLANTATIONS
Sri Lanka is the world's second largest exporter of tea—China is the largest. The crop was brought to the island by the British in 1824. Tea is grown at 3,000–8,000 ft (900–2,400 m) and is hand-picked, mostly by female workers.

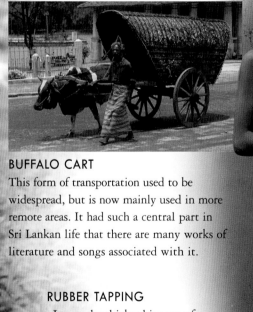

BUFFALO CART
This form of transportation used to be widespread, but is now mainly used in more remote areas. It had such a central part in Sri Lankan life that there are many works of literature and songs associated with it.

RUBBER TAPPING
Latex, the thick white sap of the rubber tree, is collected by cutting a spiral groove into the bark of the tree and suspending a metal cup below it. An expert tapper can handle as many as 400 rubber trees in a day.

Puppets are used to enact stories from the Hindu epic, the Ramayana.

Friction between the two at the end of British colonization in 1948 developed into a long war, ending in 2009. Today all Sri Lankans are rebuilding their economy and life together. The island is blessed with an excellent climate for farming, seas teeming with fish, and valuable mineral resources such as emeralds, rubies, and graphite. The national languages are Sinhala and Tamil.

Summer parade

The Buddhist festival of *Esala perahera* involves a nightly procession (*perahera*) that takes place in the summer month of *Esala*. It is an annual highlight in Kandy, a former capital of Sri Lanka nestled in the hills at the center of the country. The festivities last ten days.

TOOTH TEMPLE

When King Kit Siri Mevan brought one of the Buddha's teeth to his capital city, Kandy, from India in 313 CE he paraded it through the streets in a custom that continues annually to this day. The tooth is not only an object of great devotion, but also an important symbol of Buddhist Sinhalese identity.

MALIGAWA TUSKER

Heavily ornamented and flanked by two other elephants, the Maligawa Tusker is the highlight of the procession. This elephant carries a golden casket holding the sacred relic—the Buddha's tooth.

A Kandyan dancer holds a spectacular mask. It may have been made in Ambalangoda in the south of the island, a town famous for its mask-makers.

TRADITIONAL DANCERS

Under the caste system dancers were born into their professions, which they learned from their parents. Royal patrons supplied them with land in return for dancing and performing other religious rituals. Now that dancers are hired only for special occasions, their numbers are diminishing.

Guarding the family seat

A TRADITIONAL SRI LANKAN FISHING TECHNIQUE

THE INDIAN OCEAN AND THE NEARBY SEAS have the largest number of active fishermen in the world. International agreements determine how far into the Palk Straits—the body of water that separates Sri Lanka from India—fishermen from the respective countries may fish. There are disputes and violent, sometimes tragic, misunderstandings between fishermen out at sea in small boats from both countries. Meanwhile, closer to the shore, other fishermen simply wade out to their wooden perches and wait for the fish to come to them in the shallows. Nobody knows where this peculiar technique originated, but the spots are handed down from father to son and jealously guarded.

The People of East Asia

EAST ASIA CONTAINS the most populous and the least populous regions in the world. China has the highest population of any one country, whereas parts of Siberia and the Tibetan plateau are virtually uninhabited. The people of East Asia practice a wide range of religions and have a rich tapestry of ancient cultures, as well as thriving industrial economies.

TECHNOLOGY

Within the last 50 years countries such as Japan, China, and the Republic of Korea have taken off in terms of technology and industry. Seoul, the capital of the Republic of Korea, is now a sprawling, industrialized city.

MARTIAL ARTS

These famous fighting disciplines from Asia have become popular all over the world as forms of self-defence and self-discipline. Among many others, Tae kwon do comes from Korea, Judo comes from Japan, and Kung fu comes from China.

FESTIVAL

The people of East Asia are renowned for their large, colorful festivals which can last for weeks on end—in China, the Lunar New Year can last up to 15 days. The majority of festivities are religious. Below, towering fruit and flowers are carried at Mengwi Festival, Bali.

Tai Chi is a slow martial art that many Chinese people practice for exercise.

RICE FARMING

Although wheat and tea are widely grown in northern Asia, rice is the chief food of the continent, with more than one-fifth of the world's rice grown in Southeast Asia. Numerous farming villages and shimmering rice paddy fields are scattered across the landscape.

The arts

East and Southeast Asia have a rich tradition of performing arts, from music to drama and dance, or a combination of all three. Shadow puppets are a popular form of entertainment in Indonesia and Malaysia; silhouette puppets behind a sheet perform everything from love stories to battle scenes.

CRAFTS

The people of East Asia are renowned worldwide for their beautiful crafts. These include richly colored silks from Thailand and batik designs from Bali. The Chinese are skilled at kite-making, jade carving, and paper-making, and products such as these beautiful parasols are popular all over the world.

RELIGION

Although Buddhism was founded in Nepal and India, it quickly spread across East Asia and has become one of the main religions in China, Japan, and Southeast Asia. Indonesia is predominently Islamic with the exception of Bali, which is Hindu, and Philippines and Timor, which are Roman Catholic. The Asiatic part of Russia is also Christian. Other minority religions include Shinto in Japan and a Korean religion called Chondogyo.

Buddhist monks are allowed few possessions and spend much of their time meditating.

HINDUISM ON BALI

The majority of Balinese practice a unique form of Hinduism called *Agama Tirtha*. It is predominently Hindu, with Buddhist elements that were added to preexisting religious customs.

FOR THOUSANDS OF YEARS TIBETAN PEOPLE have been living in

TIBETANS

Tibet and areas that are now part of China, India, Nepal, and Bhutan. The Tibetan culture, in particular their written language

AN ANCIENT BUDDHIST PEOPLE

Tibetan nomads

The Tibetan Plateau lies north of the Himalayas and is a huge, rugged plain where an estimated one million nomads live. The land cannot be farmed so the nomads are the only inhabitants. Some nomads have a winter home and travel with livestock at various times during the year.

THE CAMPS
There is little or no wood on the plains of Tibet, so when the nomads move their herds around they set up tents made of black yak hair. Wood for the winter cabins is brought up from the lowlands. Lake water is too salty to drink so they camp by springs.

The storms are sometimes so severe on the Tibetan plateau that they can blow a man off the back of a yak.

THE ESSENTIAL ANIMAL
For centuries the nomads have been leading sheep, goats, and yaks from pasture to pasture. The animals are used for food, transportation, clothes, and wool products. Cashmere wool from the goats has recently been lucrative because of the demand for cashmere in the West.

YAK MILK
Tibetan nomads live mainly on the foods derived from their animals, such as milk products. They use yak milk to make their butter tea, which consists of yak butter and salted black tea mixed together into a kind of broth.

and shared faith in Buddhism, unite the people living in these countries. Since Tibet's incorporation into the People's Republic of China many of these people have been influenced by modern Chinese culture. However, most still practice Buddhism and retain many of their traditions. Ngari and Ü-Tsang make up the Tibetan Autonomous Region where two-thirds of Tibetans live.

Tibetan Buddhism

By the eighth century Buddhism had already been introduced from India and it grew into a unique branch of the religion in Tibet over the following centuries. Tibetan monks have spiritual leaders called Lamas who belong to groups of monasteries.

EDUCATION

A typical course of study in the Tibetan monastery lasts between 18 and 25 years and children begin as young as eight years old. During these years trainee monks study Buddhist philosophies as well as poetry, medicine, and art.

PRAYER WHEELS

The practice of spinning prayer wheels and hanging prayer flags is common in Tibetan Buddhism. Prayer wheels are cylindrical wheels filled with rolls of paper that are printed with mantras (sacred texts) and prayers. Devotees spin the wheel clockwise while reciting the mantras and prayers.

TIBETAN MONASTERIES

The Chinese invaded Tibet in 1949 and destroyed more than 6,000 monasteries. Since then many have been reconstructed and other schools reestablished in India. The monks here are debating—a popular part of their education.

DUNG-CHENS

Dung-chens are 10-ft (3-m) -long horn trumpets used in Buddhist rituals. The bass tones are said to resemble the sound of elephants calling.

MONGOLIA IS ONE OF THE HIGHEST countries in the world. The permanently snow-capped Altai mountains are to the west, and the Gobi Desert—an area of land that is in places almost completely

MONGOLIANS

THE NOMADIC HORSE PEOPLE

Mongolian horses

It is impossible to imagine the Mongolians without the horse. It is the most beloved animal of the Mongolian people and the symbol of the Mongolian nation. Their small horses are stocky and spirited, with powerful necks, dense coats, and thick legs. They are very hardy animals and can run for hours without tiring. They stay outside on open pastures all year.

THE *DEEL*

Mongolia has seen some westernization but traditional clothes, such as the *deel* (a long textile gown with a sash) are still worn. The *deel* is heavy and very warm, protecting against cold temperatures and bitter winds.

MONGOLIAN SCRIPT

Neglected for more than half a century, the beautiful Mongolian script has resurfaced and is now recognized as an important aspect of national culture.

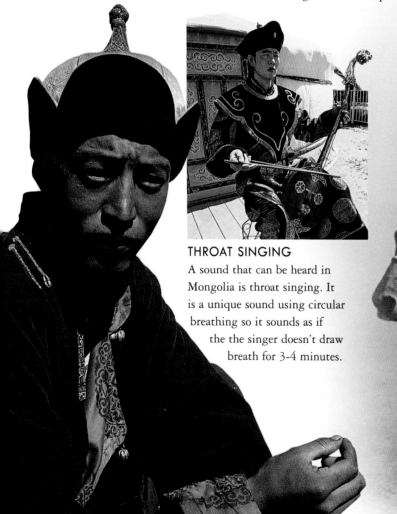

THROAT SINGING

A sound that can be heard in Mongolia is throat singing. It is a unique sound using circular breathing so it sounds as if the the singer doesn't draw breath for 3-4 minutes.

Both good riders and horses are held in high esteem, but the prestige largely goes to the horse.

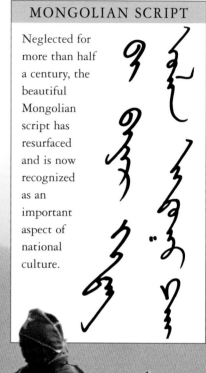

uninhabitable—is to the south. Lying between these regions are the breathtaking grasslands, or steppes. Roughly two-thirds of the 3 million people in Mongolia live in cities and towns. The rest live as nomads always moving their herds to different seasonal pastures. Cursed with bitterly cold winters and a short growing season, the steppes have attracted few new people and much of the grasslands have changed little over hundreds of years.

LIVESTOCK
As well as horses, the Mongolians breed yak, sheep, cattle, goat, and the hardy, two-humped camel, for milk, meat, wool, leather, and transportation. The nomads live mainly on flour, meat, and milk products; anything green or leafy is considered to be animal food. The horses are kept for riding and milk.

NAADAM FESTIVAL
The biggest festival in the Mongolian calendar is the *Naadam* festival held in July. For three days the nation enjoys a spectacle of horse racing, archery, and wrestling. People feast, tell legends, and sing ancient melodies.

The jockeys who race at the festival are normally between the ages of four and ten.

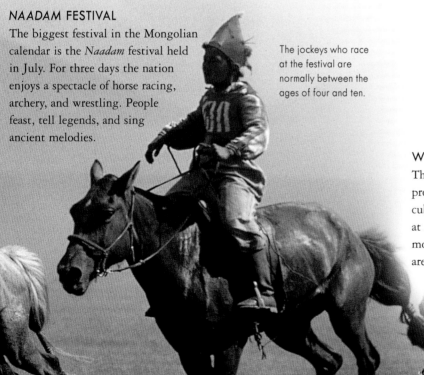

THE HOME
The Mongolian home is a large, white tent called a *ger*, which can be moved easily and quickly and erected in half an hour. Even the city Mongolians often live in gers. The door of a ger always faces south.

1 Building the frame
The frame is made up of supporting poles and wooden latice work, standing in a ring. They are fastened with leather thongs and studs.

2 Covering the *ger*
The frame is then covered with thick, white felt and fastened with ropes. Every *ger* has an opening at the top for light and ventilation.

3 Inside the *ger*
The insides of the finest *gers* are spectacular. The furniture is painted in bright colors and intricate patterns.

WOLF HUNTERS
There are strict hunting rules that prohibit the shooting of she-wolves or cubs in the winter when wolf's fur is at its thickest. The Mongolians ride motorcycles when they are hunting wolves.

City of the steppes
MONGOLIA'S THRIVING CAPITAL

SURROUNDED BY MOUNTAINS, HIGH ON THE MONGOLIAN PLAINS sits Ulanbaatar. It is the economic heart and transportation hub of Mongolia, lying on the route of the Trans-Siberian express, which has long linked it to the rest of the world. The city is on the Tuul River and was established as the capital in 1924. It is a fascinating mix of the old and the new with people living in modern housing developments alongside others pitched in traditional *gers*. Ulanbaatar is the coldest capital in the world but its bright blue skies are often polluted with smog due to industrial emissions collecting in the river valley. Since 1990, Mongolia's economy has grown and many stores and restaurants have opened in the city, along with an amusement park for children in the center.

YAKUT

IMAGINE THE COLDEST WEATHER you have ever known, then triple it, and you are somewhere near the kinds of temperatures the people in Siberia have to endure. The town of Verkhoyansk lies in the area of the

LIFE IN THE WORLD'S COLDEST TOWN

Verkhoyansk

Traditionally, the Yakut way of life revolves around reindeer herding, and also, more unusually in the Arctic, horse and cattle raising. Most Yakut people today are urban dwellers and live in towns like Verkhoyansk. Farming in this area is difficult due to the freezing conditions. However, because of the continental climate, the temperatures do rise in the summer so grass can be made into hay and vegetables can be grown.

HORSE RAISING

The horses that the Yakut use are extremely hardy animals. They have a thick layer of fat and thick fur. They survive the winter on natural pastures without being fed by humans. The Yakut people wear horse skins to keep them warm as well as reindeer fur.

TOWN

The area around Verkhoyansk is rich in natural resources, including diamonds, gold, silver, coal, natural gas, tin, and much more. These are a major source of income for the Russian economy, so there is a lot of industry and mining in the area. A lot of the Yakut people have given up their traditional ways to work in industry.

THE BOREAL FOREST

In order for a town to function in such bitterly cold temperatures, enormous amounts of wood have to be burned. Verkhoyansk lies in the vast boreal forest region of Siberia. Filled with larch and pine trees the forest provides plenty of wood.

Republic of Sakha, Siberia, and is considered the chilliest region in the Northern Hemisphere. The town is the coldest in the world and has been described as the most uninhabitable place on Earth. The lowest temperature ever recorded was a staggering -90°F (-68°C). One group of indigenous people who choose to live and survive in this chilly town are the Yakut people, who are one of the only Arctic peoples to keep horses.

Everyday survival

The temperatures in this part of Siberia can get so cold that the moisture in a person's breath can freeze in the air and fall to the ground. Parts of the body can freeze incredibly quickly if they are not wrapped up warmly. The Yakut make clothes from a mixture of animal furs.

A COZY HOME
Keeping a house warm is difficult if every time a door is opened, the cold air rushes in. For this reason some of the houses have three doors. Once you are through the first door you close it and go through the second, close it, and the third door takes you in. Warm rooms are essential.

MILK STORAGE
In a town where everything is frozen, often the best way to keep food fresh is to leave it outside. Cows are milked inside sheds and the milk is then poured into any available pot. The milk freezes in minutes, it is then taken out of the pot, and stored as round chunks.

Simply melt the milk block to drink it.

BURSTING PIPES
Water pipes are susceptible to freezing in cold climates like that in Verkhoyansk. This pipe has burst and forced water up into the air. Because of the incredibly low temperatures it has frozen in midair, the water creating a huge ice sculpture.

WATER COLLECTING
It may seem extraordinary in a snowy climate, but collecting water is more difficult than you might imagine. Snow does not provide a large volume of water so ice is generally collected. The people take a horse and sled to a frozen river and chisel off huge chunks of ice. The ice is then kept outside and used when needed.

The ice never melts when left outside in the winter.

CHUKCHI

LIVING ON THE EASTERN TIP OF SIBERIA

THE CHUKCHI PEOPLE LIVE IN THE FURTHEST northeastern part of Siberia both on the coast and inland. The administrative language of the area is Russian but some people still speak Chukchi. Because of the rising

Divided people

The Chukchi are divided into two groups: the *Coastal Chukchi*, who have permanent homes on the coast, and the *Inland Chukchi*, who breed reindeer and migrate with them between summer and winter pastures in the boreal forest. There has always been a friendly alliance between the two, which comes in handy when trading items, such as fish and reindeer skin.

THE PEOPLE ON THE COAST

The coastal Chukchi live in settlements along the coast on the very northeastern part of Siberia. They survive by fishing and hunting marine animals, such as seal and walrus. They still use traditional walrus skin boats, called *umiak*, that are made on wooden frames. In the winter it is sometimes necessary to drag the *umiak* miles over the ice to the water.

These boats can vary from about 9 to 30 ft (3–9 m) long and up to 8 ft (2.5 m) wide.

HOME OR AWAY

Most Chukchi live in small towns scattered along the coast and inland, such as this town of Uelen, which is famous for carvings. Some of the inland Chukchi, however, are seminomadic, moving with herds of reindeer biannually from the tundra to the taiga and back.

The Chukchi use hessian-filled bags as saddles when riding reindeer.

CHUKCHI SEASONS

The Chukchi divide the year into five seasons according to natural phenomena such as the rising and setting of the sun, numbers of mosquitoes, and the state of the snow. *Leleng* is their winter, which they then subdivide into three. So it could be said that the Chukchi have seven seasons.

importance of Russian culture in the region, Chukchi has become an endangered language, meaning its speakers are growing older and the children are increasingly not learning to speak it. Although the area that they live in is now inhabited by other peoples as well, some Chukchi have remained very traditional in their way of life. The word "Chukchi" itself means "rich in reindeer."

Spiritual belief

Like many Arctic peoples, the Chukchi have an animistic religion—they believe that every object, whether animate or not, possesses a spirit or life-force that may be beneficial or harmful. They believe that these spirits roam the Earth, and everyday tasks, such as hunting and fishing, include certain customs intended to make the hunt successful and all the spirits happy.

IVORY LEGENDS

The Chukchi people are well known for their beautiful carvings and engravings. They carve figures from myths and legends out of walrus ivory or whale bone. The people of the tundra tell many folk stories that involve personified wild animals, such as the raven and the Arctic fox.

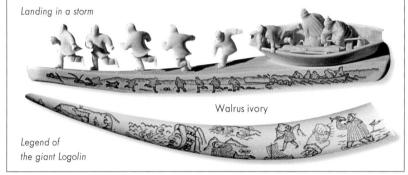

Landing in a storm

Walrus ivory

Legend of the giant Logolin

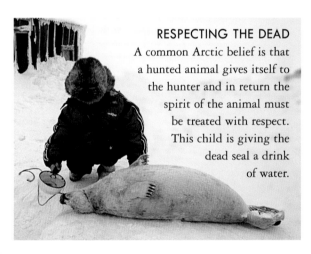

RESPECTING THE DEAD
A common Arctic belief is that a hunted animal gives itself to the hunter and in return the spirit of the animal must be treated with respect. This child is giving the dead seal a drink of water.

SHAMANISM
Traditional Chukchi people believe in shamans, figures who are capable of communicating directly with spiritual powers, often in ecstatic states. The drum is the only instrument that the Chukchi people have and it is always used in conjunction with a shaman.

Wooden icon

REINDEER PROTECTION
The Chukchi make reindeer icons out of deer skin and wood, and sometimes decorate them with beads. These icons are created to protect the reindeer and keep them from harm. If one of the herd gets lost, the Chukchi take out the icons and beat them in the belief that this encourages the spirits to send the reindeer back unhurt.

The drum is made out of reindeer skin.

CHINESE

WITH A POPULATION OF 1.4 BILLION, China has more people than any other country on Earth. One person in five in the world is Chinese. The country has a recorded history beginning 4,000 years ago with the

THE WORLD'S OLDEST CIVILIZATION

FARMING
There are many cities in China, but a third of the people live in the countryside and farm the land. The main crops are rice, wheat, and potatoes but China also produces much of the world's soy, millet, and tea.

City living
For many years the communist Chinese government had control of all industry. However, since the 1980s the government has given greater freedom to people starting businesses and encouraged international trade. As a result, the cities have gone through an economic boom, with industry starting to draw in millions of workers from the countryside. Modern architecture stands alongside ancient buildings.

CHINESE NEW YEAR
Chinese New Year is the first day of the first month in the lunar calendar. Festivities go on every day until the 15th day, which is the Lantern Festival, when people decorate their homes with beautiful, richly-coloured lanterns.

TRADITIONAL CULTURE
Old ways of life are still very much evident in China, and some have even spread throughout the world. Chinese herbal medicine and the ancient art of acupuncture are now commonly used worldwide, and Chinese food is popular in many countries, brought in by immigrant Chinese communities.

TAI CHI
Many Chinese people practice Tai Chi, which is a martial art that can also be performed slowly and used to decrease stress and maintain physical health. Every morning, in parks all over China, people can be seen practicing Tai Chi forms.

Shang dynasty and over these thousands of years China has developed a rich culture. Ninety-two percent of the country are Han Chinese. The rest of the population belong to other ethnic minorities, each of which has varied traditions, languages or dialects, and religions. Most Chinese live in the eastern part of the country.

Chinese minority groups

There are 56 official minority ethnic groups in China, in addition to the Han majority. Almost all have their own spoken languages and many their own script. Mandarin is the official state language. Most ethnic minorities are found in the west, southwest, and northwest.

HAN

The Han Chinese are the largest ethnic group in the world. The Han culture is incredibly old and the language of the Han, commonly known as Mandarin Chinese, is spoken by the largest number of people in the world and it is also one of the most ancient languages.

DAI

The Dai people live in the southern part of Yunnan Province and have a rich, colorful culture. They live in bamboo houses and have a history stretching back over 1,000 years.

BAI

The two million Bai people live mostly in the Bai Autonomous County of Yunnan Province. They are known for their house decorations, painting beams with birds, flowers, and mountains.

The Uighur people have their own language and alphabet.

UIGHUR

The Uighur (Uyghur), a Turkic people, number around 11 million in China but are spread around central and east Asia. In China, they live in the northwest, many at the foot of Mt. Tianshan, and rely on agriculture as their main means of survival. Uighurs follow the Islamic faith and speak their own Turkic language.

MIAO

AN ANCIENT CHINESE CULTURE

WITH A POPULATION OF OVER NINE MILLION in southwest China, the Miao people also have a diaspora of over two million around the world. They can trace their ancestors back over 4,000 years. The Chinese term

The Long-Horned Miao

One clan of the group are the Long-Horned Miao, who are famous for their unique costumes and horned headpieces. They are from a village called Longga in southwest China, and it is only since the highway to the village was built in 1994 that these amazing people and their culture have been revealed to the world.

Houses on the hillsides are often built on stilts with the animals living beneath them.

FABRIC DESIGN

The Miao people specialize in batik and embroidered fabrics, which are evident in their everyday dress. A girl learns to work with fabrics from the age of six or seven, and her skills greatly increase her future prospects.

HORN HEADPIECES

The women wear extraordinary headpieces that consist of hair wrapped around animal horns protruding from each side of their head. To keep the horns in place they wrap their own hair and an elongated bun made from linen, wool, and hair from ancient ancestors around them, and fix it all with white cord. The headpiece can be up to 10 ft (3 m) long and weigh up to 4½ lb (2 kg).

Miao is different from their own names for themselves, which include Hmong. Many different clans live in this mountainous area, each with its own individual characteristics, dialects, and names. All, however, share a culture that has developed from a common root. The Miao are known for their beautiful arts and crafts, particularly their fabric designs, and for their spectacular festivals and celebrations filled with song and dance.

THE SHENG

A popular instrument in the Miao culture is the *sheng*, a wind instrument made from a bundle of different lengths of bamboo. It can produce chords as well as single notes and is thought to have been used up to 3,000 years ago in China.

Farming

Much of the Miao area is hilly or mountainous, drained by several rivers. The weather is mild with plenty of rain so farming is a large part of the people's lives. The staple crop is rice, supplemented by corn, wheat, and all sorts of fruit and vegetables. Men mainly do the farming and hunting while women raise livestock and keep the home.

THE DRAGON

Many Miao still follow their traditional religion. They believe that spirits in the shape of dragons protect them, and often decorate fabrics with the beautiful, mythical creatures.

Traditionally the headdress was solid silver but these days only the smaller ornaments tend to be.

SILVER JEWELS

Women's headdresses have special importance in Miao culture. When a girl is born, her family starts to save money to buy silver head ornaments that are worn for special occasions. Each clan has slightly different designs and at festivals the women dance in them, showing off their family's wealth.

KOREANS

KOREA TAKES THE FORM OF A PENINSULA stretching southward, like a thumb, from the center of the northeast coast of Asia. Since 1955, the country has been divided into North and South Korea, North

A COUNTRY DIVIDED

Education

One of the most important elements in Korean life is a good education—teachers are deeply respected and trusted. Children are expected to study hard and parents are encouraged to offer full support for their child's education. Schools are regarded as a sort of extended family.

PLANT A TREE
Each year, school children from all over the Republic of Korea take part in a relatively new annual event, Tree Planting Day. Every child must plant a tree in order to protect the environment.

INDUSTRY
In the 1960s, the Republic of Korea started to change from an agriculturally based country to an industrial one. The incredibly rapid success of their electronics, shipbuilding, communications, and car industries has turned Korea into a model for development worldwide.

The capital of the Republic of Korea is Seoul, a bustling, modern city packed with shops and businesses.

Korea being communist, and South Korea, or the Republic of Korea, being an industrial nation. Despite the separation, however, the Koreans have many shared traditions and beliefs. The landscape ranges from high mountains to lowland forests and plains and the summers are warm, while the winters can be bitterly cold. The predominant religions in Korea are Buddhist or Confucian, with some Shamanism and Christianity.

A traditional life

Although Korea has changed dramatically in the last 50 years, the people still retain many aspects of their traditional life. Music is a large part of their culture and they claim to have 60 types of traditional instruments. They also have a long history of paper craft and make all sorts of objects with paper, including mats, bowls, and even furniture.

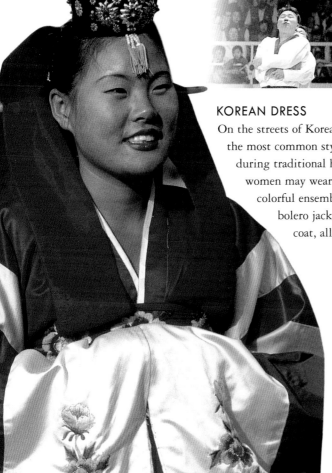

TAE KWON DO
The national sport of Korea is Tae kwon do, which was invented in Korea and dates back 200 years. This self-defensive martial art uses the whole body and not only strengthens it but cultivates a good mental attitude.

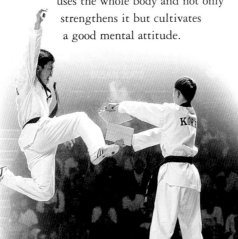

KOREAN DRESS
On the streets of Korea, westernized clothing is the most common style of dress seen. However, during traditional holidays and celebrations women may wear the traditional *hanbok*, a colorful ensemble of wrap-around skirt, bolero jacket, and sometimes, a long coat, all beautifully embroidered.

RURAL KOREA
Even though Korea was predominantly agricultural for many years, its mountainous terrain meant that little of the land could be cultivated. Rice is the staple food grown in the foothills in paddyfields.

KIMINCHI

For thousands of years Koreans have been eating pickled vegetables, such as kiminchi, or fermented cabbage. It is rare in Korea to eat a meal without it.

A farm woman carries a large bundle balanced on her head.

JAPANESE

JAPAN IS MADE UP OF FOUR MAIN volcanic islands and more than 6,000 smaller islands situated to the east of mainland Asia. Nearly 75 percent of the country is rugged and mountainous and virtually uninhabitable, and the

ANCIENT MEETS MODERN

The modern city

Tokyo, the capital of Japan, is a fast-paced, energetic city that never seems to rest. The city, and its surrounding area, houses a population of 37.5 million and covers approximately 5,000 sq miles (13.5 sq km). Much of the capital was destroyed in the Second World War and today is filled with high-rise office buildings and sprawling suburbs.

HOT SPRINGS

The islands that make up Japan are volcanic, and like a giant sponge, Japan leaks from thousands of hot springs, or *onsen*. For over 2,000 years the Japanese have enjoyed hot outdoor baths in the naturally warm waters.

Rush hour in Tokyo.

A MODERN WORLD

Japanese children and teenagers are very much a modern generation, listening to western pop music and keeping up with fashions.

ROBOT TECHNOLOGY

Few people in the modern world are unaffected by the technological ideas of Japan, from cars to computers. High-tech toys and games have been at the forefront of Japanese technology since the 1970s. Japan is a leading country in manufacturing robots.

majority of what is left is farmed. This means that a huge amount of the population live in urban areas. Japan is still a country of remarkable ethnic and cultural purity. Non-Japanese people make up less than two percent of the population. The cities of Japan are busy with traffic and industry but traditions still survive and deep-rooted appreciation of traditional arts flourishes throughout Japan from the tea ceremonies to sumo wrestling.

Traditional Japan

Japan's oldest religion is Shinto, and most Japanese still observe Shinto rituals alongside Buddhist practices. Manners and customs are of utmost importance in Japan, and the old respect and humility are practiced in the home as well as in the modern office.

TEA CEREMONY

The Japanese tea ceremony, or *chanoyu*, was established in the 16th century and is much the same today. It is the ritual way of preparing and drinking green tea and is considered an art as well as a way to purify the soul.

STREET FESTIVALS

The Japanese celebrate a huge number of festivals, many of which include street parades, such as this one. In May, when the spectacular "Children's Day" is celebrated, colorful carp banners are flown.

KIMONO

The kimono is the traditional dress of Japan. Today, Japanese women rarely wear kimonos except for special occasions, such as weddings. Children's kimonos are similar to the adults ones but often much brighter in color. Because of the complex material shape, it can take an hour or more to dress a child in a kimono.

SAPPORO SNOW FESTIVAL

The Sapporo Snow Festival is one of Japan's largest winter events. For seven days in February the main street in Susukino is transformed with myriad ice sculptures and ice buildings. Many countries take part in the ice-sculpting competition.

Sumo

SUMO WRESTLING is the extraordinary and exciting national sport of Japan. Its roots go back nearly 1,500 years and the ritual has changed little. The sport reflects many values that the Japanese hold dear, such as respect and rank, and sumo wrestlers are considered living heroes. There are six Grand Tournaments every year, each one lasting for 15 days.

THE WEIGHT

In sumo, the larger the man the better. There are no weight limits so it is possible for a wrestler to find himself fighting an opponent twice his weight. The average weight of a wrestler is about 325 lb (148 kg). One of the largest wrestlers ever was 700 lb (317 kg)!

Large banners announce sumo tournaments.

PREPARATION

Before the match each sumo wrestler's hair is tied into a top knot, called a *mage*. The knot is slightly different according to the seniority of the wrestler. The *mawashi*, or loin cloth—the only piece of clothing worn during the match—is made from 32 ft (10 m) of black silk.

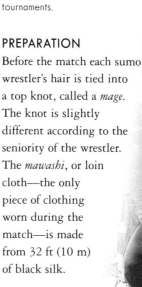

THE RITUAL OF SUMO

A sumo match is filled with symbolism, even before the fighting starts. The rituals for the top sumos are allowed to go on for four minutes before the judges make them begin to fight. The ritual fires up the spectators to feverish excitement.

1 The purification

At the start, the sumo rinses his mouth with water, the source of purity, and wipes his body with a paper towel. He then scatters a handful of salt into the ring to purify it.

2 The leg lift

The wrestler repeats certain ritualistic motions, such as raising his arms to the side as well as raising a leg up high and stamping it down hard on the ground.

3 The glare

The contestants then face each other and, crouching forward, place their fists on the floor. They then glare fiercely at each other before hurling themselves together for the fight.

DOHYO-IRI

The formal ceremony held in the ring at the start of the match is called the *Dohyo-iri*. The sumo contestants each wear an apron made of silk, beautifully decorated with rich embroidery and hemmed with gold, which they will remove for the fight. The senior judge, the *gyoji*, wears a traditional kimono. The wrestlers form a circle around the ring, then in turn, each one claps his hands to attract the attention of the gods, then performs movements to drive evil from the ring.

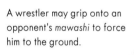

A wrestler may grip onto an opponent's *mawashi* to force him to the ground.

THE FIGHT

A bout of sumo is won by a wrestler forcing his opponent out of the ring or hurling him to the ground within it. No part of the body may touch the ground except the feet. Slapping, pushing, tripping, and judo-style flips are allowed.

PADAUNG

THE LAND OF THE LONG-NECKED WOMEN

THE PADAUNG PEOPLE OF MYANMAR number around 10,000 but have attracted attention over recent years due to their practice of placing brass coils around women's necks, giving a stretched, elongated appearance. The wrapping begins at age five or six when the first coils are placed around the child's neck and then more are added gradually as she gets older. The custom is more than a rare expression of feminine beauty, it is also considered to be a mark of status and wealth for the family. Today fewer women continue this practice, partly because the brass coils are too expensive.

THAIS

A BUDDHIST CULTURE

THE ETHNIC THAI PEOPLE ARE MADE UP OF FOUR core groups: Central Thai, Thai-Lao, Northern Thai, and Southern Thai. The 68 million Thais all descend from the natives of Yunnan province in China and

City life

The streets of the capital city, Bangkok, are filled with traffic, from cars, bicycles, and taxis, to the traditional three-wheeled vans known as *tuk-tuk*.

THAI SILK

Thailand is rich in crafts but perhaps the most famous is Thai silk, which is dyed to produce rich colors.

BUDDHISM

About 95 percent of Thais are Buddhists. They do not visit the temples regularly, but more often worship in their own homes at a shrine in front of a Buddha image. When believers are in a temple, tradition dictates that the head is lower than the Buddha image, or any Buddhist monks present, so they sit on the floor.

FLOATING MARKET

A number of narrow canals run through Bangkok. These are filled with narrow boats selling anything from food and drinks to souvenirs. Almost all of the boats are paddled by women wearing blue with flat hats called *muak ngob*. The floating markets are still important commercial centers for those living along the banks.

officially emerged as a people in 1238. Other Thai-speaking people live in China, Laos, and Myanmar. Thailand has a royal family, whose history dates back 700 years. The monarchy of Thailand prides itself on constantly adapting to ensure that it fits in with the modern world, its people, and society. Thai culture has a distinctiveness that the people are very proud of. Almost all share the Buddhist faith, which helps bind them together.

Rural life

The towns of Thailand are surrounded by small farming villages, many of which have developed different traditions and styles of dress. The villages are made up of family groups or clans ruled by a headman and his council.

FARMING VILLAGES

The villagers cooperate with each other, becoming like a large, extended family. Every village has a temple, or *wat*, used as a meeting place as well as for worship.

THAI BOXING

Muay Thai, or Thai boxing, is one of Thailand's most popular sports. The roots of this martial art can be traced back to medieval times, and it is not just a sport but an extravagant event. Before every match, the two fighters dance to special boxing music to honor and pay respect to the trainer, family, and to the sport.

AKHA HEADDRESS

The Akha people who live in the hilly regions of northern Thailand are known for their elaborate headdresses. These are adorned with silver balls and colored beads and are worn regularly by the women, not just on ceremonial occasions.

YAO PEOPLE

The Yao people are best known for their clothing. The women wear a black turban, a long tunic with a large red ruff sewn into the front, and heavily embroidered trousers. The embroidery itself is a craft tradition of which the Yao are particularly proud.

IBAN

PEOPLE OF THE LONGHOUSES

THE EAST MALAYSIAN PROVINCE OF SARAWAK in the northwest of the island of Borneo is a maze of endless rivers making their way through dense, steamy rain forests. It is here that the Iban people live,

Longhouses

The Iban live in longhouses, which are at the very center of communal life in Sarawak. Most longhouses are riverside dwellings and are therefore built on stilts to avoid flooding. The entire community lives under one roof.

An Iban bride wears a full silver headdress.

VILLAGE LIFE

The longhouses are divided into apartments and when a new couple is married, often they will simply add another building onto the end of the house. Some longhouses have hundreds of rooms under one roof. A long communal balcony runs along the side of the house with the doors to the apartments along it.

The agom is a carved wooden figure that is placed on the pathways to rice fields to protect the crop.

CARVING AND WEAVING

The Iban people learn to weave and carve from an early age. The men carve and the woman weave and the gifted continue all their lives and are highly valued. They believe the objects they make protect them from evil spirits.

JEWELRY

Large earrings and gold teeth show that a girl comes from a well-to-do family. The teeth are sometimes inlaid with precious stones. Heavy earrings create large, elongated earlobes.

forming 30 percent of the state's population, and existing by hunting, fishing, and growing rice in the thick jungle. Sarawak is known as "the land of the hornbill" after a majestic bird believed by the Iban people to be a messenger from the spirit world. The majority of the Iban these days are Christian, but they still practice traditional rituals, which are a mixture of animistic and Hindu-Buddhist beliefs.

Hunting

The Iban hunt and eat a wide variety of forest animals, including birds, squirrels, monkeys, lizards, and barking deer. But the most prized game animal is the bearded pig. Sometimes weighing more than 220 lb (100 kg), one of these animals can supply enough meat to feed a group for several days.

To shoot the dart fast and accurately, the breath must be blown from the chest and stomach rather than just the mouth.

HEADHUNTERS

Until about 70 years ago, the Iban were noted headhunters, a practice then found among most people of the area. Formerly a ritual activity, now outlawed, a captured head symbolized strength and was thought to bring blessings.

BLOWPIPES
The traditional hunting weapon of the Iban is the blowpipe. It is lighter and more accurate than a shotgun and the darts kill silently, allowing a hunter take a second shot should the first miss. The darts are dipped in poison made from tree sap, which kills by causing suffocation. The dose is carefully chosen to suit the prey.

LONGBOATS
The Iban travel on the rivers and waterways in longboats. They are not only for transportation but also to show off the owner's carving skills and status among the villagers. Well-carved paddles are also used for ceremonial occasions.

BAJAU

THE PEOPLE OF THE SEA

COMMONLY KNOWN TO WESTERNERS AS SEA GYPSIES, the Bajau boat dwellers have lived scattered over the water off the Philippines for thousands of years. Some live a nomadic life in outrigger houseboats and others settle in stilt houses at the water's edge. The Bajau people are famous for their pearl diving. Today, they retain rights to the pearl beds in the area, which are used by the modern pearl industry. The Bajau pearl fishers freedive to depths well beyond the safe limits of normal scuba diving. They can dive down to over 130 feet (40 meters) and hold their breath for up to 13 minutes.

BALINESE

THE ISLAND OF BALI IS PART OF INDONESIA, lying in the archipelago to the east of Java. The small island is a cluster of high volcanoes that drop straight to the sea with very little flat land between. The Balinese practice the

LIFE ON PARADISE ISLAND

COMMUNITY LIFE

Family and community ties are one of the most important factors in Balinese life. All families in a village worship a common ancestor, the village god, which binds the community together. Villages regularly organize festivals and participate in music and dancing.

Rice culture

According to Balinese legend, the island orginally only grew sugarcane. Then, out of pity for the human race, the god of fertility and water came to Earth and delivered rice. Rice to the Balinese is therefore a gift from God and is treated with great respect. From planting to harvest, the rice is watched, tended, and worshipped.

Men carry the rice in two baskets on their shoulder and the women carry it in baskets on their heads.

FARMING RICE

Rice is grown on every piece of land that is accessible to water. Irrigation is difficult, but the Balinese have developed an elaborate system of canals, dams, bamboo pipes, and tunnels to control the water.

1 Watering fields
First the terraces and fields are filled to the brim with water, which makes the land look like giant mirrors reflecting the sky.

2 Planting seeds
When the earth has turned to mud, the seeds are sprinkled on the ground. They will grow into a thick green carpet.

3 Harvesting grain
As the grain ripens, the rice plants turn a golden color. Both men and women work hard to collect the rice at harvest time.

THE RICE RITE

The Balinese perform many rituals and ceremonies to make the rice grow well. They pray for enough water, and the prevention of pollution to the land, and perform rituals to keep pests, such as mice, away.

Hindu religion, which is unusual in a country that is predominantly Muslim. They are proud of having preserved their unique Hindu culture and this is seen in the large number of beautiful temples on the island and numerous festivals and celebrations held. The island is visited by thousands of tourists and although this has led to many changes, the Balinese have sustained a vibrant and fascinating culture.

MARKETS

The colourful Balinese markets are not only a necessity to the people, but also attract a large number of tourists keen to buy their beautiful crafts.

ART

Textiles and carvings represent a mark of cultural identity to the Balinese. Their clothes are beautifully designed and famous the world over. Woodcarving is at its best as part of temple and palace architecture in Bali.

MUSIC

A traditional Balinese orchestra is known as the *gamelan*. It is almost completely made up of percussion instruments, such as gongs, cymbals, and xylophones. The Balinese believe that the *gamelan* is of divine origin and the instruments are treated with the greatest respect.

Balinese cremation

The people of Bali see a cremation ceremony as a joyous occasion rather than one of mourning. Hundreds of people carry beautifully decorated towers, sometimes 60 ft (18 m) high, containing the body to the place of cremation. The body is then placed inside a wooden casket and the whole thing, with the decorations, is set alight in order to liberate the soul to a higher world.

An impressive cremation adds greatly to the prestige of a wealthy family, giving occasion for extravagant festivities.

THE PEOPLE OF
The Pacific and Australia

pacific *adj* peacemaking; appeasing; inclining towards peace; peaceful; mild; tranquil; of or relating to the ocean between Asia and America, so called by Magellan, the first European to sail on it, because he happened to cross it in peaceful conditions.

THE PACIFIC ISLANDS AND AUSTRALIA COVER AN AREA larger

THE PACIFIC AND AUSTRALIA

than Asia but the landmass is smaller than Europe's. At over

A CONTINENT AND THOUSANDS OF ISLANDS

PACIFIC AND AUSTRALIA FACTS

PLACES

Number of countries ....14 +dependencies
Highest point ....Mt. Wilhelm, Papua New Guinea,
14,793 ft (4,509 m)
Lowest point ....Lake Eyre, Australia
-49 ft (-15 m)
Biggest country ....Australia
2,969,976 sq miles (7,692,202 sq km)
Smallest country ....Nauru
8 sq miles (21 sq km)

PEOPLE

Population of continent ....40 million
Proportion living in urban areas 70%

The Pacific Islands

Many of the islands in the Pacific became
European colonies in the 19th century.
Some are still colonies or are administered
under international agreements, but
most have recently grouped together
to form small independent nations.

Micronesia
This area includes the
Marshall Islands, Nauru,
and Palau.

Northern Mariana
Islands
(to US)

Wake
Island
(to US)

Mariana Islands

M   i   c   r   o   n

Saipan

e

s

*Philippine
Sea*

Guam
(to US)

i

Bikini Atoll

**MARSHALL
ISLANDS**

a

Yap

M I C R O N E S I A

Pohnpei

Babeldaob

Chuuk

C a r o l i n e   I s l a n d s

Kosrae

PALAU

M   e   l   a   n   e   s   i   a

NAURU

PAPUA NEW GUINEA

New Ireland

*Bismarck
Sea*

*New
Britain*

Solomon Islands

New Guinea

*Bougainville
Island*

**SOLOMON
ISLANDS**

*Solomon
Sea*

Guadalcanal

*Santa Cruz
Islands*

Arafura Sea

Torres Strait

*Coral
Sea*

VANUATU

*Timor
Sea*

*Joseph
Bonaparte
Gulf*

*Gulf of
Carpentaria*

Coral Sea Islands
(to Australia)

Efate

New Caledonia
(to France)

NORTHERN
TERRITORY

QUEENSLAND

P   A   C   I

Norfolk Island
(to Australia)

INDIAN OCEAN

A U S T R A L I A

WESTERN   AUSTRALIA

*Lake Eyre
North*

SOUTH AUSTRALIA

Lake Torrens

NEW
SOUTH WALES

Lord Howe Island
(to Australia)

AUSTRALIAN
CAPITAL TERRITORY

Australia
Two-thirds of
Australia is a
great plateau
of deserts and
mountains.

*Great Australian
Bight*

VICTORIA

*Tasman
Sea*

Bass Strait

TASMANIA

Tasmania

New Zealand
This country
comprises two islands
—North Island and
South Island.

S   O   U   T   H   E   R   N

40 million, its population is the smallest of any continent. The area is made up of Australia, New Zealand, Papua New Guinea, and thousands of islands in the Pacific Ocean. These islands are divided into three main areas: Micronesia, Melanesia, and Polynesia. Australia is too large to be called an island and is today considered a continent in its own right, with the other islands known as Oceania.

The world's biggest atoll is Kwajalein, in the Marshall Islands. An atoll is a ring of coral enclosing a central lagoon.

Melanesia
Five main island groups make up Melanesia—Papua New Guinea, Fiji, Vanuatu, New Caledonia, and the Solomon Islands.

Polynesia
This area covers the Cook Islands, French Polynesia, Easter Island, and Pitcairn Islands, among other small island groups.

French Polynesia consists of 130 islands and covers 10.5 million sq km (4 million sq miles).

Map labels:
PACIFIC OCEAN
Tarawa
Tungaru
KIRIBATI
TUVALU
Phoenix Islands
Kingman Reef (to US)
Palmyra Atoll (to US)
Tabuarean
Kiritimati
Jarvis Island (to US)
Line Islands
Malden Island
Starbuck Island
Tokelau (to NZ)
Northern Cook Islands
Penrhyn
Manihiki
Millennium Island
Flint Island
Marquesas Islands
Wallis and Futuna (to France)
American Samoa (to US)
SAMOA
Cook Islands (to NZ)
Vanua Levu
Viti Levu
Lau Group
FIJI
TONGA
Niue (to NZ)
Southern Cook Islands
Rarotonga
Society Islands
Tahiti
Tuamotu Islands
French Polynesia (to France)
Îles Australes
Mururoa
Îles Gambier
Pitcairn, Henderson, Ducie and Oeno Islands (to UK)
Pitcairn Island
PACIFIC OCEAN
Kermadec Islands (to NZ)
NEW ZEALAND
North Island
Bay of Plenty
Cook Strait
South Island
Stewart Island
Chatham Islands (to NZ)
Auckland Islands (to NZ)
POLYNESIA
OCEAN

Facts and figures

POPULATION BY COUNTRY
Although Australia has the largest number of people, with 24.7 million inhabitants, it is also by far the largest country and has a small population for its size. Papua New Guinea is the next most populous country, with 8.4 million people.

LANGUAGES
There are an extraordinary number of languages spoken in this part of the world. The people of Papua New Guinea alone speak 841 languages. There are 237 languages spoken in Australia and 122 in the Solomon Islands.

URBAN POPULATION
Australia and New Zealand dominate the largest urban areas, but compared to the rest of the world, they have small populations. Sydney and Melbourne are the most populous cities with 4.8 million inhabitants. Auckland in New Zealand has 1.6 million.

RELIGIONS
The majority of people in this region choose to follow Christianity, which was introduced by the missionaries and colonists. A significant number of people still follow indigenous beliefs.

The People of the Pacific and Australia

THE FIRST INHABITANTS of this area were the Aboriginals and Torres Strait Islanders of Australia, Tongans, Tahitians, Samoans, Micronesians, Melanesians, and the Polynesians—such as the New Zealand Maori. They are thought to have originated from Southeast Asia, arriving as far back as 50,000 years ago.

A fifth of Australia's population lives in Sydney.

COLONIZATION

During the late 18th century, Europeans started to pour into Australia, attracted by gold and "a new life," and much of the region was colonized. Today, Australia and New Zealand have a rich mixture of ethnic groups from Europe and Asia.

CITY LIFE

The number of people in Oceania is very low. Australia is one of the least densely populated areas on Earth. Eighty percent of Australia's population live within 25 miles (40 km) of the coast, most in cities such as Melbourne, above, and Sydney.

SPORTS

One popular sport in the area is rugby. Teams in Australia, New Zealand, and Pacific Islands such as Fiji and Samoa boast world-class players. Here New Zealand's All Blacks perform their traditional pre-game *haka* (see p.296).

FARMING

Mining and farming are important in Australia and New Zealand but most people work in service industries.

Island people

Over 20,000 islands are scattered over the vast expanse of the Pacific
Ocean. Some are large, such as New Guinea; others are little more
than tiny coral islands. Only a few thousand are inhabited today.

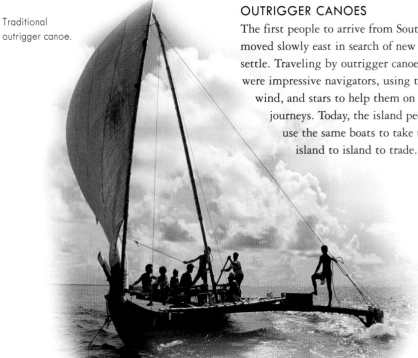

Traditional
outrigger canoe.

OUTRIGGER CANOES

The first people to arrive from Southeast Asia
moved slowly east in search of new islands to
settle. Traveling by outrigger canoe, they
were impressive navigators, using the sun,
wind, and stars to help them on their
journeys. Today, the island people still
use the same boats to take them from
island to island to trade.

ISLAND INDUSTRY

Small scale industries, such
as fishing and some mining,
are found on the Pacific
islands. However, due to
the stunningly beautiful
beaches and lagoons,
fabulous diving, and fine
weather throughout the
year, tourism is the main
source of income.

FOREIGN INFLUENCE

Tolai
dancers
wearing
ceremonial
masks in
Papua New
Guinea.

Many islanders became Christian when the missionaries arrived
in the late 18th century and have since absorbed much foreign
influence. Some villages in Papua New Guinea, however, have
had little contact with the outside world, and have developed
totally different languages and cultures from each other.

LANGUAGE

English is widely spoken throughout Australia,
New Zealand, and on many of the Pacific
Islands. However, Papua New Guinea
lays claim to over 800 different languages!

AUSTRALIANS

AUSTRALIA IS AN ENORMOUS COUNTRY. It is the sixth largest country in the world, but very little of the land is inhabited. There is less than one person per square mile and, although Australia is

A MIXED NATION OF PEOPLE

A way of life

Australians enjoy a hot climate all year round and spend a lot of time outdoors playing land and sea sports. Surfing and diving are two of the most popular pastimes. Team sports, such as rugby union and cricket, are also widely played. The country's teams are world famous—sport is almost a religion.

CULTURAL MIX
For thousands of years Aboriginal people and Torres Strait Islanders were the only inhabitants of Australia. In the 18th century British colonists arrived and the discovery of gold in the 1850s brought a rush of people from Europe, China, and the US. After the Second World War more people immigrated there and today about a quarter of Australian residents were born in another country.

AUSTRALIAN RULES
Australian Rules is a game unique to the country and is a mixture of rugby and Gaelic soccer. It is played in every state and territory, and players are household names and treated as stars.

THE GOLD COAST
With about 300 days of sun a year, the Gold Coast that stretches down the eastern side of Australia is a true surfers' paradise. The sprawling region has grown up around an extensive stretch of beautiful beaches, which makes the area a very attractive tourist destination.

THE BIGGEST SCHOOL IN THE WORLD

Children who do not live in the cities of Australia and grow up on farms—often hundreds of miles from a town—attend the "school of the air." The children stay at home and receive instruction over the air by radio and, more recently, over the internet. This "air school" covers thousands of square miles of Australia.

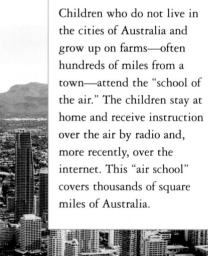

almost as big as all of Europe, it has less than 3 percent of the population Europe has. About 80 percent of people live in cities along the coast—mostly the east and southeast coasts—and most of the area in the center of the country is desert. Australia is proud to be a multicultural nation. The first inhabitants, the Aboriginal people, now make up nearly 3 percent of the population.

The outback

The area between the coasts and the desert of Australia is known as the *outback*. It is one of the hottest, driest areas in the world and is very difficult to grow crops on. However livestock, such as sheep and cattle, can survive and are kept on huge farms there.

If someone on an outback farm becomes sick or injured, the flying doctor arrives by plane.

FARMING BIG STYLE

Less than 5 percent of the population are farmers, yet over half of the land is used for grazing. A single sheep or cattle station is sometimes so big that it can take three or four days to travel across it.

1 Finding the herd
Because of the huge areas that the cattle and sheep are free to roam, farmers frequently use motorcycles or quadbikes to monitor their animals.

2 Rounding up
Beef cattle graze on dry grass and drink water drawn from wells. When they need to be herded back to the station, helicopters are used.

3 Closing in
Helicopters communicate with farmers in ground vehicles and between them help drive the cattle into large enclosures.

The great reef dive

SWIMMING AROUND THE WORLD'S LARGEST LIVING STRUCTURE

SCUBA DIVING IS ONE OF THE MOST POPULAR SPORTS in Australia. Thousands of tourists flock there each year to see the world's largest living structure, the Great Barrier Reef, which stretches down just off the east coast and covers an area about the size of New Mexico. There are over 3,000 separate reefs, 1,500 species of fish, and 400 types of corals amid the crystal-clear waters. During the Sydney Olympic Games in 2000, the torch featured the first-ever underwater leg of its journey through the Great Barrier Reef.

ABORIGINALS

FOR 50,000 YEARS THE ABORIGINAL PEOPLE OF AUSTRALIA have lived in every incredibly different region of this enormous country. There is variety among the different groups of indigenous Australians that

THE ANCIENT PEOPLE OF AUSTRALIA

Arnhem Land

In 1931, Arnhem Land in the northeast of the Northern Territories, was made an Aboriginal Reserve. Most of its population are indigenous people and the region is large and isolated, enabling them to revive and continue their culture. The area is known for its art, like bark paintings, which often promote Aboriginal rights.

FAMILY LIFE
The Aboriginal family unit is large and extended. Raising children is not just the duty of the parents but of the entire community. These family systems are central to the way each society is organized and the close family ties ensure that the traditional culture is kept alive. Elders are treated with great respect—they are the bridge between past and present.

CITY LIFE
Not all Aboriginal Australians live a traditional way of life. Many of them now live in major cities, such as Sydney, and lead more westernized lives.

MODERN CONVENIENCES
Although the people of Arnhem Land choose to live very traditionally, they also make good use of the modern world. These men are using one recently installed telephone to check that neighbors will be turning up for a ceremony.

BUSH TUCKER
The Aboriginal people only take from the "bush," or land, what is needed and always make sure that game and plants can regenerate. Children are taught to hunt while quite young.

have developed over time but all share an intimate knowledge and understanding of their environment. They were displaced and diminished by the colonial powers but in the 20th century their human rights were recognized to a greater extent. Australian Aboriginal people have learned to adapt to change and have survived to become some of the oldest living cultures in the world.

WEAVING

The women make mats, baskets, and other containers by weaving many materials together, such as pandanus, palm fronds, bark, grasses, and even human hair. The items are colored with natural dyes made from roots or bark and are sometimes decorated with feathers or pieces of cloth. The Aboriginal people are famous for their arts: woven products as well as their paintings are sold throughout Australia.

THE NGANGIYAL

This tentlike basket is called a *ngangiyal*. It is made of woven pandanus and is used for what the Aboriginal people refer to as "private women's business." As these children show, it's also fun to play with!

THE BOOMERANG

Boomerangs are curved wooden throwing sticks used as hunting weapons and as clapsticks during ceremonies. They are cleverly designed to return to you when thrown. They are made from many types of wood and are often decorated.

The two children on the left are accompanying the didgeridoo player with their clapsticks.

THE DIDGERIDOO

A musical instrument, the didgeridoo is a long, thin tree trunk, usually from a eucalyptus tree that has been hollowed out by termites. The trunk is cut to three feet (1 m) or so in length and fitted with a waxy mouthpiece. When blown it makes low rumbling notes. It is very difficult to play, but experts can make it sound like the calls of certain birds and animals.

Dreamtime

The Aboriginal people believe that their knowledge, faith, and practices are linked to the stories of creation, which are known as *Dreamtime* or *Dreaming*. Ancestral spirits came to Earth and created the land, animals, and plants. They taught the people how to live with the Earth and to respect it. The Dreamtime stories are still told today and are central to Aboriginal culture.

STORYTELLING

The Dreamtime stories explain how people should behave, live, and respect the land. These stories are passed down from generation to generation and relate to a large part of everyday life. The elders take every opportunity to teach children about the way of life of their people and, through story and song, have kept alive their traditions and heritage over thousands of years.

ULURU

All over Australia there are many sacred sites and *Dreamtime tracks*, which are the paths taken by the spirits when they created the land. Uluru is a sacred rock for the Aboriginal peoples of the Central Desert. It is rich in mythology and the caves are filled with ancient rock art depicting Dreamtime stories. In 1985, the site was returned to the Aboriginal Australians and the caves can only be visited by initiated people.

MIMI

The Mimi are spirits believed to live in Northern Australia. They are always carved or painted as tall, thin beings. When the first people arrived in Australia it is said that the Mimi spirits taught them how to live off the land. They showed them how to hunt, cook, and respect the Earth that they live on. They also taught the people how to paint. The Mimi are believed to be mischievous, but harmless spirits.

Dreamtime today

When Australia was colonized, the Aboriginal way of living was misunderstood and colonials made attempts to change the way the indigenous people lived. These days the culture is accepted and many Aboriginal people are returning to their traditional ways.

Uluru was called Ayers Rock by the British colonizers. It is the largest stone monolith on Earth.

AN ANCIENT ART
Modern painting and ancient rock art often depict the Dreamtime stories. The Rainbow Serpent is a spirit shared by many communities across Australia. It is the protector of land and people, and the source of life, but it can be destructive if it is not respected.

WALKABOUT
To enter manhood an Aboriginal boy will take a journey alone to prove he can survive in the wilderness in the traditional way. It is often referred to as a "walkabout." These boys are demonstrating a traditional way of drinking that does not disturb the water.

INITIATION CEREMONY

In some Aboriginal communities in Australia, boys have to go through an initiation ceremony to enter manhood. They are taught songs and dances, decorate their bodies, then perform rituals that can go on for weeks.

MIDDLE SEPIK

RIVER PEOPLE OF PAPUA NEW GUINEA

THE SEPIK IS A LONG RIVER THAT RUNS through mainland Papua New Guinea, from the highlands to the coast, and all along it live different clans. The people of the Middle Sepik live along the river, inland from the

LIVING ON STILTS

The houses along the Sepik river are mainly built on stilts. This is so that during the rainy season, when the water level rises, the houses are in no danger of flooding. The stilts also prevent too many mosquitoes and rats from infesting the houses.

The river

The Sepik River is roughly 700 miles (1,100 km) from source to mouth and is navigable for almost its entire length. It is vital to the local people who live on its banks—they use it for transportation, and as a source of water and food. Many of the legends in the area are connected to the river and it is regarded as a spirit itself.

COLLECTING FOOD

Men, women, and children all share the fishing jobs in the Middle Sepik area. They use long dugout canoes to catch large eels and crocodiles, and set traps in the water or use spears to catch fish. They make flour from sago palms in the swamps and keep chickens and pigs in the villages.

THE CROCODILE

The Sepik people honor the crocodile and there are many myths and legends surrounding it. The people have lots of spirits or gods and the crocodile is one such spirit of the river. When making canoes, the Sepik people often carve the head of a crocodile on the prow.

Two dugout canoes negotiate one of the many narrow waterways on the river.

coast, and their land stretches up to the beginning of the highlands. They share many cultural similarities from village to village, such as the elaborate initiation rites and the highly developed art and architectural styles. Secrecy is an important part of life; the older males get, the more they are allowed to learn. Older men often hold debates challenging each other's knowledge of the secret and magical names.

Male initiation

The process of men initiating boys into manhood is of enormous importance in Sepik societies and there are many rites connected to it. The initiation has many levels where each boy is taught obligations and secret rituals, and learns about the mythical journeys of his ancestors. It is often years before a boy becomes a man.

HAUS TAMBARAN

Every village has a spiritual house called a *haus tambaran*. The building can have one or two stories and contains many intricate carvings. It is where the young boys learn rituals that will take them to manhood. Women are not allowed to enter.

SEPIK MASKS

The Middle Sepik people are famous for their art and carvings. Spirit houses are filled with masks depicting ancestors, mythical beings, and nature spirits. Each mask has complex meanings and many different spiritual purposes. Some masks, such as this one, have tongues sticking out as a sign of aggression toward enemies of the clan.

INITIATION SCARRING

In some Sepik groups a young male must learn about pain—this involves scarring. This boy has had his skin cut deeply and made to resemble crocodile skin. Afterward, the wounds are rubbed with a mixture of ashes, oil, and mud to ensure that the pattern, which is considered to be highly attractive, is permanent.

Only certain powerful men may lower the *savi masks* from their storage in the *haus tambaran*.

HULI

THE WIG PEOPLE OF THE HIGHLANDS

PAPUA NEW GUINEA IS THE EASTERN HALF of a large island in the Pacific Ocean with a number of islands surrounding it. The western half of the island is Irian Jaya—part of Indonesia. The inland central area rises

The Huli

The Huli people live in the central mountains of Papua New Guinea in rain forest that is so dense that no outsider knew they existed until the 1930s. Like many of the peoples on the island, ceremonies and festivals are a major part of life—they are not only important within the group, but also for forming alliances with different clans. Self-decoration is a large part of the ceremonies.

This girl has painted her face with ocher and wears feathers in honor of the birds the Huli revere.

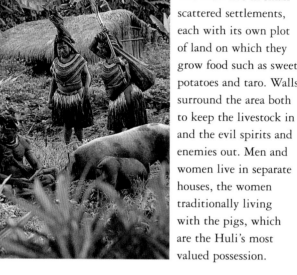

EVERYDAY LIFE

The Huli live in small scattered settlements, each with its own plot of land on which they grow food such as sweet potatoes and taro. Walls surround the area both to keep the livestock in and the evil spirits and enemies out. Men and women live in separate houses, the women traditionally living with the pigs, which are the Huli's most valued possession.

THE HULI WARRIOR

From the day a Huli boy is born he is taught how to be a warrior and to defend his family. Clans often have disagreements, mainly over land, women, or pigs, which can lead to fighting. Pigs are often exchanged to settle disputes and compensate for injury or death.

into a wide ridge of mountains known as the highlands, a territory that is so densely forested that the island's local peoples remained isolated from each other for thousands of years. As a result, incredibly, there are as many as 800 different languages in Papua New Guinea. One of the many peoples that live in the Highlands are the extraordinary Huli, famous for their spectacular head adornments.

Huli wig school

One interesting feature about the Huli people is their elaborate wigs. As teenagers, the boys are taken from their homes to live in and attend wig school for several years. They learn to be efficient warriors and good community members but, most importantly, they grow and tend to their hair, which will one day be cut and made into spectacular wigs.

The students at wig school put cassowary wing feathers through their noses.

WIG CARE

It is essential to look after the growing hair in order to keep it in prime condition. Without magical rites, the instruction of a hair trainer, and constant grooming, men cannot grow their hair sufficiently to satisfy traditional wig requirements. They even sleep with their heads propped up to avoid flattening the shape.

THE FINISHED WIG

When the hair is considered long enough it is cut and, while still keeping the mushroom shape, it is decorated with bright feathers, daisies, and even possum fur.

SING SING

The ceremonial wigs are worn during *sing sings*—ceremonies that include initiation rites and weddings. Neighbors are sometimes invited to attend *sing sings* and clans and families have a chance to show solidarity and exhibit wealth. They perform dances in their groups and feast on pigs.

These men are painting their faces—using car side-view mirrors to aid them! A small sign of modern influence.

PAPUA NEW GUINEA

A GATHERING OF TRIBES

EACH YEAR MORE THAN 50 cultural groups from all over Papua New Guinea gather together in the West Highlands province for the spectacular and flamboyant Mount Hagen Cultural Show. It was originally started as a way to calm tribal animosities and to celebrate the enormous diversity of traditional ways. All the groups dress up in their most colorful displays of makeup and ornamentation to impress the other clans. The whole show is such a visual extravaganza that it has become a huge tourist attraction. Up to 50,000 people have been known to descend on the area. The Asaro clan in this picture are famous for their extraordinary mud masks and mud body paint.

TROBRIANDERS

THE PACIFIC ISLANDS OF PARADISE

THE TROBRIAND ISLANDS ARE A SPRINKLING of coral islands situated in Melanesia in the Pacific Ocean. Since 1975, the islands have been considered part of a larger area known as the Massim

Ancient ways

When the Christian missionaries arrived in the early 20th century, they tried to quell many traditions on the islands, such as body decoration and the wearing of grass skirts. However, in time the islanders reverted to their old customs and, although most claim to be Christian, the religion doesn't impinge on traditional beliefs.

THE KULA EXCHANGE

Kula is the inter-island, ceremonial trading network that involves the Trobriands and surrounding islands. It has been in action for over 500 years and is a means of trade. Each time a person arrives on an island to trade, they must offer either shell armbands or necklaces with elaborate ceremony. The *soulava*, shell necklaces, only ever travel in a clockwise direction around the islands and the armbands, *mwali*, only travel in a counterclockwise direction. The same items have been in circulation for hundreds of years.

FISHING

Outrigger canoes are used for fishing. The Trobrianders use nets, spears, and baited hooks to lure fish; they catch turtles using their hands. In deep water they dive down to incredible 30 ft (10 m) depths and cling onto coral with one hand while spearing with the other. Fish are caught as food for the village or for trade with other islands.

BANANA LEAF CURRENCY

There are many kinds of valuable items that are used as currencies in Papua New Guinea, including money made from shells. Trobrianders also have a kind of currency made from banana leaves.

District of the Nation of Papua New Guinea, although the people's culture and traditional ways are still valued. The islands are beautiful tropical paradises with bleached white sand, coconut palms, dugout canoes, thatched fishing huts, and little or no traffic. Many of the islands don't even have electricity. The islanders are best known for their extraordinary method of exchange and trade with each other, known as the *Kula*.

TROBRIAND CRICKET

Cricket was introduced to the Trobriand Islands by Christian missionaries to discourage ritual warfare. The Islanders took to it with enormous enthusiasm and added many of their own rules. They perform special dances for every point they gain and have dispensed with the bails.

YAM STORAGE

The yam is prized in the Trobriand Islands. It grows well in the thin soil and is a staple food. The islanders build elaborate and beautiful yam houses to store and show off their prized vegetables, which sometimes grow to more than three feet (1 m).

The yam houses stand in the center of the village. More care goes into the building of these than of real houses.

THE YAM FESTIVAL

Yams are more than just a food: they represent wealth and are a symbol of life. During the annual yam festival, which lasts over a month, the yams are picked and stored and the islanders hold dance competitions and cricket matches. Beauty, body ornamentation, and magic are a large part of the festival.

SING SING

Dance festivals, or *sing sings*, are an important part of Trobriand life. Often the men and women dance separately. The girls perform a seductive *cassava* dance, swaying their hips in short grass skirts and snaking their hands from side to side. The men, in contrast, stamp on the sand to the rhythmic sound of drums.

YAPESE

THE SEAFARING ISLANDERS

SITUATED IN THE HEART OF MICRONESIA in the Pacific Ocean lie the 134 islands—most of them unpopulated—that make up the State of Yap. The islands are scattered over 600 miles (1,000 km) of ocean, but the

THE BUILDINGS

There are three different types of buildings on the Yap Islands—the family house, the men's house, and this one, the *pebay*, which is the community house. It is a place where people get together for dances and meetings, and also acts as a school house.

YAP DAY

On the first of March each year the islanders celebrate Yap Day—a festival commemorating the rich culture and lifestyle of the islands. All the villages perform dances that tell stories, and contests are held to find the best sportsman and the provider of the finest local produce. The dances are prepared and practiced all year and are always performed in large groups.

Yap Island

The main town on Yap is Colonia, which is situated around a bay. Although it is the center of tourism and government, most Yapese people live in villages located outside the town, where they lead a unique lifestyle. The main occupations of the people on the island are farming and fishing.

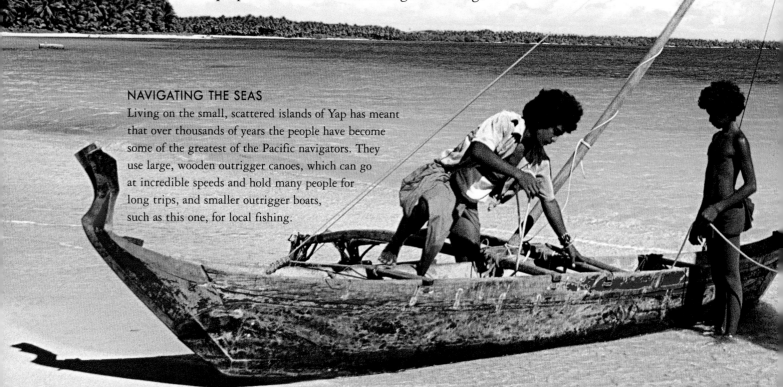

NAVIGATING THE SEAS

Living on the small, scattered islands of Yap has meant that over thousands of years the people have become some of the greatest of the Pacific navigators. They use large, wooden outrigger canoes, which can go at incredible speeds and hold many people for long trips, and smaller outrigger boats, such as this one, for local fishing.

main four populated islands are clustered together. The temperature throughout the seasons on the islands tends to remain at approx 80°F (27°C) but in May, June, and November typhoons strike, causing huge storms. Over hundreds of years various people, such as traders and missionaries, have settled on these islands, but the Yapese have always clung with determination to their original customs and traditions.

The coins have holes in the center so they can be carried. Two people are needed to carry each coin.

STONE CURRENCY
Yap coins are the biggest in the world. They are round chunks of stone that range from 1 ft (0.3 m) to 12 ft (3.5 m) tall. But the stone does not come from the Yap Islands. It comes from volcanic islands 300 miles (550 km) away. Over hundreds of years, Yapese sailors have risked their lives to bring back the stones in outrigger canoes.

This man sings and blows into a conch to announce a successful catch.

STAR COMPASS
This simple diagram of stones and leaves is actually a star compass. The outer rim of stones represents constellations, showing when they rise and set on the horizon, and the leaves inside represent the swell of the waves and the canoe. Together they help the navigator find his way.

NI-VANUATU

THE REPUBLIC OF VANUATU IS MADE UP of 80 islands scattered over the Pacific Ocean in a "Y" shape. Most of the islands are volcanic in origin, while a few are coral atolls. There are frequent earth tremors in the area

THE PEOPLE OF THE VOLCANO

Vanuatu Cultural Centre

The people of Vanuatu are fiercely proud of their cultures and many value a traditional way of life. The Vanuatu Cultural Center was started in 1955 and has more than 80 volunteers. They travel all over the islands collecting information about local cultures. They then write up literature about them to document and preserve them, and to promote the islands all over the world.

The preparation of kava for the men of the village.

MOUNT YASUR

Tanna Island, part of Vanuatu, is a place where the culture and custom remain strong. The island is volcanic and explosions occur regularly on Mount Yasur. Most local people believe that the volcano is the house of spirits and rituals are held to honor it.

KAVA

All over Vanuatu a favorite drink is kava. At dusk men start gathering and preparing the kava root. They chew it, then spit it into a bowl and add water. They always drink it fresh and, because it is a potent drug, it aids their sleep.

ISLAND MUSIC

The Ni-Vanuatu pride themselves on their musical instruments. This young boy, wearing a loincloth and decorative leaves, holds a long bamboo tube. While he sings, he thrusts the bamboo against a wooden board, creating rhythmic, musical sounds.

UNITED IN DANCE

These dancers on Tanna Island wear grass skirts, colorful scarves, and feathers. During the *toka* festival, women from many villages dance all night, then men take over at sunrise.

and the islands are home to nine active volcanoes. There are over 100 indigenous languages in Vanuatu, but most people speak or understand a form of pidgin, based on English. Vanuatu is home to a rich Melanesian culture full of tradition, magic, and ritual, and each tribal group on the islands has its own identity and customs.

The great Pentecost jump

Every April, when the yam crop is ready for harvest, the people of Pentecost Island build a 100 ft (30 m) high tower. Over the next few weeks boys and men jump from the top with vines tied to their feet, believing this will make the ground fertile. According to legend, a woman did the first jump, then both women and men, but now only men take part.

LIFE OR DEATH

The men choose their own length of liana vine and, because they must aim for the vine to tighten as near to the ground as possible, the length is of vital importance. A vine just 4 in (10 cm) too long could mean serious injury or death.

1 The first jump
A boy jumps for the first time when he enters manhood, and from then on jumps regularly. His ankles are tied tightly with the vine, which is attached to the top of the tower.

2 Reach for the sky
The land diver always stretches his arms toward the sky before jumping. The divers believe that the higher the jumpers dive, the higher the crop will grow.

3 The jump
With the whole community watching, the diver then hurls himself off the top of the tower. There are injuries and sometimes a man dies from the fall.

BUNGEE JUMPING

Modern-day bungee jumping was inspired by the ancient Pentecost jump. The only difference is that the modern jumpers use elastic, which is a great deal safer!

SAMOANS

THE PEOPLE OF WESTERN SAMOA

THE ISLANDS OF SAMOA ARE A GROUP OF ACTIVE volcanic islands that lie in the Pacific Ocean between New Zealand and Hawaii. The only large town on the four inhabited islands is Apia, the capital.

Fa'a Samoa

The Western Samoans follow a more traditional way of life, known as *fa'a Samoa*, a moral code on how to live life. It teaches about church, community, family, and, most importantly, respect. The *aiga*, extended family, is all-important and each is led by a *matai*, selected for life, who runs the family's social, economic, and political affairs.

FOOD ON SAMOA

The families all own garden plots, where they grow fruit and vegetables such as bananas and taro. They also keep chickens and pigs and marinate raw fish by a method known as *oka*.

THE HOME

Samoan homes, called *fale*, have wooden frames, thatched sugarcane canopies, and coconut-leaf blinds that roll down the sides to shade against the sun or protect against wind and rain. They are completely open and everyone sleeps together on woven mats. Twenty or more people may all sleep in a *fale* at one time.

DANCING

One of the things the Samoans are best known for is their dancing, one area of culture that has changed little from contact with western civilization. The dances are performed by individuals or groups either sitting or standing.

The rest of the settlements are some 400 coastal villages. In the 19th century, Germany and the US divided the island chain into Western and Eastern Samoa and took them as their territories. In 1962 Western Samoa became an independent nation once again. Both Western and Eastern, or American, Samoa rely heavily on tuna canning but also tourism, civil service, and agricultural products.

SAMOAN TATTOOS

The Samoans are probably the most famous tattooists of the South Pacific with their striking patterns and designs. Not many Polynesian words have entered the English language, but one that has is *tattoo*.

1 Tattooing ceremony
Traditional tattoos are done using boar-tooth needles dipped in soot-based ink. Songs are often sung to the recipient to take their mind off the pain.

2 Soothing the tattoos
After the tattoo is finished, the tattooist rubs coconut oil into the designs. Traditional tattooing can take many weeks to complete, but these days they use methods that take a shorter time.

3 The designs
The male tattoos stretch from the knee up to the lower back and the stomach, resembling a pair of shorts. The female tattoos tend to be on the wrists or above the knee.

FISHING IN PAOPAO

Traditional fishing gear—fish hooks and octopus lures—are still used on Samoa, especially in villages. The skills are passed on through experience and practice and learned from generation to generation. The boats they use are *vaa'alo* (outriggers) and the smaller *paopao*.

RELIGION

The Samoans are devout Christians and have been ever since the Christian missionaries arrived in about 1830. Samoa's motto is "Samoa is founded on God." Churches tend to be the grandest buildings in the village and everyone wears white to the services.

TOURISM

The tourist industry is one of the most important income generators to the economy of Samoa, and the government puts heavy emphasis on it. The Samoans welcome tourists into their homes and allow them to become involved in ceremonies and the traditional way of life.

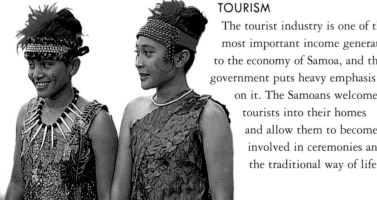

Samoan women wear traditional dresses made from woven matting or leaves.

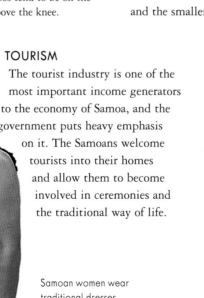

NEW ZEALANDERS

NEW ZEALAND IS MADE UP OF TWO MAIN ISLANDS, North Island and South Island, and a scattering of smaller islands situated in the Pacific Ocean to the

A LAND OF SHEEP AND SPORTS

A CLEAN LAND

New Zealand has some of the most beautiful landscapes in the world, and some of the cleanest. The people do not support nuclear power. Instead they use hydroelectric power and have few industries.

CITY LIFE

Only 15 percent of the population of New Zealand live in the countryside—the rest live in towns and cities. The capital, Wellington (right), is situated on the south of the North Island. Auckland, however, is the largest city and is home to almost a third of the total population.

A LOVE OF SPORTS

With over half the population signed up to sports clubs, New Zealanders are close to obsessed with playing or simply watching—whether it is rugby union, netball, cricket, or yacht racing. The country is also well known for its extreme sports including bungee jumping, rafting, mountaineering, skiing, and snowboarding.

southeast of Australia. It is sparsely populated and the people, known as "kiwis," are mostly of British descent. The indigenous Maori people make up about 14 percent of the population. The beautiful scenery in New Zealand, ranging from towering mountains with volcanic geysers and glaciers to long beaches and lush green fields has in recent years attracted film-makers from all over the world who use it as a spectacular photographic location.

THE GREAT OUTDOORS

New Zealand is home to glacial mountains, huge forests, and long beaches, and is a haven for outdoor pursuits. *Tramping*, or hiking, is a very popular pastime, with many people rushing into the great outdoors on weekends.

Industry

New Zealand is an agricultural country, and its farm products are sold widely abroad. More than half of the land is used as sheep pasture, with lamb and wool being major exports. Other exports include dairy products, fish, fruit, and lumber to be made into paper.

SHEEP SHEARING

There are approximately 4.7 million people living in New Zealand and an estimated 39 million sheep—that means a lot of shearing. Each year major sheep-shearing championships are held where people gather from all over the country to witness this fast and highly competitive sport—an experienced shearer can shear one sheep in just a few minutes.

KIWI FRUIT

Kiwi fruit originated in China, but was brought to New Zealand in the 20th century and grown in gardens as the Chinese gooseberry. When New Zealand began exporting it, the fruit was called kiwi, borrowed from the native kiwi bird.

Saving lives on the beaches

THE LIFEGUARDS OF NEW ZEALAND'S COASTLINE

NEW ZEALAND IS A MECCA FOR THRILL SEEKERS from all over the world, particularly those looking for thrills on or in the water. Everything from jet-boarding, white-water sleding, rafting, kayaking, and diving, to, in particular, surfing and windsurfing are experienced in all weathers nearly all year round. With so much activity on the water, *Surf Life Saving New Zealand*, established in 1910, is an essential organization on the beaches. In their time, the life savers have saved many tens of thousands of lives. Competitions between life savers are held annually, and lifeguards in this picture race across a beach in the North Island during the *Ironman Surf League* finals. The competition includes rescue events and surfboard races.

MAORI

A CULTURAL REVIVAL

THE MAORI WERE THE FIRST SETTLERS IN NEW ZEALAND,

arriving from Polynesia in the late 13th century. They occupied almost every area of New Zealand, and there were over 6,000 Maori villages long before European

CULTURE

The Maori culture is a heritage passed down through the generations. The people have documented their history and expressed their feelings through art for hundreds of years. The traditional Maori greeting is a nose-to-nose touch called the *hongi*.

Haka

The word *haka* means "Maori dance," one that was traditionally performed at the onset of war to unite the people in anger and courage. It is a disciplined dance ritual where the hands, feet, legs, body, voice, and tongue all play a part, blending together to issue a challenge. There are several types of *haka*, but *Ka Mate* is the most popular.

This is the traditional Maori *Haka*. The New Zealand *All Blacks* rugby team has adopted the moves, which they perform before matches.

HANGI

The traditional, ancient Maori way of cooking is called *hangi*—cooking a meal underground using heated stones. The *hangi* is still popular with a lot of Maori people today.

1 Digging the pit
A large pit is dug into the ground and stones are laid at the bottom. The stones are heated and covered in cabbage leaves or watercress to stop the food from burning.

2 Into the steam
Mutton, pork, chicken, potatoes, and sweet potatoes are lowered into the pit in a wire basket. The food is covered with wet sheets and earth to keep in the steam.

3 Ready to eat
The food takes about three hours to cook. When it appears it has a soft texture as if steamed, and an earthy, slightly smoked flavor.

TA MOKO

The ancient practice of Maori tattooing is called *ta moko*. The use of full facial tattoos has recently become an art form again in Maori culture, many men now tattooing their faces as well as their bodies.

settlers first arrived. The original homeland was called Hawaiki but the European explorers renamed it New Zealand. The Maori still have a very strong culture of their own, even though many of them now live a western lifestyle. Their numbers are now rising after a long period of decline and there are currently more than 700,000 Maori, about 15 percent of the population. The Maori language is also increasingly used.

The *Marae* is often named after an ancestor. The ridgepole that holds the roof symbolizes the spine, with the rafters as ribs. Each rafter has an ancestral lineage carved into it.

THE SPIRITUAL MARAE

The center of every Maori community is the *Marae* —a meeting house with a surrounding courtyard, which may include a church. It is used as a political and ceremonial place where important decisions are made and rituals held. Within the *Marae* the Maori language, *Maoritanga*, is spoken. Even urban communities have a *Marae*.

POI DANCE

The Maori *poi* dance is generally performed by women. A *poi*, which means "ball" is attached at each end of a piece of flaxen string. The *pois* are then twirled and whirled rhythmically. The design is based on an ancient weapon and the length of them can vary from 1–3 feet (0.3–1 m). They are swung around the body in various patterns that suggest forces of nature such as birds in flight, waterfalls, or summer rain. The whole effect can be quite hypnotic.

The dancers wear flax skirts and traditionally woven bodices or *pari*.

A traditional greenstone, or jade, pendant.

Index

Acknowledgments

DK WOULD LIKE TO THANK Vanessa Bird for compiling the index; John Friend for proofreading; and Jo Walton for picture research.

The publisher would like to thank the following for their kind permission to reproduce their photographs:
Key: a-above; b-below/bottom; c-center; l-left; r-right; t-top

PICTURE CREDITS

1 **Getty Images:** Sia Kamobou/AFP. 2 **Bryan And Cherry Alexander Photography**: tr. 2-3 **Justin Barton** c. 2 **Corbis:** Patrick Ward br. 2 **Getty Images**: Carlos Navajas cra. 3 **Alejandro Balaguer**: b. 3 **Corbis:** Alan Schein Photography cla. 3 **Getty Images**: Christopher Arneson t. 4 **Alamy Stock Photo:** Bill Bachman t. Getty Images: John van Hasselt/Corbis b. 5 **Alamy Stock Photo:** Joerg Boethling b; Michele Burgess tr; Ei Katsumata tl. 8-9 **Corbis:** Alan Schein Photography. 10 **Corbis:** Keren Su bl, b; Martin Rogers tl. 10 **Panos Pictures**: Penny Tweedie tr. 11 **Corbis**: Bob Krist tr; Richard Cummins bl. Getty Images: Klaus Vedfelt br. 12 123RF.com: Vasilis Ververidis tl. **Corbis**: David Batterbury; Eye Ubiquitous tr; 12 **Still Pictures**: John Maier b. 13 **Corbis:** Christine Osbourne bl; David Turnley br; Michael Cole tl; Roger Ressmeyer tr. 14 **Alamy Stock Photo:** Lorne Chapman tl; imageBROKER tr. 14 **Corbis:** Bob Krist bl; Charles O'Rear crb; Dave G Houser bc; David Samuel Robbins tc; David Stoecklein cra; Dewitt Jones br; Kevin Fleming cla; Ted Spiegel clb; William Manning c. 15 **Corbis:** Bettmann cla; Jeff Curtes bl; W. Wayne Lockwood, M.D. tl; Warren Morgan clb. 17 **Alamy Stock Photo:** age fotostock bl; Martin Thomas Photography tl; Mihai Andritoiu tr; eye35.pix cl. Getty Images: Lance King br. 17 **Corbis:** Douglas Peebles cr. 18 **Corbis:** Alan Schein Photography b. 18 **South American Pictures:** Tony Morrison tr. 19 **Bryan And Cherry Alexander Photography:** tl. 19 **Corbis:** Catherine Karnow br; Peter Turnley bl; Rose Hartman tr. 20 **Corbis:** Bill Ross l; Chuck Savage tr; Joseph Sohm; ChromoSohm Inc. br; Rose Hartman cr. 21 Alamy Stock Photo: David Grossman **tr. Corbis:** Bob Krist br; Richard Cummins tl; Ted Spiegel cl. 22-23 **Corbis:** Adam Woolfitt 24 **Alamy Images:** Chuck Pefley tl; PixelPod br. 24 **Corbis:** Bob Krist tr; Farrell Grehan bl. 25 **Alamy Stock Photo:** Brian Lawrence tr; Visions of America, LLC tl. **Corbis:** Kevin Fleming cl; Owaki - Kulla clb, bl, br. 26 **Corbis:** Nik Wheeler cr; Patrick Ward tc; Philip Gould b. 26 **PA Photos:** EPA cl. 27 **Corbis:** Buddy Mays c; Nik Wheeler bl; Owen Franken tr; William Boyce br. 28 **Corbis:** Kelly-Mooney Photography bl; Kevin R. Morris br; Owaki - Kulla tl. 29 **Corbis:** Kelly-Mooney Photography tr; Kevin Fleming bc; Philip Gould r, c. 30 **Corbis:** Galen Rowell tr; James Marshall cl; Rick Doyle tc. 30 **DK Picture Library**: b. 30 **PA Photos:** tl. 31 **Corbis:** Gunter Marx Photography tr; Kevin R. Morris bl; Richard A. Cooke cl; Roger Ressmeyer tl; Tom Bean br. 32-33 **Getty Images:** David W. Hamilton 34 **Corbis:** Joseph Sohm; Richard Hamilton Smith tc; Robert Holmes cl. 34 **Getty Images:** Roger Hill / Barcroft Images / Barcroft Media (b). 35 **Corbis:** Craig Aurness tr, bc, c; James A. Sugar tc, bl; Macduff Everton br; Richard Hamilton Smith c. 36-37 **Bryan And Cherry Alexander Photography:** 38 **Alamy Images:** Andre Jenny bl; Ethel Davies tl. 38 **Corbis:** Layne Kennedy tr. 38-39 **Lonely Planet Images:** Bill Bachmann c. 38 **Rex Features:** cl; Jim Argo clb. 39 **Corbis:** David Turnley tr, cr; Joe McDonald br. 40 40 Alamy Stock Photo: Mira bl. **Corbis:** Buddy Mays bc; Danny Lehman cr; Ric Ergenbright br. 40 **Rex Features:** John Freeman tl. 41 **Corbis:** Peter Turnley br; Raymond Gehman bc; Richard A. Cooke c. 41 **Katz/FSP:** Jeff Jacobson tr. 41 **Magnum:** Hiroji Kubota tl. 42 **Corbis:** Bob Krist tl. 42 **Getty Images:** Cosmo Condina b. 42 **South American Pictures:** tr. 43 **Eye Ubiquitous:** James Davis tr. 43 **Hutchison Library:** Isabella Tree br. 43 **Impact Photos:** Material World cr. 43 **South American Pictures:** tl, cl; Tony Morrison bl. 44 **Corbis:** Paul A. Souders cl; Richard Cummins bl; Wally McNamee tr. 44 **Hutchison Library:** Robert Francis br. 45 **Corbis: Dewitt Jones** tl; Paul A. Souders bl; Richard Hamilton Smith bc; Richard T. Nowitz br. 45 **DK Picture Library:** tr. 46-47 **Alamy Stock Photo:** Lorne Chapman. 48 **Corbis:** Michael S. Yamashita br; Ted Spiegel bl. 48 **Lonely Planet Images:** Mark Lightbody tr. 49 **Rolf Bettner:** tc, cra, c, r. 49 **Corbis: Dewitt Jones** cl, b. 49 **Toronto Star:** tl. 50 **Bryan And Cherry Alexander Photography.** 51 **Alamy Stock Photo:** imageBROKER tr. **Bryan And Cherry Alexander Photography:** tl, b. 52 **Alamy Stock Photo:** Mauritius Images GmbH (bl). 52 **Bryan And Cherry Alexander Photography:** cr, b. 52 **Lonely Planet Images:** Graeme Cornwallis tc. 53 **Bryan And Cherry Alexander Photography:** bl, bc, r, t; ale c. 54 **Corbis:** Danny Lehman tr; David Cumming tl; Eye Ubiquitous; Jose Fuste Raga b. 55 **Corbis:** Bob Krist cba; Dave G. Houser br; Jeremy Horner bl; Tony Arruza c. 55 **Getty Images:** Guido Alberto Rossi t. 56 **Corbis:** Bob Krist tr; Owen Franken bl. 56 **Panos Pictures:** Jean-Leo Dugast tl; Marc French c. 57 **Corbis:** Macduff Everton r; Tony Arruza tr. 57 **Robert Harding Picture Library:** Fred Friberg bl; Sylvain Grandadam tl. 58-59 **Corbis:** Richard Bickel 60 **Corbis:** Bill Gentile bl; Jay Dickman tr, br; Kevin Schafer c. 61 **Corbis:** Bill Gentile tr; Kevin Schafer br. 61 **Philip Dennis:** tl, cla, cl, bl, bc. 62 **Corbis:** Buddy Mays tr; Charles & Josette Lenars bl; Danny Lehman br; David Samuel Robbins c. 63 **Corbis:** Bettmann c; Richard A. Cooke cl; Wolfgang Kaehler cl, r. 63 **Lonely Planet Images:** Alfredo Maiquez tl. 64 **Corbis:** Charles & Josette Lenars bl; Macduff Everton br; Roman Soumar 65c. 64 **Magnum:** Thomas Hoepker tc. 65 **Corbis:** Charles & Josette Lenars br; Dave G. Houser tr. 65 **Alamy Stock Photo:** Dmitry Rukhlenko - Travel Photos cr. **Magnum:** Burt Glinn bc. 66 **Corbis:** Charles & Josette Lenars tl; Danny Lehman cla; Hank Whitemore/Sygma cla; Jan Butchofsky-Houser crb; Pablo Corral V bl. 66 **Alamy Stock Photo:** Art Kowalsky tr; Federico Tovoli/VWPics crb. 66 **DK Picture Library:** Barnabas Kindersley cra. 66 **Popperfoto:** Bob Thomas ca. 66 **South American Pictures:** clb, br. 67 Alamy Stock Photo: Yaacov Dagan cla. 67 **Still Pictures:** Nigel Dickinson cb. 67 **Alejandro Balaguer:** b. 67 **Hutchison Library:** Felicity Nock crb. 67 **Still Pictures:** John Maier t. 68 **Alamy Stock Photo:** Vicente Quintero bl. 69 **Alamy Stock Photo:** Amazon-Images bl; robertharding tr, br; imageBROKER cr; Didi cl. 69 **Corbis:** tl. 70 **Corbis:** Adam Woolfitt bl; Alison Wright br; Tiziana and Gianni Baldizzone tl. 70 **South American Pictures:** tr. 70 **Still Pictures:** Mark Edwards cb. 71 **Alejandro Balaguer:** cr. 71 **Corbis:** Charles O'Rear tl; Stephanie Maze cra. 71 **Getty Images:** Andrea Booher tr; Angelo Cavalli b. 71 **Robert Harding Picture Library:** Victor Englebert crb. 72 **Hutchison Library:** Brian Moser tl; Felicity Nock tr, br; Titus Moser bl. 73 **Hutchison Library:** Brian Moser tl; Felicity Nock bl; Moser/Taylor r. 73 **South American Pictures:** Britt Dyer c. 74 **Corbis:** Jeremy Horner br. 74 **Robert Harding Picture Library:** Victor Englebert tr, l. 75 **Andes Press Agency:** Roberto Falck tl. 75 **Alejandro Balaguer:** br. 75 **Panos Pictures:** tr. 75 **Still Pictures:** Dario Novellino br. 76-77 **Corbis:** Jack Fields 78 **Sue Cunningham Photographic:** c, cr, bl. 78 **South American Pictures:** Index Editora br. 78 **Still Pictures:** Nigel Dickinson tc. 79 **Corbis:** Sygma t. 79 **Still Pictures:** Mark Edwards bc, r. **Sue Cunningham Photographic:** 80-81. 82 **Getty Images:** Ary Diesendruck l. 82 **South American Pictures:** tc. 82 **Still Pictures:** Julio Etchart bl. 83 **Corbis:** Jim Zuckerman br; Ricardo Azoury tl, cla; Robert Holmes cl. 83 **Still Pictures:** tr; Chris Martin bl. 84 **Corbis:** Jeremy Horner tc, tr; Owen Franken br. 84 **Getty Images:** Peter Adams bl. 85 **Corbis:** Barnabas Bosshart br; Daniel Lainé tr. 85 **Sue Cunningham Photographic:** cl. 85 **Getty Images:** David W. Hamilton bl. 86 **Aspect Picture Library:** Peter Carmichael br, t. 86 **Corbis:** Jeremy Horner cr; Kevin Schafer tl, c; Wolfgang Kaehler bl, br. 86 **Hutchison Library:** Eric Lawrie tr. 87 **Aspect Picture Library:** Peter Carmichael tl, tr, cl, br. 87 **Corbis:** Julie Houck tl; Wolfgang Kaehler tr. 87 **Hutchison Library:** Eric Lawrie br. 88 **Andes Press Agency:** Carlos Reyes-Manzo r. 88 **Alejandro Balaguer:** l. 89 **Andes Press Agency:** bl. 89 **Alejandro Balaguer:** tr. 89 **Exile Images:** br. 89 **South American Pictures:** Kathy Jarvis tl. 90 **Alamy Stock Photo:** Andrew Short br. 90 **Getty Images:** Geoffrey Clifford tl. 90 **South American Pictures:** Kathy Jarvis bl. 90 **Zefa:** Abril tr. 91 **Corbis:** b; Owen Franken tr. 91 **South American Pictures:** Tony Morrison tl. 92-93 **Impact Photos:** Christophe Bluntzer 94 **Jacek Piwowarczyk:** br. 94 Alamy Stock Photo: Federico Tovoli/VWPics tr. 94 **Still Pictures:** Edward Parker bl. 95 **Alejandro Balaguer:** tl, r. 95 **Corbis:** James Sparshatt bl. 96 **Panos Pictures:** Helen Hughes tl. 96 **Rehue Foundation:** c, br. 96 **Rex Features:** Rob Crandell l. 97 **Exile Images:** J Etchart br. 97 **Panos Pictures:** Helen Hughes tl. 97 **Rehue Foundation:** tr, c. 98 Alamy Stock Photo: Paul Brown br. 98 **Aspect Picture Library:** Horst Gossler bl. 98 **Corbis:** Bob Krist cra; Caroline Penn clb; Kraft Brooks/Sygma crb; Liba Taylor tr; Lindsay Hebberd tl; Owen Franken cla; Paul W. Liebhardt c; Sandro Vannini clb. 98 **Getty Images:** Stefanie Glinski/AFP tr; Sia Kamobou/AFP crb. 98 **Impact Photos:** Alain Evrard bc. 99 **Corbis:** Charles O'Rear tl; Earl & Nazima Kowall cla; Giraud Philippe cr; Roger De La Harpe; Gallo Images clb. 100-101 **Alamy Stock Photo:** funkyfood London - Paul Williams b. 100 **Still Pictures:** Hartmut Schwarzbach bl. 101 **Alamy Stock Photo:** Stuart Black bl; Jake Lyell tl; Charles O. Cecil cl; FS-Stock tr. 102 **Corbis:** Buddy Mays t. 101 **Getty Images:** James Marshall cr. 102 **Alamy Stock Photo:** Brian Atkinson br. Getty Images: Aurelien Meunier bl. 103 **Bryan And Cherry Alexander Photography:** tl. 103 **Corbis:** Charles & Josette Lenars cra; Peter Turnley cr. 103 **Getty Images:** Sia Kamobou/AFP tr. 103 **Still Pictures:** Hartmut Schwarzbach b. 104 **Aspect Picture Library:** Peter Carmichael cl, b. 105 **Aspect Picture Library:** br; Peter Carmichael tl, tr, cr. 106-107 **Corbis:** Paul Hardy. 108 **Alamy Stock Photo:** Paul Brown b; eFesenko tr. 109 **Alamy Images:** Christine Osbourne br. 109 **Corbis:** Christine Osborne tr. 109 **Getty Images:** Guido Alberto Rossi bl; Khaled Desouki/AFP tl; Annette Lena/Gamma-Rapho cr. 110-111 **Hutchison Library:** David Brimcombe 112 **Africancraft.com:** tl, cl, bl. 112 **Alamy Stock Photo:** Eddie Gerald tr. 112 **Robert Harding Picture Library:** Jenny Pate br. 112 **Hutchison Library:** Nick Haslam bc. 113 **Aspect Picture Library:** Larry Burrows b. 113 **Getty Images:** Education Images/UIG tl. 113 **Popperfoto:** Mike Hutchings/Reuters tr. 114 **Alamy Stock Photo:** Joerg Boethling tr. 114 **Bryan And Cherry Alexander Photography:** cl. 114 **Hutchison Library:** Sarah Errington c 115 **Bryan And Cherry Alexander Photography:** tr. 115 **Hutchison Library:** Mary Jelliffe b. 116-117 **Robert Estall Photo Library:** Carol Beckwith & Angela Fisher. 118 **Getty Images:** Stefanie Glinski/AFP. 119 **Shehzad Noorani.** 120-121 **Dena Freeman.** 122 **Alamy Stock Photo:** LOOK Die Bildagentur der Fotografen GmbH cl. 122 **Nicolas Lewis:** tr, bl, br. 123 **Nicolas Lewis.** 124-125 **Images Of Africa Photobank:** David Keith Jones 124 **Still Pictures:** Muriel Nicolotti bl. 124 **Getty Images:** Joseph Van Os tl. 125 **Corbis:** Jim Zuckerman tr. 125 **Still Pictures:** Adrian Arbib br; Muriel Nicolotti tl. 126-127 **Still Pictures:** Adrian Arbib 128 **Corbis:** Roger De La Harpe; Gallo Images br. 128 **Still Pictures:** Roger de la Harpe t, br. 129 **Alamy Stock Photo:** M.Sobreira bl. Getty Images: Gary Bernard/AFP tr. 129 **Eye Ubiquitous:** Tovy Amsel tl. 129 **Impact Photos:** Gold Collection br. 130-131 **Africa Imagery:** b. 130 **Corbis:** Louise Gubb/SABA t. 130 **Images Of Africa Photobank:** Ivor Migdoll bl. 131 **Africa Imagery:** tl, tr. 131 **Images Of Africa Photobank:** Jeremy Van Riemsdyke br. 132 **Corbis:** Anthony Bannister; Gallo Images br. 132 **N.H.P.A.:** Anthony Bannister tl, c. 132 **Panos Pictures:** David Reed bl. 133 **N.H.P.A.:** Anthony Bannister tl, tr, cr, clb, b. 134 **Aspect Picture Library:** Horst Gossler bl, br. 134 **Giacoma Pirozzo:** t. 135 **Hutchison Library:** Christina Dodwell tr, cra. 135 **N.H.P.A.:** Daniel Heuclin br. 135 **Panos Pictures:** Jean-Leo Dugast crb, l. 136-137 **N.H.P.A.:** Martin Harvey. 138 123RF.com: Alberto Bin cb; Iurii Sokolov clb. **Alamy Stock Photo:** Andrew Wilson tl. **Getty Images:** Frans Lemmens crb;Gent Shkullaku/AFP bl. 138 **Corbis:** Brian A. Vikander ca; Catherine Karnow tr;Christine Osbourne cra; SETBOUN br. 138 **DK Picture Library:** Peter Wilson cla, br.

PICTURE CREDITS CONTINUED

138 **Popperfoto:** Desmond Boylan/Reuters tr. 139 **Alamy Stock Photo:** robertharding bl; Tom Till cl. 139 **Eye Ubiquitous:** James Davis tl. 140 **DK Picture Library:** l. 140 **Getty Images:** Steve Sarushek br. 141 **123RF.com:** Aleksandrs Tihonovs tl. Alamy Stock Photo: Novarc Images cr; Peter Russian cl; Robin Weaver bl; Anna Stowe Landscapes UK b. 141 **Corbis:** David Turnley tr. 142 **Corbis:** Matthias Kulka bc; Peter Turnley t; Ray Juno bl. 142 **Panos Pictures:** J. C. Tordai br. 143 **Alamy Images:** Chad Ehlers cl; Diogo Baptista bl. 143 **Corbis:** Palmer/Kane, Inc. br; Patrick Ward clb; Peter Turnley tr. 143 **Rex Features:** Action Press tl. 144-145 **Corbis:** Catherine Karnow b. 144 **Getty Images:** Harald Sund tr. 144 **Hutchison Library:** Robert Francis tl. 144 **Arctic Images:** bl. 145 **Corbis:** Catherine Karnow bl; Dave G. Houser tl. 145 **Eye Ubiquitous:** Judith Platt tr. 146 **Alamy Stock Photo:** LS Photos cb. 146 **Corbis:** Adam Woolfitt bl; Anthony Nex tl. 146 **Scotland in Focus:** Willbir r. 147 **Corbis:** Bo Zaunders br; Farrell Grehan bc; Hubert Stadler tl. 147 **Scotland in Focus:** MacSween Haggis tr. 148 **Corbis:** Chris North; Cordaiy Photo Library Ltd. bc; Michael S. Yamashita c; 148 **Foodpix:** tr. 149 **123RF.com:** Iurii Sokolov clb. 149 **Corbis:** Adam Woolfitt tl; Michael Nicholson br; David Cumming; Eye Ubiquitous tr; Robert Estall bl. 150-151 **Charles Tait Photographic:** 152 **Corbis:** Chris Lisle bl; Galen Rowell tl; Hubert Stadler tr. 152 **DK Picture Library:** Barnabas Kindersley br. 153 **Alamy Stock Photo:** Realimage clb; roger tillberg tr. 153 **Corbis:** Stephanie Maze tl. 153 **Lonely Planet Images:** Anders Blomqvist b. 154 **Bryan And Cherry Alexander Photography.** 155 Alamy Stock Photo: ton koene crb. 155 **Bryan And Cherry Alexander Photography:** tr, br, l. 156 **Corbis:** Charles & Josette Lenars br; Michael S. Yamashita cr. 156 **Getty Images:** Monica Dalmasso bl. 156 **Rex Features:** Kainulainen; Lehtikuva Oy/ Ritola tr. 157 **Alamy Stock Photo:** imageBROKER crb. 157 **Corbis:** Layne Kennedy tr; Stephanie Maze cr. 157 **Lehtikuva Oy:** Matti Kolho tl; Pekka Sakki br. 158-159 **Corbis:** John Garrett 160 **Corbis:** James A. Sugar bl; Owen Franken br. 160 **Lonely Planet Images:** Guy Moberly t. 161 **123RF.com:** belikova tl; lois poppleton tr. Getty Images: Naeblys bl. 161 **Corbis:** Dave G. Houser cl. 162-163 **Corbis:** Hans Georg Roth 164 **Alamy Images:** Photolocate cr. 164 **Getty Images:** Bruno De Hogues r; Ian Shaw bl; Jazz Archiv Hamburg\ullstein bild tl. 165 **Alamy Stock Photo:** Andrew Wilson clb. Getty Images: Lucas Barioulet/AFP tl. 165 **Corbis:** Richard Bickel bl. 166 **Corbis:** Craig Aurness l; Owen Franken tr, br. 167 **Alamy Images:** Robert Harding World Imagery tr. 167 **Corbis:** Owen Franken tl. 167 **Getty Images:** Jean-Pierre Pieuchot b. 168 Alamy Stock Photo: Peter Schickert br. 168 **Corbis:** Uwe Walz tl. 168-169 **Rex Features:** Action Press 168 **Still Pictures:** Andreas Riedmiller bl. 169 **Corbis:** Bob Krist br; Dave G. Houser tr. 169 **Getty Images:** Michael Rosenfeld bl. 170 **Corbis:** Gideon Mendel br; Richard Klune bl. 170 **Still Pictures:** Andreas Riedmiller tr. 171 **Corbis:** Gunter Marx Photography tl; Jose Fuste Raga tr. 171 **Still Pictures:** Andreas Riedmiller cl, cr, b. 172-173 **Alamy Stock Photo:** Deco. 174 **Getty Images:** Frans Lemmens tl. 174 **Christof Sonderegger, Fotograf:** bl, br. 175 **Bryan And Cherry Alexander Photography:** bl. 175 **Eye Ubiquitous:** James Davis tl. 175 **Getty Images:** Hans Wolf cr. 176 **Alamy Stock Photo:** Delphotos tr; Tom Till bl; Art Kowalsky cr. 177 **Associated Press AP:** Mikhail Metzel tl. 177 **Bryan And Cherry Alexander Photography:** tr. 177 **Eye Ubiquitous:** James Davis c. 177 **Alamy Stock Photo:** Alexander Blinov br; ITAR-TASS News Agency bl. 178 **Corbis:** Bernard Bisson/Sygma tr; David Turnley bl; James Marshall br. 179 **Corbis:** Raymond Gehman t; Setboun br. 179 **Lonely Planet Images:** Krzysztof Dydynski bl. 180 **Network Photographers Ltd.:** Laurie Sparham bl. 180 **Panos Pictures:** Peter Barker tl. 180 **Art Directors & TRIP:** J. Bartos br. 181 **Popperfoto:** Dimitar Dilkoff/Reuters br; Petr Josek/Reuters l. 181 **Art Directors & TRIP:** M. Maclaren tr. 182 **Corbis:** Gary Trotter; Eye Ubiquitous tr; Richard Bickel b. 182 **Getty Images:** Gent Shkullaku/AFP crb. 182 **James Kyllo:** cr. 182 **Rod Shone:** tl. 183 **Corbis:** Richard Bickel b. 183 **Rod Shone:** tl, tr. 184 Alamy Stock Photo: imageBROKER br; Hermes Jankone 2 bc. 184 **Corbis:** Bettmann tc; David Hanover bl; Enzo & Paolo Ragazzini c. 185 **Corbis:** David Lees tl; Geray Sweeney bl; Owen Franken r; Vittoriano Rastelli c. 186 **Corbis:** Jeffrey L. Rotman tr. 186 **Getty Images:** Francesco Ruggeri br. 186 **Magnum:** Ferdinando Scianna l. 187 **Corbis:** Jonathan Blair cl; Vittoriano Rastelli bc, br. 187 **Lonely Planet Images:** Ionas Kaltenbach tl. 187 **Alamy Stock Photo:** Simone Genovese bl. 188-189 **Shutterstock.** 190 **Alamy Stock Photo:** Art of Travel tl.190 **Getty Images:** Nicolas Economou/NurPhoto tr. 190 **Corbis:** Sheldan Collins bl. 190-191 **Eye Ubiquitous:** James Davis. 191 **Getty Images:** Bernard Grilly tr. 191 **Impact Photos:** David Slimings bcr. 191 **Art Directors & TRIP:** M. Nichols cr. 192-193 **123RF.com:** Jordan Rusev. 194 **123RF.com:** Aliaksandr Mazurkevich crb. Alamy Stock Photo: D Lomax/Robert Harding World Imagery clb; Yaacov Dagan bl; Komkrit Suwanwela cla; Steve Davey Photography bc; Andrey Vishin br; Eddie Gerald tr. Getty Images: Vyacheslav Oseledko/AFP tl. **Robert Harding Picture Library:** tc. 194 **Bryan And Cherry Alexander Photography: ca.** 194 **Corbis:** John Hicks clb. 195 **Corbis:** Dean Conger cl; Tiziana and Gianni Baldizzone tl. 195 **Panos Pictures:** John Miles bl. 196 **Corbis:** Keren Su bl, b. 197 **Corbis:** Jed & Kaoru Share tl; Michael Freeman cl; Steve Raymer tr. 197 **Alamy Stock Photo:** eye35.pix br; robertharding crb; PawelBienkowskiphotos bl. 198 **Alamy Stock Photo:** halil ibrahim kurucan tl; Jan Wlodarczyk br. 198 **Corbis:** Helen King bl. Getty Images: Kaveh Kazemi tr. 199 **Alamy Stock Photo:** Melvyn Longhurst clb. 199 **Corbis:** Chris Lisle br; David H. Wells c; Lindsay Hebberd bl; Richard Powers t. 200 **Alamy Stock Photo:** Eddie Gerald bl. 200 **Corbis:** Annie Griffiths Belt tl, tr; Hanan Isachar br. 201 **Associated Press AP:** Nati Harnik tr. 201 **Corbis:** Hanan Isachar tl. 201 **Rex Features:** ASAP b. 202 **Corbis:** Charles & Josette Lenars bl. 202 **Magnum:** Ian Berry c, br. 202 **Art Directors & TRIP:** V Kolpakov tr. 203 **Alamy Stock Photo:** mikle15 tl; Kasia Nowak cl. 203 **Armenia Week:** cr, br. 203 **Jon Spaull:** tr. 204-205 **Corbis:** Nik Wheeler 206 **Alamy Stock Photo:** Andrey Vishin bl. 206 **Associated Press AP:** Vahid Salemi tr. 206 **DK Picture Library:** br. 207 **Alamy Stock Photo:** Germán Vogel br. 207 **Associated Press AP:** tr; Enric Marti c; Hasan Sarbakhshian tl, bl. 208 **Associated Press AP:** Ruth Fremson tc. 208 **Getty Images:** Nevada Wier cl, bl. 209 **Alamy Images:** D Lomax/Robert Harding World Imagery t. 209 **Getty Images:** Frans Lemmens bl. 209 **Jon Spaull:** br. 210 **Corbis:** Keren Su tr. 210 **Hutchison Library:** Sarah Errington tr. 210 **Panos Pictures:** Alain le Garsmeur b. 211 **Alamy Stock Photo:** Eddie Gerald tr. 211 **Corbis:** Nevada Wier bl. 211 **Hutchison Library:** Sarah Errington cl, br; Trevor Page tl. 212 **Bryan And Cherry Alexander Photography.** 213 **Alamy Stock Photo:** Gerner Thomsen tr. 213 **Bryan And Cherry Alexander Photography:** tl, c, br. 214-215 **Getty Images:** Vyacheslav Oseledko/AFP. 216 **Corbis:** Alison Wright tr; Christine Kolisch br; Tiziana and Gianni Baldizzone cr. 216 **Still Pictures:** Hartmut Schwarzbach bl. 217 **Corbis:** Galen Rowell tl; John Noble b; Kurt Stier tr. 218 **Getty Images:** Andia/UIG tc. 218 **Robert Harding Picture Library:** Christopher Rennie bl, c; James Strachan bc. 219 **Robert Harding Picture Library:** David Beatty tr, br; Maurice Joseph tc. 219 **Panos Pictures:** Dermot Tatlow bc. 220 **Corbis:** Bennett Dean/Eye Ubiquitous bc. 220 **Robert Harding Picture Library:** F Jackson c. 220 **Saif Saifuddin:** tr. 221 **Alamy Stock Photo:** Steve Davey Photography tr. 221 **Corbis:** Ric Ergenbright bc. 221 **Robert Harding Picture Library:** F. Jackson tl, bl. 221 **Lonely Planet Images:** Richard L'Anson br. 222 **123RF.com:** Aliaksandr Mazurkevich b. Alamy Stock Photo: Andy Dossett tl. 222 **Corbis:** Baldev/Sygma tr. 223 **Corbis:** Brian A. Vikander cl. 223 **Lonely Planet Images:** Sara-Jane Cleland tl; Stephen Saks r. 224 **Hutchison Library:** Jeremy Horner cr, bl. 224 **Panos Pictures:** Jeremy Horner tr; Peter Barker tc. 224 **Still Pictures:** Shehzad Noorani br. 225 **Alamy Stock Photo:** Mamunur Rashid tl. 225 **Hutchison Library:** Nancy Durrell McKenna cr, cbr; Shahidul Alam tr. 225 **Still Pictures:** Shehzad Noorani b. 226-227 **Still Pictures:** Hartmut Schwarzbach. 228 **Alamy Stock Photo:** Danita Delimont tr. 228 **Corbis:** Lindsay Hebberd br; Michael Busselle tl; Sheldan Collins cl; Wolfgang Kaehler c. 229 **Corbis:** Chris Lisle tc; Lindsay Hebberd cl, bl, br. 230-231 **Corbis:** Jeremy Horner 232 **Corbis:** David Ball tl; Keren Su tr, br. 232 **Hutchison Library:** Michael Macintyre bl. 233 **Corbis:** Alison Wright br; Keren Su tr; Patrick Ward bl; Paul A. Souders bl. 234 **Corbis:** Tiziana and Gianni Baldizzone bc. 234 **Hutchison Library:** tr. 234 **Impact Photos:** Christophe Bluntzer c. 234 **Still Pictures:** Thomas Kelly l. 235 **Corbis:** Michael S. Yamashita b; Tiziana and Gianni Baldizzone tl. 235 **Impact Photos:** Christophe Bluntzer tr. 235 **Still Pictures:** Thomas Kelly cr. 236 **Hutchison Library:** Sarah Murray c; Stephen Pern tc. 236 **Impact Photos:** David Gallant bl. 236-7 **Still Pictures:** Stephen Pern 237 **Corbis:** Adrian Arbib cra; Jacques Langevin/Sygma tl. 237 **Hutchison Library:** Stephen Pern tr. 237 **Still Pictures:** Adrian Arbib cla; Stephen Pern bl. 238 **DK Picture Library:** bl. 238-239 **Still Pictures:** Adrian Arbib 240 **Bryan And Cherry Alexander Photography:** tr, br, l. 241 **Bryan And Cherry Alexander Photography:** tl, tr, cr, b. 242-243 **Bryan And Cherry Alexander Photography.** 244 **Corbis:** c; Bill Varie bl; Keren Su tl; Liu Liqun tr; Michael S. Yamashita br. 245 **Corbis:** John Slater c; Keren Su br; Robert van der Hilst bl. 245 **Lonely Planet Images:** Bradley Mayhew tr. 246 **Corbis:** Keren Su tl, tr, bl. 246-247 **Panos Pictures:** Penny Tweedie 247 **Alamy Images:** Robert Harding World Imagery tr. 247 **Corbis:** Keren Su tl, b; Steve Raymer bl. 248 Getty Images: SeongJoon Cho/Bloomberg cl. 248 **Robert Harding Picture Library:** Sassoon tr. 248 **Impact Photos:** Philip Gordon b. 249 **Corbis:** Dave Bartruff bl, br. 249 **DK Picture Library:** Barnabas Kindersley cr. 249 **Hutchison Library:** Michael Macintyre tr. 249 **popperfoto.com:** Marwan Naamani/AFP tl. 250 **Alamy Stock Photo:** Komkrit Suwanwela c. Getty Images: Toshifumi Kitamura/AFP br; Frédéric Soltan/Corbis bl. 250 **Corbis:** Michael S. Yamashita tr;. 251 **Corbis:** Bob Krist c; Haruyoshi Yamaguchi/Sygma br; Michael Freeman bl; Michael S. Yamashita tc. 252 **Corbis:** Bernard Bisson/Sygma tr. 252 **DK Picture Library:** l. 252 **Robert Harding Picture Library:** br. 253 **Corbis:** Michael S. Yamashita tl; Steve Crise clb. 253 **Robert Harding Picture Library:** tr. 253 **Still Pictures:** Kyodo News cl, b. 254-245 **Impact Photos:** M. Huteau/ana 256 **Robert Harding Picture Library:** tr. 256 **Hutchison Library:** Jeremy Horner c; Liba Taylor l. 256 **Lonely Planet Images:** Chris Mellor br. 257 **Corbis:** Wolfgang Kaehler br. 257 **Impact Photos:** Alain Evrard bl; Robert Hind tl. 257 **Panos Pictures:** Jean-Leo Dugast tr. 258 **Corbis:** Chris Hellier tr; Reinhard Eisele bc. 258 **Robert Harding Picture Library:** l; Richard Ashworth c. 258 **Panos Pictures:** Chris Stowers bl. 259 **Corbis:** Dallas and John Heaton tr. 259 **Hutchison Library:** Michael Macintyre br. 259 **Panos Pictures:** Chris Stowers tl. 259 **Still Pictures:** Chris Caldicott bl. 260-1 **Corbis:** Albrecht G. Schaefer 262 **Corbis:** Ludovic Maisant cr; Patrick Ward br; Paul A. Souders bl. 262 **Robert Harding Picture Library:** Maurice Joseph cra. 262 **Hutchison Library:** Jakum Brown tl. 262 **Panos Pictures:** Chris Stowers tr. 263 **Robert Harding Picture Library:** Sylvain Grandadam tr. 263 **Hutchison Library:** J.G. Fuller tl; Michael Macintyre b. 263 **Lonely Planet Images:** Gregory Adams tc. 264 **Alamy Stock Photo:** jackie ellis bl; European Sports Photographic Agency br; Travelscape Images bc; Eric Lafforgue ca. Corbis: cla; Craig Lovell cb; Mark A. Johnson tl; Owen Franken cra; Paul A. Souders tr. Getty Images: Eric Lafforgue/Gamma-Rapho clb. 264 **Focus New Zealand:** crb. 264 **Panos Pictures:** Penny Tweedie cr. 265 **Alamy Stock Photo:** imageBROKER tl; Martin Valigursky bl. Getty Images: Eric Lafforgue/Art In All Of Us/Corbis cl. Corbis: Anders Ryman cla. 266 **Corbis:** Mark A. Johnson bl. 267 **Alamy Stock Photo:** Friedrich Stark br. Getty Images: Eric Lafforgue/Art In All Of Us/Corbis bl. 267 **Corbis:** Casa Productions tr. 268 **Corbis:** Albrecht G. Schaefer bc; Royalty-free tl. 268 **Getty Images:** Tom Cockrem tr. 268 **Popperfoto:** Reuters bl. 269 **Alamy Stock Photo:** Eric Lafforgue bc. 269 **Bryan And Cherry Alexander Photography:** tl. 269 **Corbis:** Charles & Josette Lenars bl. 270 **Alamy Stock Photo:** Martin Valigursky b. 270 **Corbis:** Dimitri Lundt; TempSport tl. 270 **Getty Images:** Zigy Kaluzny c. 270 **Panos Pictures:** Penny Tweedie br. 270 **PA Photos:** tr. 271 **123RF.com: Andrey Moisseyev bl. Corbis:** Patrick Ward crb; Paul A. Souders cr, br, t. 272-273 **Lonely Planet Images:** Nigel Marsh 274 **Panos Pictures:** Penny Tweedie tr, c, bl. 274 **Getty Images:** Louis Grandadam cl. 275 **Corbis:** Dallas & John Heaton bl. 275 **Panos Pictures:** Penny Tweedie tl, tr, br. 276 **Corbis:** Yann Arthus-Bertrand c. 276 **Getty Images:** Penny Tweedie tr. 276 **Panos Pictures:** Penny Tweedie bl. 277 **Panos Pictures:** Penny Tweedie tr, cr, br. 278 **Alamy Stock Photo:** jackie ellis tr. 278 **Corbis:** Michael S. Yamashita tl; Wayne Lawler; Ecoscene br, b. 279 **Corbis:** Bob Krist tr; Bojan Brecelj cl; Chris Rainier b. 280 **Corbis:** Chris Rainier br. 280 **Getty Images:** Eric Lafforgue/Gamma-Rapho bl. 280 **Michele Westmorland:** tr. 281 **Corbis:** Albrecht G. Schaefer bl; Kevin Schafer cl. 281 **Michele Westmorland:** tc, tr. 282-283 **Corbis:** Chris Rainier 284 **Corbis:** Caroline Penn c, br. 284 **Hutchison Library:** Andre Singer tl. 285 **Corbis:** Caroline Penn br. 285 **Eye Ubiquitous:** James Davis bl. 285 **Robert Harding Picture Library:** tl. 285 **Impact Photos:** Caroline Penn tr. 286 **Bryan And Cherry Alexander Photography:** tl, tr, b. 287 **Bryan And Cherry Alexander Photography:** tr, br. 287 **Corbis:** Anders Ryman bl; Charles O'Rear tc. 288 **Alamy Stock Photo:** Jan Butchofsky br. 288 **Corbis:** Anders Ryman bl; Roger Ressmeyer tl, tr. 289 **Corbis:** Anders Ryman tl, cl, bl, r; Paul A. Souders bc. 290 **Corbis:** Catherine Karnow tl; Earl & Nazima Kowall tr. 290 **Eye Ubiquitous:** James Davis bl, b. 291 **Corbis:** Anders Ryman tl, cla, cl; Jack Fields tr, br. 292 **Corbis:** Paul A. Souders c, b. 292 **Getty Images:** Jess Stock tl. 292 **Lonely Planet Images:** Grant Somers tr. 293 **Corbis:** Craig Lovell tl; Kevin Fleming tr, br. 294-295 **Corbis:** Paul A. Souders 296 **Corbis:** Anders Ryman bl; Neil Rabinowitz br; Paul Almasy crb. 296 **Eye Ubiquitous:** James Davis tr. 296 **Focus New Zealand:** tl. 296 **Robert Harding Picture Library:** Caroline Washington cra. 297 **Corbis:** Anders Ryman b; Macduff Everton tr; Wolfgang Kaehler tl. 299 **Bryan And Cherry Alexander Photography:** 300 **Robert Harding Picture Library:** G. Corrigan. 303 **Hutchison Library:** Isabella Tree.